Resentment's Virtue

Resentment's Virtue

Jean Améry and the Refusal to Forgive

Thomas Brudholm
Foreword by Jeffrie G. Murphy

Temple University Press
Philadelphia

Temple University Press
1601 North Broad Street
Philadelphia PA 19122
www.temple.edu/tempress

Cloth edition published 2008
Paperback edition published 2010
Printed in the United States of America

∞ The paper used in this publication meets the requirements of the American
National Standard for Information Sciences—Permanence of Paper for Printed
Library Materials, ANSI Z39.48-1992

Library of Congress Cataloging-in-Publication Data

Brudholm, Thomas, 1969-
  Resentment's virtue : Jean Améry and the refusal to forgive / Thomas Brudholm ;
foreword by Jeffrie Murphy.
      p. cm. — (Politics, history, and social change)
  Includes bibliographical references and index.
  ISBN 13: 978-1-59213-566-0 (cloth: alk. paper)
  ISBN 10: 1-59213-566-8 (cloth: alk. paper) 1. Forgiveness. 2. Resentment.
3. Reconciliation. 4. South Africa. Truth and Reconciliation Commission. 5. Améry,
Jean. I. Title.
  BJ1476.B78 2007
  179'.9—dc22
                            2007018931
  ISBN 13: 978-1-59213-567-7 (paper : alk. paper)

Contents

Foreword

We live in a time in which the virtue of forgiveness (conceived as transcending certain resentments) risks becoming distorted and cheapened by various movements that advocate it in a hasty and uncritical way. Selective and considered forgiveness may indeed reveal virtue in victims of wrongdoing, may legitimately free those victims from being consumed by unhealthy resentments, and may aid in restoring relations that are worth restoring. None of this, however, shows that forgiveness is always a virtue, that all resentments are unhealthy, and that all relationships are worth restoring. Some wrongs and some perpetrators of those wrongs may be unforgivable, some resentments may be justified and healthy, and some ruptured relationships may be utterly unworthy of restoration—a point that may be missed when the often uncritical boosters of universal forgiveness (a group that sometimes includes the famous and influential South African Bishop Desmond Tutu) heap praise on what they take to be the moral, spiritual, and mental health exhibited by those who forgive, and thereby tacitly condemn even those who will not forgive grave wrongs by unrepentant perpetrators as exhibiting serious moral, spiritual, or even psychological problems. This final charge comes as no surprise, of course, in a culture that is increasingly dominated by therapeutic language and often uses that language as though it is equivalent to moral and religious language. The old theological concept of "cheap grace" comes to mind—at least to my mind—when inspiring (to some) platitudes and slogans about forgiveness and its virtues take the place of critical and disciplined moral, religious, and psychological thought on the topic.

In recent years there have been some voices expressing criticism of hasty and uncritical endorsements of forgiveness. These voices—still a small minority in the vast literature (both scholarly and self-help) on forgiveness—have come from religious writers, philosophers, and even psychologists. Psychologist Sharon Lamb and I, for example, co-edited in 2002 the book *Before Forgiving: Cautionary Views on Forgiveness in Psychotherapy*, a book to which scholars from both philosophy and psychology contributed essays, and my own *Getting Even: Forgiveness and its Limits* was published in 2003.

These books, along with most of the others that seek to introduce some skepticism into the discussion of forgiveness, are concerned mainly with *interpersonal* forgiveness—forgiveness of betrayal by a friend or lover, forgiveness by a crime victim of the perpetrator of that crime, or even the problems involved in asking God for forgiveness for one's own personal sins—something often modeled on the analogy of a child asking a father for forgiveness.

As important as the topic of interpersonal forgiveness is, a topic of equal importance—one that has become particularly vivid in the twentieth and early twenty-first centuries—is what might be called *group* forgiveness: members of certain groups (victims and survivors) considering whether they ought to forgive members of other groups (perpetrators or even their descendants) who have victimized them—victimized them as perpetrators or as in some other way manifesting complicity in what has come to be called *mass atrocities*. Here are three obvious examples of such atrocities (and, alas, many more could be given): the Holocaust, the slaughter of hundreds of thousands of Tutsis by Hutus in Rwanda, and the torture and killing of blacks by the South African apartheid government.

Unfortunately, the same kind of boosterism of uncritical forgiveness that often infects discussions of interpersonal forgiveness is also present in many discussions of forgiveness for mass atrocities. Consider the South African Truth and Reconciliation Commission (TRC). There have been some balanced discussions of the virtues and shortcomings of that commission—Martha Minow's 2002 book *Between Vengeance and Forgiveness*, for example—but for the most part the workings of that commission have been portrayed almost as a Platonic form of how morality, religion, psychology, and basic human decency can combine to produce a nearly perfect response to mass atrocity. In his less cautious moments Bishop Tutu has served as a cheerleader for this interpretation of the TRC. Most influential, however—on countless numbers of American high-school and college students—has been the film *Long Night's Journey into Day*. This purports to be an accurate documentary of the workings of the TRC and the response of South Africans, both black and white, to the commission. It is in fact, however, little more than a sentimental propaganda film that shows mainly the bright side and little of the dark side of the process. It does not document, for example, the way in which the Steve Biko family deplores the TRC because its process simply ignores the fact that many victims and survivors of the atrocities of the apartheid government are mainly interested in just punishment for the perpetrators of those atrocities and, prior to the administration of such punishment, are not much interested in even discussing the forgiveness of them or reconciliation with them.

It may, of course, be the case that the TRC was the only possible way, compatible with future peace and democratic government, of dealing with transitional justice in South Africa. The transfer of power was, after all, the result of a negotiated settlement to avoid a violent revolution, and it is unlikely that members of the apartheid government would have agreed to a settlement that would have rendered them open, like the criminals at Nuremberg, to severe punishment. Political necessity, however, should not be confused with forgiveness. It is important to remember that the TRC required from perpetrators only disclosure and admission of responsibility as conditions for amnesty. It did not require expressions of repentance or apology from them and did not base its decisions on whether the victims themselves (the only ones really in a position to grant forgiveness) wished to forgive. So it strikes me as absurd, whatever the other considerable merits of the TRC, to glamorize it as an exercise of the virtue of forgiveness, and it is indecent to portray those who do not wish to forgive and reconcile as lacking in either virtue or mental health.

With perfect timing this wonderful book by Thomas Brudholm now arrives on the scene. Drawing on extensive research on the TRC, he explores some of the myths surrounding it and exposes the way in which Bishop Tutu has encouraged those myths. Not only does Brudholm expose the flaws in the claim that the TRC is an exercise of forgiveness proper, he goes an important step further and argues for the legitimacy of a posture of *nonforgiveness* on the part of victims of atrocity—one response (though, of course, not the only one) that can preserve their dignity and self-respect and even mental health. While in no sense wishing to condemn those victims who choose to forgive, he fights against the all too common tendency to condemn those victims who choose to retain their resentments and *not* forgive.

Brudholm's exploration of the TRC takes up the first part of his book. Valuable as this part is, however, the second part is—in my judgment—even more valuable. In this section he explores in detail the thought of the writer and intellectual and Holocaust survivor Jean Améry—a man who retained his resentments not just against the perpetrators of the Holocaust but also of those German survivors of the war who seemed to him to remain far more successful and self-satisfied than was consistent with the legacy of evil that they had inherited: a legacy that had marked Améry and that had provided him with only sustained resentment as a way to try to hold his own sanity and self-respect together. I am somewhat embarrassed to admit that, in spite of all my research and writing on forgiveness and resentment, I had never before encountered Améry's thoughts on these matters—thoughts best expressed in his book *At the Mind's Limits*—until introduced to his writings a few years ago by Thomas Brudholm. I remain deeply grateful for this introduction.

Let me close by noting that Brudholm's book should be of interest not only to those interested in responses to mass atrocity (or in other issues of transitional justice) but also to those philosophers and psychologists interested in the moral emotions—particularly its analysis of resentment. Before becoming acquainted with Améry's writings, I had thought that Bishop Joseph Butler's 1726 sermon, "Upon Resentment," when combined with contemporary philosopher Peter Strawson's seminal essay, "Freedom and Resentment," made a case for the nature and value of resentment that could not be improved on. I had also thought that Nietzsche and Max Scheler had said pretty much all that needed saying on *ressentiment*—an emotion generally portrayed as a narcissistic and self-destructive perversion of legitimate resentment. I learned from Brudholm's discussion of the relationship between resentment and *ressentiment* (and the way in which Améry seeks to show that *ressentiment* may not be just a perversion after all), and I think that this discussion will enrich the thought of anyone interested in the moral emotions.

Richard Rorty once said that the best way to judge the value of a work in philosophy is to determine if it "advances the conversation" on the topic at issue. Judged by this standard, Brudholm's book is a work of genuine value.

Jeffrie G. Murphy

Jeffrie G. Murphy is Regents' Professor of Law, Philosophy, and Religious Studies at Arizona State University. He is the author of numerous books and articles on the morality of punishment, mercy, forgiveness, and the moral emotions. His most recent book is *Getting Even: Forgiveness and Its Limits*.

Preface and Acknowledgments

T his is a book about *unforgiveness*. More precisely, it is about the moral dimensions of victims' resentment and resistance to forgiveness in the aftermath of mass atrocities. Drawing on the works of Jean Améry, it aims to demonstrate that the "negative" emotions and attitudes are not only understandable but that they can also possess a moral component. This moral component is all too often ignored by the boosters of forgiveness, healing, and reconciliation. When I first began studying responses to mass atrocities, I was neither aware that the unwillingness to forgive was an issue in need of examination, nor did I harbor any prior interests in the ethics of emotional responses to being wronged. Being a philosopher by training, I was instead much excited about the invention and ongoing development of legal and political responses to legacies of collective violence. I had no idea that I would end up arguing that the preservation of resentment or the refusal to forgive may itself reflect a moral protest and ambition that might be as permissible, admirable, or humane as the willingness to forgive. Quite to the contrary, as I became interested in questions about transitional justice and reconciliation, I had in mind a more "constructive" examination of concepts like "political forgiveness" and "restorative justice." Like so many others, I was particularly fascinated by the proceedings of the South African Truth and Reconciliation Commission and by the ways in which they challenged given accounts of how nations could or should deal with an atrocious past.

The turning point in my interests is not easy to identify, but most influential was my reading an essay collection written by an intellectual and survivor of the Holocaust named Jean Améry. I stumbled on the thin little book—entitled *At the Mind's Limits*—as I quickly browsed a London bookshop for literature on the Holocaust. Quotes on the cover promised pages to be read "with almost physical pain" and the "testimony of a profoundly serious man." Although somewhat discouraged by the strong pathos, I let the book slip down into my already over-filled basket. Little did I know that in it were indeed the most interesting and thought-provoking essays of an "extraordinarily acute conscience"[1] and that the introduction of Améry to debates and conferences about transitional justice would become a central endeavor of mine. What seemed to me particularly compelling was the essay *Resentments* in which Améry defends the Nazi victim's preservation of a special kind of resentment in the face of calls to forget, forgive, or look to the future. Reading about forgiveness and reconciliation with the reflections of Améry in the back of my mind, my attention was soon captured by a certain insufficiency in discourses and institutions devoted to the promotion of forgiveness and reconciliation. What I found missing was a lack of interest, nuance, and fairness with regard to victims who are unwilling to forgive or let go of resentments, and I gained the desire to give a fairer hearing to such "negative" attitudes and actors. Feeling that enough had been written about healing and forgiveness, I wanted to explore the unpleasant attitudes as human responses worthy of examination in their own right—not just to learn more about how to overcome them and not only as an indirect path to a deeper understanding of forgiveness. As always, the result is not final or comprehensive. Yet, I hope that it represents a challenge worth taking seriously and that it will contribute to a more balanced treatment of negative emotions and unforgiving victims in current thinking about responses to mass atrocity.

The book is a revised version of my PhD thesis (Brudholm 2005), which I could still be trying to revise, had it not been for the pragmatic sense of my advisor at the Danish University of Education, Anne-Marie Eggert Olsen. I would like to thank her for that and for her close readings of the original drafts. My gratitude also goes to Peter Berliner, Nigel Biggar, Lars Buur, Norbert Frei, Arne Grøn, Dietrich Jung, Preben Kaarsholm, Peter Kemp, Martin Mennecke, Natan Sznaider, Ruti Teitel, Margaret Walker, and Thomas Wamsler. Without the benefit of advice from philosophers as well as scholars with a background in history, law, theology, psychology, sociology, or anthropology, I would never have dared to undertake a project that goes well beyond the boundaries of a traditional philosophical study. The book is in part based on untranslated German publications. For the translations of several quotes from German to English, I am grateful to Claudia Welz. I owe a special debt to Tom Cushman and Jeffrie Murphy. In certain stressful moments their wit kept me going, and without them, the writing of the book would certainly have been a more solitary experience. Conversations with Murphy shaped the whole project significantly, and Cushman generously devoted an issue of the *Journal of Human Rights* to a special issue on the negative emotions in post-conflict societies. Also many thanks to series editor John Torpey and to a whole line of professionals affiliated with Temple University Press who have helped bring this book into existence. The French philosopher Blaise Pascal once mentioned that authors talking about their books as "my book" should rather say "our book" because our writings are always influenced by others. This rings to me true in general, but it is particularly pertinent in relation to my wife, Sara Paludan, and I would like to express my gratitude for successive attentive readings and for the patience with which she endured extended periods where her husband could think of nothing except the problems of his study. Finally, the study behind this book was made possible by a PhD fellowship granted by the Danish Research Agency and the Danish Center for Holocaust and Genocide Studies and carried on by the Danish Institute for International Studies.

1

Transitional Justice and the Ethics of Anger

My first thought was for the commander who gave the order to attack. I hope he burns in the hottest corner of hell. My second thought was for the soldiers who loaded the breeches and fired the guns. I hope their sleep is forever punctuated by the screams of the children and the cries of their mothers

(MAASS 1996:189)

Sometimes when I sit alone in a chair on my veranda, I imagine this possibility: one far-off day, a local man comes slowly up to me and says, "Bonjour Francine. I have come to speak to you. So, I am the one who cut your mama and your little sisters. I want to ask your forgiveness." Well, to that person I cannot reply anything good. A man may ask for forgiveness if he had one Primus too many and then beats his wife. But if he has worked at killing for a whole month, even on Sundays, whatever can he hope to be forgiven for?

(HATZFELD 2006:196)

Every morning when I get up I can read the Auschwitz number on my forearm, something that touches the deepest and most closely intertwined roots of my existence. . . . My neighbor greets me in a friendly fashion, Bonjour, Monsieur; I doff my hat, Bonjour, Madame. But Madame and Monsieur are separated by interstellar distances; for yesterday a Madame looked away when they led off a Monsieur, and through the barred windows of the departing car a Monsieur viewed a Madame as if she were a stone angel from a bright and stern heaven, which is forever closed to the Jew.

(AMÉRY 1999:94)

Dwelling on the Negative

A re the strongly vindictive desires expressed in the first quote above by the witness to a massacre of civilians in Sarajevo fundamentally undesirable or unjustified? Would it have been more commendable if he had rather expressed a desire to see justice done in order to prevent such atrocities from happening again? Or should one at least hope that he has since then been able to transform vindictiveness to a more compassionate attitude to the perpetrators of the heinous crime: hating their acts, but forgiving the agents? What is the moral significance of the experience and expression of anger in the face of evil?

And what should we think about the attitude of Francine, a survivor of the genocide in Rwanda in 1994, which is expressed in the second quote. During the massacres, she witnessed people being hacked to death, she herself barely survived, and her family was brutally murdered. Equally dismissive of both forgiveness and vengeance, Francine hopes that justice could bring some share of peace of mind (Hatzfeld 2005:21–28).

Advocates of forgiveness sometimes argue that forgiveness would be meaningless if it only forgave the forgivable, that forgiving is not just a sign of personal virtue but also brings healing to the victim and is a prerequisite for social reconciliation. Moreover, the unforgiving victim is typically represented as consumed by bitterness and a lust for revenge. Indeed, this is why there is allegedly no future without forgiveness. Yet, how does all of this seem to apply to Francine and her refusal to forgive? Would a more forgiving and conciliatory response to the returnee have been testimony of a more generous and admirable character? Is there something about forgiveness that she has not understood, and is her wish for some measure of justice really just a disguised thirst for revenge?

Finally, with the third quote, there is Jean Améry. He wrote this passage twenty years after his liberation from the Nazi death camps. Yet in it he speaks as if the past was still present, and it seems that his identity as a former Nazi victim had become the defining feature of his existence. Was he so traumatized that it had become impossible for him to let go of the past? Or was he wallowing in his grievances, obsessed perhaps with his victimhood? When societies try to "move on" after mass atrocity, victims who cannot or will not abide with the call to forgive and reconcile are often pictured as "prisoners of the past": traumatized, self-preoccupied, resentful, and vindictive. To be able to forgive or forget is generally taken to be morally and therapeutically superior to harboring resentment and other "negative" emotions. But, perhaps, sometimes, when one is dealing with extreme horrors and evildoers, it could be the other way around. Possibly, there are circumstances in which forgiving is a temptation, a promise of relief that might be morally dubious. Indeed, the refusal to forgive may represent the more demanding moral accomplishment. Perhaps even long-standing resentment has to be judged differently when societies abandon survivors and grant amnesty to the perpetrators of heinous deeds.

Questions like those posed above are rarely taken seriously in current discourses of forgiveness and reconciliation after mass atrocity, which assume that forgiveness and compassion are morally superior to anger and resentment. Indeed, in the context of efforts to promote forgiveness and reconciliation, anger and resentment are often seen not merely as inferior emotions. More than that, they connote self-preoccupation, weakness, and danger insofar as they are seen as intimately connected to desires for revenge. Atrocity survivors[1] who express their willingness to forgive or who testify in court with decorum are commonly admired and appreciated. They incarnate magnanimity, strength, and humanity—and they provide reasons to hope that recovery and reconciliation are possible even in the worst of cases. For example, in his reflections on the proceedings of the Truth and Reconciliation Commission (TRC) of South Africa, Desmond Tutu has repeatedly marveled and expressed his exhilaration at victims who were willing to let go of anger and to forgive despite having been injured grievously. But what about those who would not forgive? They demonstrated, according to Tutu, "the important point that forgiveness could not be taken for granted; it was neither cheap nor easy" (1999:271). Thus he pays attention to the unforgiving others only as a means of expressing even more admiration for those who were willing to forgive. To the extent that current discourses of forgiveness and reconciliation focus on emotions and attitudes of people who have been seriously wronged, a similar picture prevails: forgiving is studied and promoted with a nuanced attention to its nature and benefits, but anger and resentment are either rejected without serious analysis or examined mainly to understand what forgiveness is and why it is desirable (Govier 2002:50).

As Tutu puts it, the study of forgiveness has become a "growth industry" (1999:271). This book offers a counterpoint to the near-hegemonic status afforded to the logic of forgiveness in the literatures on transitional justice and reconciliation (Fletcher and Weinstein 2004:574, Kritz 1995, Teitel 2000).[2] It is meant to complement the scores of writings in which outrage, resentment, and refusals to forgive or reconcile are hastily rejected as the negative to be overcome: the irrational, immoral, and unhealthy or understandable but unfortunate attitudes of victims who are not—at least not yet— "ready" or "capable" of forgiving and healing.

I do not deny the possibility that the refusal to forgive and reconcile and the preservation of anger and outrage *can* be pathological and morally unjustifiable. People sometimes are consumed by anger, and anger sometimes leads to dehumanizing and heinous acts of excessive revenge. Equally real is the dwelling on or wallowing in litanies of suffering: "the temptations of grievance and victimhood" (Govier 2002:152). The point is simply that the negative aspects of anger and resentment are already much referred to and already well known. Similarly, the rhetorical attention to excess and pathology has overshadowed the fact that negative emotions are not only understandable in the aftermath of mass atrocity but that they also possess a moral component that is often ignored by the boosters of reconciliation. I hope to contribute to an undoing of notions that victims' resistance to calls for forgiveness is always the sign of a lust for revenge or some kind of personal deficiency or failure. Although I am sympathetic to the need for more complex accounts of the avenger and of vengeance and vindictiveness, the focus in this book rather lies on the moral significance of various kinds of resentment (for books on vengeance cf. French 2001, Jacoby 1988, Murphy 2003, Phelps 2004, Solomon 1999, Tobias & Zinke 2000, R. Wilson 2001).[3] I argue that, in some circumstances, the preservation of outrage or resentment and the refusal to forgive and reconcile can be the reflex expression of a moral protest and ambition that might be as permissible and admirable as the posture of forgiveness. When this possibility is neglected and when advocates or scholars arguing the case for forgiveness and healing lose sight of the contestability of the values they promote, they also lose sight of the possible moral legitimacy of some victims' preservation of resentment. This neglect is not fair—and in fact it can be deeply offensive.

In short, I hope to contribute to a more complex and philosophically nuanced understanding of the negative emotions and attitudes of anger and resentment. I dwell on the negative to show that there is more to the harboring of resentment and resistance to forgiveness than advocates of the value of forgiveness, healing, and reconciliation commonly acknowledge. This is, in a nutshell, the *raison d'etre* of this book. The overall undertaking involves continuous discussion with the philosophical tradition, as well as a critical reappraisal of Desmond Tutu's advocacy of forgiveness. Most important, this challenge to current thinking about resentment and reconciliation is built on a careful reading of Jean Améry's essays on the condition of the Nazi victims and on their resentment in particular.

A theologian speaking of compassion and forgiveness once told me that his work was an attempt to contribute to an ethics for judges and those who judge others. If the following examination is to be seen as the development of an ethics directed at any particular group, it must be to those who act as conciliators and those who encourage the wronged (or their relatives) to forgive others.

Alchemies of Reconciliation after Mass Atrocity

Moral questions about the nature and value of the negative emotions arise in a broad variety of contexts: for example, in our daily life and personal relations, in courtrooms, during practices of mediation, and in the context of psychological counseling. This book's focus is limited to the aftermath of mass atrocities and to the question of how to think about the emotions and attitudes of people who have survived genocide, persecution, or torture and who endure the loss of loved ones, safety, health, and less tangible elements, such as hope or a sense of trust in the world.

In the literature on transitional justice or responses to collective violence, the terms "mass atrocities" and "atrocity crimes" typically encompass the most grave and massive crimes in international law: genocide, crimes against humanity, and serious war crimes (see Appendix 2 for an explanation of the concepts of genocide and crimes against humanity). Cases of mass atrocities include the Holocaust and the genocides in Cambodia, Rwanda, and Bosnia. The large scale and extreme gravity of such crimes leave behind a legacy with which individuals and societies, institutions, and organizations can struggle for decades.

This study is focused on the time *after* the violence has been brought to an end. "After" connotes that something is finished, over, or done with. Yet, although mass killings have been stopped, camps have been opened, and restitution has been offered, the past is often still intensely alive long after the actual atrocities take place—in the lives of the survivors, bystanders, and perpetrators, as well as in the postconflict societies in which they live.[4] The blurred borders between past and present also mean that one should take care not to adopt a too narrow perspective on victims' resentment. The cluster of violations that evoke their resentment may involve more than the granting of amnesties, the violations of human rights, denial and forgetfulness, and the attitudes that government institutions and societies may direct toward the victims when reconciliation is on the agenda. In various ways, the resentment occasioned by such postatrocity conditions is connected to the resentment related to the original atrocities. Whereas the legitimacy or propriety of outrage in response to the horrors of mass atrocity is beyond question, it is more difficult to gain clarity about the moral nature and value of responses to the policies and attitudes of the aftermath. Is it not, at some point, legitimate or appropriate to expect victims of mass atrocity to overcome their resentment against perpetrators? Communities can lose patience with survivors and relatives who seem stuck in grievances or who appear to nurse their victimhood (perhaps for political reasons). At some point, societies can tire of survivors' talk of the past and demands on the present.[5] Their rage, some may say, *was* understandable, but it has had its time. Prosecutions were necessary and legitimate, but after several decades prosecutorial zeal may come to be seen as merely the expression of sheer vengeance.[6] "Now" it is time to let go; true grief and anger have an end. The past cannot be changed anyway, and it is more reasonable to accept loss and begin to look ahead. Indeed, the passing of time often seems to explain or justify the changing of attitudes. Indeed Chapter 9 focuses on the moral significance of the passing of time.

A study of conflicting normative perspectives on emotions and attitudes might seem completely irrelevant to the concerns that are central to studies of transitional justice and reconciliation after political mass violence. Indeed, the emotional aspects of transitions are a neglected area, and this book seeks to establish a recognition of the role of emotions in the transitional justice literature.[7]

Over the last couple of decades, the question how emerging democracies should address mass violations of human rights in their pasts has become the subject of a global conversation. A continuously growing scholarly literature of transitional justice studies addresses the hard choices facing such societies. At the same time, the topic is eminently practical and political and of concern to practitioners as well as occupying powers, foreign ministries, and policy institutes. An interdisciplinary scholarly undertaking, transitional justice as a discipline is still under development. Its emergence is related to the upsurge of innovative legal institutions, most prominently the truth commissions and the international criminal tribunals in South America, Africa, and Europe.[8] Because the field is focused on institutions, justice, law, policies, and instruments, it seems mainly to call for legal and sociological studies, policy papers, and the like. However, whether one considers the discourses of the practitioners or the scholarly works on transitions and reconciliation, it is clear that emotions—and the politics or therapy of the emotions—do matter.

Most discussions of how societies can deal with past mass atrocity share the assumption that people who have been seriously wronged will be seething with a lust for revenge. This lust is commonly pictured as manifesting in *cycles* of hatred, violence, or revenge,[9] which is one reason why the transformation of victims' emotional responses to injustice and injury is a central concern of efforts to promote reconciliation after mass atrocity. Yet, even though recent empirical studies of what victims desire in the aftermath of mass atrocity do mention revenge, it is only one such want or desire: victims also demand to know the truth of what happened, public acknowledgment of the criminal nature of the events, and legal punishment for the perpetrators (Stover 2003, Walker 2006). Thus, the importance given to the picture of the victim craving revenge is empirically misleading and testifies to the need for a much closer examination of the nature and significance of emotions like outrage and resentment. Moreover, across the field one often finds the use of therapeutic language and aspirations.[10] The "wounds" caused by past atrocity have to be "cleansed," and the goal is often thought of as the healing of victims and societies. More precisely, notions of the overcoming or taming of emotion inform many conceptions of the process of reconciliation.

Therefore, one can talk of *alchemies* of reconciliation, because notions of cathartic emotional transmutations sometimes seem more like wishful thinking than conceivable outcomes.[11] For example, both trials and truth commissions have been pictured as vehicles of emotional healing and cathartic transformation. It is commonly hoped that trials will channel or placate victims' and relatives' retributive emotions. For example, the Victims' Trust Fund of the International Criminal Court claims that trials are beneficial, because (among other things) they can express the community's abhorrence of the atrocities committed and "can placate a victim's desire for vengeance."[12] Or, as Antonio Cassese, former president of the International Criminal Tribunal for the Former Yugoslavia (ICTY), has said, when lobbying in 1994 for the tribunal before the General Assembly of the UN, "Only international justice can dissolve the poisonous fumes of resentment and suspicion, and put to rest the lust for revenge" (Landgren 1998). The religious-redemptive discourse cultivated by Desmond Tutu during his time as the chair of the TRC exemplifies an even more extravagant project of emotional transformation. That is, its ideal was that of victims *overcoming* their anger and desires for revenge, not appeasing them by retribution.

Despite the many references to emotions, the understanding of resentment and other negative emotional attitudes is typically tied to rationalist, therapeutic, or moralist accounts that do not give these attitudes their due. What permeates contemporary discussions of responses to mass atrocity is a consensus that one needs to *deal* with the dangerous and undesirable emotions in question. Political leaders, commissioners, and presidents of criminal tribunals often talk of the goal of "closure": the shutting of the door on the past in order to move into a more "glorious" future. The task is to release societies and individuals from the ongoing threats or emotional remainders of the past: the cycle of violence must be broken, the guilt and shame of the perpetrators and bystanders need to be acknowledged and atoned, and the persistent grief and resentment of the surviving victims and their relatives should be brought to an end to make a "new" life possible. The question is what is needed to make possible the transition to peace, reconciliation, and a new and peaceful future.

The conceptual tags themselves of these areas of study—transitional justice, forgiveness and reconciliation, or conflict resolution—express the basic sense in which the scholarly field is guided by the possibility of restoration of trust and hope in the wake of mass atrocity. "Transitional justice histories are," as Ruti Teitel ascertains, "redemptive stories, of return, of wholeness, of political unity" (2004:219).[13] There are, of course, voices within the field that caution against this general trend. For example, Elizabeth V. Spelman warns that "a voracious appetite for fixing can lead to poor judgment about what is and what is not desirable or even possible to repair" (2003:239). In a similar vein, Martha Minow asks, "When is the language of healing itself an insult to those whose devastation is inconsolable, untellable, unassimilable?" (1998:22). As a final example, Payam Akhavan, the former legal advisor for the Prosecutors Office at the ICTY, cautions that "illusory closure can easily be sought through the ritual of legal process. To imagine that the horrors of genocide can be contained within the confines of judicial process is to trivialize suffering that defies description" (2001:8).

Still, much literature on transitions and reconciliation is animated by a spirit of repair and redemption. The appetite for fixing, the spirit of forgiveness and reconciliation, and the language of healing and recovery mean that there is little interest left to consider the possible value and legitimacy of victims' negative emotions. The recent philosophical rediscovery of emotions as sources of understanding and as partly cognitive in nature has not yet found any strong spokespersons in the context of transitional justice thinking.[14] Victims' resentment and hatred are rather cast in the rationalist image as blind forces or energies: this is where the talk of the need to "tame," "channel," or "placate" the compulsive desires in question enters. Next, when negative emotions are treated from a public health perspective, they appear as "health effects" and "healthy psychological and physical functioning requires [their] overcoming" (Halpern and Weinstein 2004:562). Finally, when forgiveness, healing, and reconciliation are seen as absolute and flawless goods, the advocate may assume that the problem is only how to further their realization. When anger and resentment are overcome, nothing of any positive value is left behind.

According to Barbara Herrnstein Smith, there is no illusion more powerful "than that of the inevitability and propriety of one's own beliefs and judgments" (Smith 1997:54). In her exploration of the dynamics of belief and resistance in intellectual controversies, Smith considers how the believer deals with another person's skepticism or different belief. If what I believe is good and true, then how is opposition to it possible? As Smith points out, the two favored solutions in such situations seem to be "demonology and, so to speak, dementology":

> That is, the comforting and sometimes automatic conclusion that the other fellow (skeptic, atheist, heretic, pagan, and so forth) is either a devil or a fool—or, in more (officially) enlightened terms, that he or she suffers from defects or deficiencies of character and/or intellect: ignorance, innate capacity, delusion, poor training, captivity to false doctrine, and so on (Smith 1997:xvi).

Let us apply Smith's argument to the context of mass atrocity: *if* the unforgiving and unreconciled survivors understood more about the background of the perpetrators or about what ideals and values really counted, if they were more capable of managing their anger, and if they thought more rationally about their own good or the good of the nation, *then* they would try to forgive or let go of their resentment and engage more constructively in the process of reconciliation. Relentless, backward-looking resentment must be the sign of some kind of moral failure, personal deficiency, or malfunction. In short, much talking and thinking about postconflict justice and reconciliation have

focused on a model of an idealized actor who demonstrates a readiness to forgive and reconcile and a capacity to let go of the past in order to move ahead.
It is time to examine more closely the moral nature and value of victims'
refusal to forgive, resistance to reconciliation, and preservation of resentment.
This examination should be made not only to "understand what forgiveness is
and why it is desirable" (Govier 2002:50) but also because that resistance,
refusal, and resentment are humane responses that might be preserved for
genuinely moral reasons.

Anger, Resentment, and *Ressentiment*

"Wrath—Goddess, sing the wrath of Peleus' son Achilles." As is indicated by
the first line of the *Iliad*, anger—in its variety of forms and in its relation to
virtue and justice—has been a topic of reflection since antiquity (Harris
2001:131). Questions of the nature and value of the passions or emotions in
responses to wrongdoing have deep roots in the history of ethics. Other than
when they slumbered during the heyday of positivist and analytical philosophy, philosophers and theologians have been awake to and aware of anger and
resentment as a topic of philosophical ethics since antiquity. Seneca may be
seen as representative of a Stoic and Christian approach according to which
anger is first and foremost an unmitigated evil, sickness, or sin. Of course,
there are Christian writers and theologians who have maintained a more
ambivalent message, but they constitute an exception. Desmond Tutu, as we
shall see, seems to be thinking along the lines of the dominant tradition in
which anger is a deadly vice.[15] One can place Aristotle opposite to Seneca. Like
Seneca, Aristotle acknowledged the vice of excessive anger, but he was also
cognizant of the vice tied to a lack of anger in the face of injury. Thus, one may
position Aristotle as the "founding father" of a long line of thinkers who have
argued that anger should not be seen as absolutely bad. To the contrary, they
posit that anger—when justified and appropriate—is a valuable aspect of a
virtuous person and of life in society.[16]

The concept of resentment has a distinct history and meaning in the
Anglo-American philosophy of moral emotions and attitudes. In a long tradition that includes such classical thinkers as Joseph Butler and Adam Smith
and such contemporary philosophers as Jeffrie Murphy and Richard Wallace,
resentment is seen as a legitimate and valuable form of anger responding to
perceived moral wrongs. For example, according to Butler, resentment functions as "a weapon, put into our hands by nature, against injury, injustice, and
cruelty" (1897:121). These philosophers may differ about the conditions and
circumstances under which anger or resentment is appropriate or honorable,
but one of the distinguishing features of the philosophical approach to
resentment is the drawing of a distinction between excessive and pathological

forms of anger and resentment, on the one hand, and appropriate and valuable forms, on the other hand. Let me offer this passage from Adam Smith's *Theory of the Moral Sentiments*, originally published in 1854, as an example:

> The insolence and brutality of anger, in the same manner, when we indulge in fury without check or restraint, is, of all objects, the most detestable. But we admire that noble and generous resentment which governs its pursuit of the greatest injuries, not by the rage which they are apt to excite in the breast of the sufferer, but by the indignation which they naturally call forth in that of the impartial spectator . . . which never, even in thought, attempts any greater vengeance, nor desires to inflict any greater punishment, than what every indifferent person would rejoice to see executed (Smith 1854/2000:27).[17]

Leaping ahead to present-day philosophers, Jeffrie Murphy has argued that "resentment stands as emotional testimony that we care about ourselves and our rights" (2003:19). Not to have resentment when our rights are violated "conveys—emotionally—either that we do not think we have rights or that we do not take our rights very seriously" (Murphy and Hampton 1988:17). This does not mean that resentment may not be unjustified or that it should never be overcome, but rather that it should not be condemned in principle; it allows for the argument that resentment can be transcended too hastily or even wrongly. In Murphy's and several other philosophers' works, resentment is also seen to play a valuable social-ethical role. According to Richard Wallace, in expressing emotions like resentment we are not just venting feelings of anger and vindictiveness; rather, "we are demonstrating our commitment to certain moral standards, as regulative of social life" (1994:69). In a similar vein, Margaret Walker aims to provide an explanatory account of the moral work done by resentment in interpersonal and social relationships. According to Walker, resentment is not simply about injuries to oneself; the resentful person is not necessarily self-preoccupied. Resentment is an accusing anger that responds to threats or perceived violations of norms. A person showing resentment not only expresses an inner turmoil but also invites a response:

> The "aim" of resentment is, ideally, to activate protective, reassuring, or defensive responses in some individuals, or in a community that can affirm that the victim is within the scope of that community's protective responsibilities, or that the resenter is in fact competent in grasping and applying the community's shared norms. The transgressor can reassure the wronged party, and also the community by "getting the message": she might respond with acceptance of rebuke, with

evidence of remorse or shame, and might offer apology or amends (Walker 2006b:135).

Resentment, as it is used in this book, is distinguished not by how it feels, but by the way in which those who account for their feeling make reference to perceived injustice, injury, or violation. Thus construed, resentment is not defined by a certain (low-state) kind of emotional intensity, but can range from a momentary irritation to outrage.

The contrast between these philosophical perspectives and the talk of anger and resentment as dehumanizing forces—corrosive of humane relationships—is marked. Spanning the differences separating the approaches of the philosophers discussed here is an understanding of resentment as being part and parcel of living in humane relationships. Probably, the main source of this conception is a very influential essay by Peter F. Strawson. As Strawson put it, "Being involved in inter-personal relationships as we normally understand them precisely is being exposed to the range of reactive attitudes and feelings [i.e. resentment, indignation, gratitude etc.]" (1974:11). He argues that it is possible to adopt what he calls an "objective attitude" to the other human being; that is, to see the other person as an object of social policy, a subject for treatment, as something to be dealt with or cured. Relating to the other in such "objectivizing" ways precludes reactive attitudes like resentment. However, doing so also means not relating to the other as a fellow human being: "If your attitude towards someone is wholly objective, then though you may fight him, you cannot quarrel with him, and though you may talk to him, even negotiate with him, you cannot reason with him" (Strawson 1974:9). In other words, being susceptible to anger or resentment is inextricably tied to participation in "the general framework of human life." A social life bereft of resentment is an impossible and, insofar as it is imaginable, impoverished life.

Resentment is an ambiguous term, not just because resentment itself, as well as the anger of which it is a specific kind, can appear in so many different guises but also because of the kinship between resentment and *ressentiment*. Our understanding of the concept of *ressentiment* is strongly colored by Nietzsche's picture of the loathsome and pathological "man of *ressentiment*" in *On the Genealogy of Morals* (Nietzsche 1887). *Ressentiment* connotes self-poisoning, hypersensitivity, deceitfulness, and emotions like vindictiveness, hatred, malice, spite, and envy. Nietzsche coined the term "the man of *ressentiment*," but the type has also been described vividly in Dostoyevsky's *Notes From the Underground* (1864/1993). Here we find the "mouse-man" wallowing in a self-poisoning preoccupation with the past (11):

There, in its loathsome, stinking underground, our offended, beaten-down, and derided mouse at once immerses itself in cold, venomous, and, above all, everlasting spite. For forty years on end it will recall its offense to the last, most shameful details, each time adding even more shameful details of its own, spitefully taunting and chafing itself with its fantasies. It will be ashamed of its fantasies, but all the same it will recall everything, go over everything, heap all sorts of figments on itself, under the pretext that they, too, could have happened, and forgive nothing.

To speak of "resentment" in English is sometimes to speak of "*ressentiment*" (cf. Wallace 1994:247, n. 17). At the same time, the case for resentment has in part been argued by distancing it from *ressentiment*. As Jeffrie Murphy puts it, "*Ressentiment* is, by definition, an irrational and base passion. It means, roughly, 'spiteful and malicious envy.' It thus makes no sense to speak of rational or justified or honorable *ressentiment*" (Murphy 1999:152). Whereas there is certainly a case to be argued for resentment, it seems nearly absurd to try something similar with regard to *ressentiment* or with regard to the moral standing of its holders.

This brings us to Jean Améry and a point that has not been discussed in Anglo-American discussions of his reasoning. In the generally cogent English translation of his works provided by Sidney and Stella P. Rosenfeld and in Anglo-American discussions of Améry, "resentment" is the key term. However, in the original German text Améry uses the term *ressentiment*—this emotion is what he unabashedly harbors and what he sets out to examine and to justify. He even describes himself as a self-professed man of *ressentiment*. As he puts it: "a less rewarding business of confession cannot be imagined" (Améry 1999:64). The English translation of *ressentiment* as resentment can hide the distinct and more negative connotations that are deliberately embraced by Améry. However, reading Améry, it soon becomes clear that the *ressentiments* to be justified are claimed to be of a "special kind," known by "neither Nietzsche nor Max Scheler" (1999:71). In several respects, Améryean *ressentiments* seem close to the morally legitimate and socially valuable emotion conceptualized as resentment in the moral philosophical works mentioned above. At the same time, his reasoning also reveals certain affinities to *ressentiment* as conceived by Nietzsche and Scheler.

Therefore, in this book, I position Améryean *ressentiments between* the familiar concepts of resentment and *ressentiment*. A principal objective of Part Two is to attain clarity about the nature and value of these Améryean *ressentiments*. Améry's reflections generally manifest a tension between conventional vocabulary and the particular experiences and situation that he wants to conceptualize as precisely as possible. In his effort to address his contemporaries, Améry picks up conventional concepts (apparently applicable to him and his "kind") in order to turn them around until they come to capture more adequately the particularities of the Nazi crimes or the survivor's condition during and after the Holocaust.

All during the process of writing this book, I wondered whether to coin a new term (e.g., "ressentment" or "resentiment") to mark clearly the focus on that "something" on which Améry stands between the philosophical concept of resentment and Nietzschean notions of *ressentiment*. Using either of these terms is both partly appropriate and partly misleading, and in Chapter 14 I explain why. However, I needed to make a choice of terminology. In the close examination of Améry's reflections, I use the term he actually used—*"ressentiment"*—while consistently amending the English translation on this single point. Yet, in the chapters that do not focus on Améry's thinking, I use the term "resentment." That is, for the more general discussion of the ambiguities and moral aspects of victims' resentment, "resentment" is a more capacious and appropriate term (and thus is included in the title of this book).

Philosophy on the Border

As should be clear by now, the sources I draw from to explore Améry and the South African case are quite varied and include the following: Holocaust and genocide studies; studies in international law and the ethics of criminal law; psychological literature on trauma and recovery; works on transitional justice and studies of reconciliation processes, restorative justice, forgiveness, and the South African TRC in particular; the critical reception and discussion of the works of Jean Améry; the history of postwar Germany; and finally a host of testimonies and reflections by surviving victims of genocide and crimes against humanity. Of course, my examination of the topic is also informed by sources from the philosophical tradition. I draw on the works of a range of philosophers who have all written on the moral nature and value of the reactive emotions and attitudes to being wronged: anger, indignation, resentment, and forgiveness. Despite a number of differences, these sources share an intention to deepen and widen our understanding of negative reactive emotions and attitudes and to contradict hastily drawn pictures of the goodness of forgiveness and the badness of resentment. Several scholars—Lawrence Langer, James E. Young, and Katharina von Kellenbach—have questioned the validity and desirability of the language or logic of repair and redemption, forgiveness, and reconciliation in responses to the Holocaust. These works have all been of significant inspirational value to the inquiry. Hence, although my own background is in philosophy and in ethics in particular, *Resentment's Virtue* is not a philosophical study in any narrow sense. I have tried to write a book that is accessible to those who are interested in the given ethical issues and that cuts across what sometimes seems like gaps between empirical studies and philosophical reflection.

Unlike many philosophical books, the present one pays a lot of attention to concrete contexts and to the untidy reflections of a person whose essays have never been reprinted in a single anthology of philosophical papers. I chose the contextual approach—philosophy from the bottom up, as one might put it—for two reasons. The first one has to do with how best to think about emotions and attitudes. Even though it is possible and desirable to consider general features of resentment or the unwillingness to forgive, our understanding of the dynamics and value of these and other emotions and attitudes would benefit from case studies. Martha Nussbaum is among several philosophers who have argued that the questions we are most likely to ask about the emotions are inherently domain or case specific (cf. Bandes 1999). Does, for example, the relentlessly unforgiving victim have the right view of the situation and what is at stake in it? As Nussbaum writes, such questions "will usually be asked well only in the concrete. Anger as a whole is neither reliable or unreliable, reasonable or unreasonable; it is only the specific anger of a specific person at a specific object that can coherently be deemed unreasonable" (Nussbaum 1999:21). At the same time, as Nussbaum continues, some emotions seem "always suspect or problematic" (21). Because *ressentiment* is one of those emotions, it is interesting to consider whether Améry is able to demonstrate successfully the need for a redefinition and reevaluation of *ressentiment*.

The second reason why I chose my approach has to do with the extreme aspects of the subject matter. Primo Levi wrote that if the Nazi camps had lasted longer, "a new, harsh language would have been born" (1987:113). One cannot presume that conventional conceptualizations and categories can do justice to the phenomena and problems related to genocide. Hence, the scholar wishing to write about subjects related to mass murder needs to adopt a probing and tentative approach to existing vocabularies and at least be informed by the reflections of people who have faced atrocities or their legacies first hand. Professional philosophers who would like to contribute to the interdisciplinary study of responses to mass atrocities cannot assume that they have something deep or helpful to add only on the basis of their extensive readings in the academic philosophical literature. What has been said about the philosophical study of the Holocaust applies, I think, to philosophical studies of crimes against humanity and their legacies in general: although philosophers are neither trained nor commonly inclined to reckon with detail and particularity, that is exactly what is required here.[18] And it is required not as pedagogical illustrations or as examples on which a normative ethical theory can be tested, but rather as the concrete occasions for philosophical reflection. Hannah Arendt once said that every thought is an *afterthought,* and to the extent that this book is an exercise in philosophical ethics, it is not "applied ethics," but ethical afterthoughts on victims' resentment and resistance to forgiveness.

I am not an enemy of philosophical abstraction or the articulation of theoretical frameworks. Simply, the point I make here is that the philosophical examination of concepts, distinctions, moral issues, and frameworks has to pass through a consideration of the particular and concrete.[19] The problem is not abstraction as such, but rather what Berel Lang has called the *flight* into abstraction (2005:181). However, this book claims that the reflections of Améry are relevant to thinking about resentment and reconciliation in the aftermath of mass atrocities more generally. Offhand, this claim might itself be thought to imply an indulgence in hasty abstractions and equalizations of what is very unequal. That is, one may argue that the historical context and trends against which Améry fought are incomparable to the situations of victims in current postconflict societies; that his reflections are solely relevant to an illumination of the condition of the Nazi survivor (because of the unique features of the Nazi genocide); and indeed that to try to use his reflections in relation to a broader discussion of mass atrocities is even offensive insofar as it subsumes the Holocaust as "no more" than a mass atrocity among others. Or, finally and from an opposite perspective, one may assert that this claim is counterproductive in relation to a practical agenda because attention to the Holocaust will undermine the book's comparative relevance ("these other cases are not as bad, so . . ."). Obviously, I do not think that any of these objections apply to the present undertaking. The proof lies in the quality of the following chapters, but I also touch on the relevance of Améry's reflections in the transition between the two parts of the book and in the final chapter.

Book Outline

The study is divided into two parts. Part One explores how resentful and unforgiving victims, appearing before the Truth and Reconciliation Commission of South Africa, were seen and treated by prominent representatives and staff of the commission. The attention is primarily directed toward the "reconciliators" and their understandings of emotions and attitudes as colliding with the commission's promotion of forgiveness and reconciliation. Drawing on transcripts of the hearings of the TRC as well as on the writings of some of its spokesmen, the chapters seek to demonstrate how the reconciliators characterized victims' resistance to forgiveness and how they responded to resistance when it was explicitly articulated. This examination differs from most existing philosophical reflections on the commission in its attempt to cut across what sometimes seems like a gap between empirical studies and philosophical commentary. Thus, the exploration begins in the actual hearings of the commission and ends in the writings of its chair, Desmond Tutu. I argue that the TRC neglected or denied in various ways the moral nature and legitimacy of victims' anger and unwillingness to forgive.

The praise heaped on forgiving victims often included vilifications of the imagined alternative. Concrete resistance expressed during the hearings—for example, by victims who stated their refusal to forgive or reconcile—would sometimes be met with pressure by commissioners eager to move the victims in the direction that would fulfill the mandate of the commission. Although no one was forced to forgive, the TRC policed and directed the display of emotions and attitudes to conform with its mandate. Moving from the hearings to writings by some of its most prominent spokesmen, focus is turned to an essay by Charles Villa-Vicencio (who served as the head of the TRC's research unit), I show how therapeutic language can reduce victims' anger to trauma, a mental problem of the victim, and a sign of self-preoccupation; in other words, something that the traumatized person should deal with for his or her own sake to be able to move on and take responsibility as a co-citizen. Furthermore, in the writings of Desmond Tutu, resentment and desires for retribution appear as completely destructive and dehumanizing forces that should be "avoided like the plague." The ostensibly total disqualification of resentment seems premised on an absolute notion of social harmony that is completely devoid of conflict. It goes together with what can be called a "boosterism" of forgiveness.

The second—and longer—part unfolds as a thorough interpretation of an essay entitled "*Ressentiments*," published originally in Germany in 1966 by the writer and Holocaust survivor, Jean Améry, and included in the 1999 collection of essays, *At the Mind's Limits: Contemplations by a Survivor on Auschwitz and Its Realities.* The shift from Part One to Two brings with it a shift of geographical and historical context as well as a change of perspective. Whereas Part One was primarily occupied with the voice and reflections of those trying to encourage others to forgive and reconcile, Part Two gives voice to the victim: a shift, in other words, from the third- to the first-person perspective on resentment and unforgiveness. Challenging commonly held beliefs in the moral superiority of the forgiving person, Améry casts the preservation and voicing of resentment in the face of social pressure and in spite of the passing of time as a moral and humane accomplishment. A bias toward the future and a concern about self-preservation might be natural, but as moral beings, human beings should be expected not to simply move on as if they were a piece of unaffected nature or nothing but a part of the social body. Améry builds his case on a certain picture of the moral person and of the relationship among morality, society, and nature. He aims to show that we should respect, not chastise, the person who preserves resentment when moral repair fails to be achieved and when the voicing of resistance invites demonizing and pathologizing social responses. This kind of resentment should not be considered a moral taint on the person nor should it be reduced to an illness to be treated. Resentment can also be the reflex expression of an honorable emotional response to inexpiable evil or wrongs and legitimate moral expectations that have not been properly dealt with.

I initially chose to examine Améry's essay, "*Ressentiments,*" because of its significant value as a challenge to current studies of transitional justice and reconciliation. However, in addition to its contribution to the overall aims of this book, the purpose of Part Two is also to contribute to a more comprehensive understanding of Améry's thinking. Considering the existing critical reception of Améry's essay, one has the impression that the interpreters have read at least two entirely different essays. I try to show that these interpretations have not accounted for the ambiguities suffusing the essay and hope to open the reader to a dialectical understanding that is sensitive to the tensions within Améry's reflections.

Having to settle on a given organization of the book, I faced the dilemma whether to begin with the reading of Améry or with the exploration of the TRC. Reasons for beginning with Améry included not only the obvious beauty of following the historical timeline but, more important, of also being able to use insights drawn from Améry's reflections more explicitly in the examination of the TRC. Yet, obviously the reasons for commencing with the examination of the TRC turned out to be weightier. They included a pedagogical preference to begin and end the book in the present; the narrative "charms" of moving from a well-known case to a widely unknown treasure and from the well-known voices of prominent advocates of forgiveness to the seldom heard voice of the resentful and unforgiving victim. Moreover, the exploration of the South African case is tied to this introduction as the particular to the general. It reveals, in a more concrete way, a lack or a deficiency in the discourse of forgiveness and reconciliation, and it *exposes* the fact that the negative emotions and attitudes need a fairer hearing. In this way, the examination in Part One is meant to show in more detail why it is so important to dwell on the "negative" emotions and to bother with Améry's untidy and contra-intuitive perspective. However, in order to compensate for the postponement of the investigation of the "negative" emotions, and in order to at least provide the reader with a rough sense of the meaning of "resentment" and related concepts, I added the previous section "Anger, Resentment, and *Ressentiment.*"

Originally, I had planned to write a rather more traditional philosophical work offering a systematical philosophical argument and, in conclusion, a synthetic philosophical account of the moral significance of resentment in an ethics of reconciliation. That did not happen. The contextual analysis and critique came to occupy the ground. However, for the reasons mentioned above, I am convinced that the book *begins* where it should begin. It is a necessary first exploration on the basis of which might be constructed a more general framework or an ethics of reconciliation. Of course there is always more to be done, but as the Danish philosopher Søren Kierkegaard once insisted, when you want to build a house, you had better begin with the foundation.

I

Revisiting The Truth and Reconciliation Commission of South Africa

> *I refuse not to be angry and cannot forgive. What is even more difficult is to have someone tell me I should not still feel like this.*
>
> BRIAN MPHAHLELE, APARTHEID VICTIM†

---

† Cited in Verdoolaege Annelies. 2006. Managing reconciliation at the human rights violations hearings of the South African TRC. T. Cushman and T. Brudholm eds. 2006. *Human Rights and Negative Emotions: Special issue of Journal of Human Rights* 5 (1): 61–80.

2

Commissioning Anger

On the side of the victims, the benefits are undeniable in therapeutic, moral, and political terms, all together. Families who fought for years to know the facts were able to express their pain, vent their hatred in the presence of the offenders and before the witnesses. At the price of long hearings, they had an opportunity to tell of tortures and to name the criminals. . . . In offering public space for complaints and the recounting of suffering, the commission certainly gave rise to a shared katharsis.

(RICOEUR 2004:483–84)

I cannot begin to describe the rage I feel and have felt for the past years at her senseless killing. . . . I have not been able, despite extensive therapy and counseling, to shed the anger, rage, guilt, feelings of revenge and helpless desperation at the system that allows murderers to escape punishment.

(GRAYBILL 2002:45)[1]

Re-Viewing a Miracle

Scholars arguing the case for forgiveness or restorative justice have often expressed high praise for the Truth and Reconciliation Commission (TRC) of South Africa and the chairmanship of Desmond Tutu. Those arguing on Christian grounds are particularly praiseful, and the excerpt above from Paul Ricoeur's 2004 book, *Memory, History, Forgetting* can easily be supplemented with others stressing the nearly miraculous nature of the institution and its moral voice. For example, according to Mark R. Amstutz the TRC provides a unique context in which to explore "the quest for reconciliation through the miracle of forgiveness" (2006:182). Indeed, Amstutz declares his agreement with the assessment of another proponent of forgiveness, L. Gregory Jones, that the TRC process was "one of the most dramatic and hopeful signs of an authentically Christian contribution to political life to emerge in many years" (as cited in Amstutz 2006).[2] However, these assessments gloss over the grievances of families who fought for years to secure the prosecution and punishment of people responsible for murder, torture, and other gross human rights violations. Out of focus are also the many victims to whom participation in the hearings was a mixed blessing or a cause of deep frustration.

Yet, the rhetoric of cathartic relief or closure, which has been influential in securing support for international criminal tribunals, no less than truth commissions, is in both cases difficult to reconcile with actual surveys of victims' experiences with witnessing and truth-telling. For example, according to the Trauma Center for Victims of Violence and Torture in Cape Town, some 60 percent of those who testified in the TRC felt *worse* after testifying (cited in Shaw 2005).[3] Drawing on examples from the actual hearings of the TRC as well as on empirical studies and examinations of commissioners' writings, in Part One, I hope to cut across what sometimes seems like a gap between empirical social science and the overly optimistic assessments of philosophical and theological studies such as those referred to above.

More substantially, Part One provides a critical analysis of the place of anger and resentment in the TRC of South Africa by addressing the following questions: During the hearings, how were various kinds of anger, as well as those who refused to forgive, represented and treated? Were dissent and attitudes that collided with the praise of forgiveness treated as morally respectable possibilities? Were victims pressured to forgive? And how have these topics been treated in the speeches and writings of prominent and influential actors among the commissioners?

The examination of these questions concretizes the more sweeping assertions and broad perspectives of Chapter 1 and also demonstrates why we need to consider in such detail Jean Améry's thoughts on the victim's resentments and opposition to forgiveness. I hope that Part One also contributes to a critical examination of the advocacy of forgiveness by the TRC as well as of the moral leadership and language provided by Desmond Tutu. Yet, as a caveat, let me stress that the assessments of particular aspects of the proceedings and writings presented in Chapters 3 through 6 should not be taken as comprehensive conclusions about the TRC model or the TRC as a whole. These chapters focus mainly on the therapeutic and the religious-redemptive perspectives on forgiveness and resentment. Yet, the TRC was a huge and complex undertaking, involving around 360 people and several mutually inconsistent modes of discourse and practice. Commissioners and staff with different backgrounds and concerns (e.g., human rights advocates, lawyers, and theologians) often disagreed about key issues. In short, the main purpose of Part One is not to provide an overall assessment of the TRC, but rather to bring out for examination how the advocacy of forgiveness (even in a much-celebrated case) *can* fail the victims or their relatives in various crucial ways.[4]

The analysis of anger and unforgiving victims in the TRC context is divided into four chapters. Chapter 3 examines the actual hearings of the TRC, and Chapters 4 and 5 focus on subsequent writings by two of the most prominent leaders and theologians of the commission: Desmond Tutu, its chairman, and Charles Villa-Vicencio, the head of the commission's research unit. In Chapter 6, the final chapter of Part One, I consider whether the TRC promoted forgiveness in a way that caused new resentment in the victims. Chapter 6 also examines the way in which the Constitutional Court of South Africa characterized the resentment of the victims who persisted in their pleas for punishment. The reasoning of the court appears, or so I argue, to be a more sensitive and balanced alternative in comparison with the TRC discourse. The next section of this chapter provides a brief overview of the TRC, just detailed enough to set the scene for the purposes of this book.

The Truth and Reconciliation Commission of South Africa

From 1948 until 1993, an apartheid regime of systematic oppression and segregation ruled South Africa. Racial discrimination had been prevalent for centuries, but after 1948 it became an integral part of a legal system in which gross violations of human rights flourished. Apartheid was only dismantled through a long process of violence and negotiation. In 1993, difficult political negotiations between the African National Congress and the government of F.W. de Klerk led to an interim constitution that took effect with the first free elections in South Africa in April 1994. In 1995, the new parliament passed the Promotion of National Unity and Reconciliation Act, which created the Truth and Reconciliation Commission.[5] The TRC was mandated to provide a public record of past human rights violations (from the Sharpeville Massacre in 1960 until 1994), to grant amnesty to perpetrators, and to provide recommendations to the government concerning reparations to the victims. Given the way in which the provision of amnesty is sometimes presented as part of a superior form of justice (restorative justice), it is important to recognize that originally the amnesty provision was rather a necessary political compromise between the Nationalist Party and the African National Congress. Yet, in contrast to the general or blanket amnesties (e.g., known from several South American countries), the amnesties granted by the TRC were based on individual applications and were tied to the satisfaction of certain criteria related to the nature of the acts and the degree of disclosure offered by the amnesty applicant (remorse and apology were not required). Thus, the amnesty procedure introduced in South Africa was conditional and individualized. The interim constitution mandated this ground-breaking procedure, stating that "in order to advance . . . reconciliation and reconstruction, amnesty shall be granted in respect of acts, omissions and offences associated with political objectives and committed in the course of the conflicts of the past" (Interim Constitution 1993).

Desmond Tutu was appointed chair of the seventeen-member commission. The Commissioners and additional staff served on one of three committees, which each had separate responsibilities. The Human Rights Violations Committee was mandated to gather information about the human rights abuses of the past and to determine whom to register as victims. The public hearings of victim testimonies conducted by this committee became the most prominent face of the TRC in the media. The hearings were charged with emotional tensions, and the evils that were revealed publicly were truly horrible. In *Unspeakable Truths* Priscilla Hayner describes the three-and-one-half page single-spaced data entry list used by the TRC for a systematic registry of different categories of violations:

> The list begins with *forcible abduction, amputation,* and *beating of head against a wall,* and continues on to *pulling out of teeth, removal of fingernails, being dragged behind moving vehicle, being buried alive,* and *being burned with chemicals*—and that's all just on the first page. Another 150 terms follow on the next pages: *deprivation of sleep, head submerged in water, intentional spreading of disease, being forced to watch the torture of others, genital mutilation, gang rape, suspensions of weights from genitals, decapitation, burning of body parts,* and *disembowelment* (Hayner 2002:151).

Such acts—and many others like them—were vividly and painstakingly recalled and recounted during the hearings of the TRC. The Human Rights Committee considered more than 21,000 written victim statements and conducted a series of 160 hearings of about 2,000 victims and witnesses around the country. The opportunity for victims or relatives to relate their own accounts of the violations of the past was seen as essential to the achievement of one of the main objectives of the TRC: the restoration of the human and civil dignity of those who had been wronged. The victims were not cross-examined, and efforts were made to ensure that they were treated with dignity and compassion (cf. Phelps 2004:109 and Verdooelage 2006).

Judges led the Amnesty Committee, which was given the task to facilitate the granting of amnesty according to certain principles. As indicated by the slogan "amnesty for truth," perpetrators of politically motivated human rights violations could apply for amnesty if they gave full disclosure of all relevant facts related to their case; acts committed for personal gain or out of personal malice against the victim were not eligible for amnesty. Numbers vary somewhat depending on the calculation methods used, but approximately 7,116 persons applied for amnesty, of whom 1,312 were granted amnesty by the TRC. Once granted amnesty, ex-perpetrators are immune from criminal prosecution and cannot be sued for damages.

Finally, the Committee on Reparations and Rehabilitation was responsible for making recommendations to the government and other sectors of society on measures to provide reparations to victims of apartheid. The work of this committee has been easier to overlook because it did not have the media appeal of victim testimonies and perpetrator confessions, but the question how to secure appropriate monetary and symbolic reparations to individuals and communities was—and remains—contested and significant. That is, measures of repair and rehabilitation were seen as an important counterpoint to the granting of amnesty. The government's reluctance to grant reparations has generated widespread criticism, not the least because of the asymmetry between the immediate benefits of amnesty to the perpetrators and the cuts and delays in provisions of repair to the victims.

In October 1998, the TRC handed over the five-volume *Truth and Reconciliation Commission of South Africa Report* to Nelson Mandela. Two volumes based on the findings of amnesty hearings conducted after 1998 have been added since. The report states that victims should be provided with "the necessary space to air their grievances and give voice to previously denied feelings (vol. 1, chapter 5, para. 48). Moreover, that the resistance and hostility of some victims, directed at time at the Commission itself, required understanding and respect," and that "victims justifiably insisted that they were not prepared to forgive" (ibid.). However, these statements are undermined immediately because they are followed by the suggestion that resistance to forgiveness is premised on a wrongheaded notion of forgiveness as implying forgetting (para. 49/50). The report does not consider the possibility that forgiving could in some instances be wrong or that forgiveness may not be the most promising way to recovery for all victims.

The main work of the TRC was completed with the handing over of the report in 1998, but the Amnesty Committee did not finish operations until mid-2001 and the TRC did not end formally until December 2001. Still, there remains much unfinished business. Even a cursory glance at the public debate in the South African press (around 2006) reveals unsettled questions about the provision of reparations and the criminal prosecutions of TRC-related cases. Police generals, military men, and others who should be prosecuted enjoy retirement in freedom, and apartheid victims have brought compensation claims against multinational companies (cf. Carter 2006 and Terreblanche 2006).

3

The Hearings

*Many indeed most of those who have suffered and who have come to
testify before the Commission have amazed us—have amazed the
world with their readiness to forgive with their nobility and generosity
of spirit. They are the people who have made possible the miracle that
is this new South Africa.*

DESMOND TUTU, OPENING STATEMENT IN THE HUMAN RIGHTS VIOLATION
HEARING, JUNE 18, 1996[1]

*Commissioners never missed an opportunity to praise witnesses who
did not express any desire for revenge. . . . The hearings were structured
in such a way that any expression of a desire for revenge would seem
out of place. Virtues of forgiveness and reconciliation were so loudly
and roundly applauded that emotions of vengeance, hatred and
bitterness were rendered unacceptable, an ugly intrusion on a peaceful,
healing process.*

(R. WILSON 2001:120)

"This Is Not a Court of Law"

Truth and reconciliation commissions are often claimed to be more
victim-friendly than criminal trials. Indeed, being cross-examined
by Slobodan Milosovic or simply being exposed to the intrinsic
harshness of the adversarial criminal justice process is not likely to be
"healing" to participating victims. In criminal courts, victims' testimony is
constantly cut short, and they are asked to focus on the forensic details.
Indeed, the main reason for their presence in court is not to tell their story
and have it validated publicly, but rather to provide a piece of the evidence
in relation to which the question of the guilt or innocence of the defendant may be decided. At the same time, genocide trials from Nuremberg
to The Hague have been blessed or plagued, depending on one's point of
view, with the practical repercussions of trying to do much more than
achieve justice in the traditional sense of determining guilt and providing
a sentence. In addition to this most basic task, different genocide trials
have to different degrees pursued other ambitions: to provide a history lesson to a given nation or country, to contribute to reconciliation, or to be
a cathartic or healing force for participating victims and societies at large.

In several cases, the pursuit of pedagogic, therapeutic, or political objectives has resulted in a loosening of ordinary rules of relevance and evidence, which has had both positive and negative effects on witnesses. On the one hand, this loosening has allowed more victims to bear witness in a wider sense than would otherwise have been possible. On the other hand, loose rules of evidence also give more free rein for an aggressive defense to harass witnessing victims on the basis of hearsay, dubious character assessments, and inflammatory material (cf. Landsman 2005). Perhaps, the criminal trial is inherently not a victim-friendly setting.[2]

Therefore, some advocates have looked to truth commissions as a more victim-friendly forum. Raquel Aldana (2006:108) summarizes these proponents' arguments, which claim that victims regain their dignity through a restorative process that "(1) invites victims to tell their story in an open and receptive environment, (2) reveals a comprehensive truth of what transpired, and (3) promotes reconciliation between perpetrators and victims."

At the Human Rights Violations (HRV) hearings of the TRC, the differences between the TRC's treatment of victims and the experience of witnesses at a criminal trial were emphasized repeatedly. The TRC commissioners welcomed the victims personally. The witnesses were not cross-examined, and they were allowed to pose questions directly to the perpetrators. Witnesses were told that the purpose of the actual proceedings was to help them regain their dignity, allow them to provide testimony, and receive official and public acknowledgment of their suffering. As the TRC Report put it, the emphasis was on "the validation of the individual subjective experience of people who had previously been silenced or voiceless" (1998:111). As one commissioner told a victim: "Now, please be free. This is not a court of law; it's just a place where you want to come and ventilate your truth" (Verdoolaege 2006:67).

Yet, the fact that the commission was not a court of law did not mean that it did not praise, remind, encourage and discourage, admonish, and guide the victims according to its values, actors, and rituals. According to anthropologist Richard Wilson (2001), for several months the TRC routinely asked the victims at the end of their testimony whether or not they forgave their perpetrators.[3] As Annelies Verdoolaege (2006:74) notes, "A manual counting of all of the HRV hearings suggests that in about 70% of the testimonies the concept of reconciliation was either evoked by the commissioners themselves, or the commissioners urged the victims to express a willingness to forgive and reconcile." When victims in public appearances did deviate from the pro-forgiveness party line, they were guided back by the commissioners.[4]

This chapter brings to light some of the ways in which the discourse and practices of the TRC actively discouraged and denounced victims' display of resentment and refusals to forgive. The chapter is divided into two parts. First, it presents an analysis of how commissioners characterized the alternative to the willingness to forgive. The second part examines the TRC's responses to victims who explicitly refused to forgive or reconcile.[5]

Forgiving and Its Alternatives

During the HRV hearings, victims and relatives who expressed their willingness to transcend anger and desires for retribution in order to forgive or reconcile were regularly praised publicly as magnificent models of the kind of generosity that South Africa needed. As evidenced in the TRC Final Report, which stresses that forgiveness "is about seeking to forego bitterness, renouncing resentment, moving past old hurt" (1998, vol. 1, ch. 5, para. 50), the hearings proceeded on the assumption that forgiveness involves the overcoming of resentment. Thus, it is not surprising that commissioners' praise of forgiving victims is intertwined with references to the set of negative emotions supposedly foregone. Here are two examples of such praise directed to individual victims during the HRV hearings[6]:

> COMMISSIONER: I have been particularly touched by your last paragraph where you say that you are not being driven by vengeance and a desire for revenge, but you are gladdened to coming before the Commission, because you have got this quest for real reconciliation.... You have touched us and I suppose that all who have listened to you this morning are going to be equally, are being equally touched by the spirit in which you have made your submission (HRV hearing, East London, June 11, 1997).
>
> COMMISSIONER: According to your statement you do say that in spite of all this you still don't hate any one, and you don't hold any grudges against anyone, and you are prepared to forgive everyone who comes to you. That we appreciate a great deal because only a few people think that way. After all the ordeals that you have gone through you are still prepared to shake hands and talk to people and look at things positively (HRV hearing, Durban, Vryheid, April 17 1997).

The commissioners are moved not only by the positive qualities of the forgiving and conciliatory victims. Their praise is also tied closely to what the forgiving and conciliatory victims had allegedly transcended, what they were allegedly *not* driven by or what they did *not* feel, do, or desire: they did not harbor vengeance, hatred, or grudges.

A similar rhetoric runs through Desmond Tutu's writings and speeches on forgiveness, as he expresses his exhilaration at those victims of apartheid who "instead of lusting for revenge . . . had this extraordinary willingness to forgive" (Tutu 1999:86); he asks in wonder, what makes victims "ready to forgive rather than wreak vengeance?" (31). He consistently praises the readiness to forgive or reconcile; he perceives that as something touching and highly appreciated. Given the nature and contours of the imagined alternatives—hatred, bearing grudges, all-consuming bitterness, a lust for revenge, and the like—one understands his exhilaration.

An analogous rhetoric of extreme opposites is nearly endemic in religious leaders' advocacy of forgiveness. As Pope John Paul II put it in his message for the World Day of Peace, "The deadly cycle of revenge must be replaced by the new-found liberty of forgiveness" (Amstutz 2006:66). Or, as Lewis Smedes put it in *The Art of Forgiving*: "The fact is that forgiving is the only way for any fairness to rise from the ashes of unfairness" (1997:556). The rhetoric supports the misguided assumption that forgiving and reconciliation are "the only truly viable alternatives to revenge, retribution and reprisal" (Tutu 2004:204), because the alternative is presented as something that only immoral or deluded actors could possibly choose. The normative conclusion is inevitable: "Without forgiveness there is no future" (Tutu 1999).

This stark dichotomy of either forgiveness or vengeance-hatred-bitterness does not do justice to the actual spectrum of possible attitudinal responses between those two emotional poles. The rhetorical evocation of vengeance as forgiveness's demonic other does not appropriately capture the position of victims who seek just legal prosecution and punishment of the wrongdoers. Some victims calling for trials and objecting to the advocacy of forgiveness might be driven by desires for revenge, but it is equally possible that they simply want legal justice. To talk as if a desire for punishment or retribution, on the one hand, and revenge, on the other hand, were one of a kind, fails to acknowledge a difference of moral significance to many survivors. Similarly, the discourse of either forgiveness or vengeance reduces criminal prosecution and punishment to its "backward-looking" retributive dimension—which is, again, reduced to a lust for revenge (for a critical comment, see Kiss 2003:85, Tutu 1999:31). Retribution, however, is not reducible to revenge, and criminal justice is definitely about more than giving the criminals what they deserve.[7]

One might even add that the rhetorical use of "revenge" or "vengeance" as the totally immoral, demeaning, and irrational alternative to forgiving is unfair to victims who might positively desire revenge, who consciously desire satisfaction of their vindictive passions directed toward the perpetrators. Several books have been written to bring more nuance to our grasp of revenge and the avenger (see Ignatieff 2001, 2003, Jacoby 1988, Phelps 2004, Solomon 1999, 2003, Tobias and Zinke 2000, R. Wilson 2001). There is absolutely no need to romanticize anger and revenge, but it is equally wrong to identify anger only with its excessive and bloody instances. "Boundless vindictive rage is," as Susan Jacoby once put it, "not the only alternative to unmerited forgiveness" (1988:362). In short, the simplified picture of the alternatives available to survivors of mass atrocity leaves no space for victims who neither want to forgive nor to wreak vengeance. This is wrong not only because it misrepresents what unforgiving victims may feel or desire, but it also might push people to forgive when they are not ready to do so:

> If the possibilities for addressing conflict are represented as "vengeance or forgiveness," victims may feel, or may actually be, pressed to take an undemanding, or even a forgiving stance, even where this frustrates their needs for vindication or forecloses any of the varieties of vindication that might satisfy their needs to have their dignity restored, their suffering acknowledged, or their losses compensated (Walker 2006a:99).

Facing Resistance

To encourage forgiveness, commissioners thus represented the emotions that the forgiving victims had overcome or were willing to abandon in a negative way. What happened when commissioners came to face real resistance to, or dissent from, the rhetoric of forgiveness from victims who refused to forgive or reconcile or express their acceptance or support of the granting of amnesty? During the hearings, such angry protests were sometimes simply ignored and sometimes met with attempts to goad the "dissenters" in the right direction by reminding them of their earlier declared commitment to reconciliation.[8]

At an amnesty hearing in Johannesburg on October 21, 1996, a whole row of bereaved mothers and widows were met by a kind of condescending questioning. The attorney representing the amnesty applicants had opened the hearing in high style, expressing that the time had passed for deception, denial, conflict, repression, hatred, and the like. His opening speech culminated in the declaration that, now, it "is time for reconciliation. It is time for healing. It is time for forgiveness. It is time for truth. It is time for confession." However, the mothers and wives of those who had been killed were of another opinion. When asked what they felt,[9] the women not only stated their resistance to the granting of amnesty and their refusal or inability to forgive. They also explained that the plea for amnesty came too late or that they felt co-opted by the government's support of amnesty for the perpetrators, who had never approached the women on their own initiative to ask for forgiveness.

It is interesting to look at the commissioners' responses to the women's dissent. They ranged from a brief question—"Is there anything else you would like to add to that?" (and the subsequent excusal of the bereaved relative) —to an inquiry that seemed to presume that the source of the women's resistance was a lack of knowledge about the ongoing nation-building project. Here is an example of such an inquiry, variations of which were repeated throughout the hearing:

> Q.: Let me put it this way; you do read newspapers and watch TV, not so?
> A.: Yes I do read newspapers and I do watch television.
>
> Q.: I assume that you know about this Truth & Reconciliation Commission that is going on, of which Amnesty is part thereof?
> A.: Yes I heard.
>
> Q.: Do you know that this is done by the Government to foster or to promote reconciliation in the country?
> A.: Yes I do know that.
>
> Q.: What is your attitude about this reconciliation process?
> A.: I don't have any comment on that one.
>
> Q.: Do you believe in reconciliation?
> A.: Yes I do believe.[10]

The witness's refusal to forgive or to support the granting of amnesty thus is met with attempts to convince her that her attitude will harm her country's rebuilding efforts. A more harsh interpretation—based on the possibility that the commissioner did not really seek to move the witness by invoking national reconciliation efforts—is to see the exchange of questions and answers as motivated by a wish to publicly shame or belittle the unforgiving relative by attempting to position her as "unenlightened." In any event, the questioning aims to pressure or intimidate the witness. It is striking that we hear no words that could reassure dissenters that their sentiments and demands are legitimate as such and that the TRC, despite its preference and support of the suspension of those demands, could still recognize them as genuinely moral in nature. It is also worth noting that giving up resentment and a *desire* for retribution or revenge does not imply a support for amnesty—unless of course one assumes that the only reason for the state to punish criminals is to satisfy the crime victim's desires for vengeance or even punishment proper. The contrast between the warm and welcoming responses given to forgiving victims and the range of responses given to their unforgiving counterparts can also be illustrated with the following example. During Bettina Mdlalose's testimony about the killing of her son in an HRV hearing in Durban, Vryheid, on April 16, 1997, the following exchange occurred:

> COMMISSIONER: But one other thing that's an objective of this Commission is that after we have ventilated about the atrocities that were committed to us, is that we should reconcile as the community of South Africa at large. The perpetrators, those who committed those atrocities to you, killed your son, according to our records haven't come forth for amnesty, or perhaps sending us to you for forgiveness. But one question I would like to ask is that, if today those perpetrators could come forth and say, "Commission, because you exist today, we would like to go and meet Mrs. Mdlalose to ask for forgiveness," would you be prepared to meet with the perpetrators? I know they haven't come forward, they have not even admitted an application for amnesty, but still we would like to ask from you, to get a view from you that if they come to you and ask for forgiveness would you be prepared to sit down with them, shake hands with them, and reconcile with them? Would you be prepared to talk to them?
>
> MRS. MDLALOSE: I don't think I will allow such an opportunity.
>
> COMMISSIONER: Thanks. Thank you for responding, because you just told us what you feel from inside. But do not feel bad . . .[11]

Another relevant case is the HRV hearing of Margaret Madlana in Alexandra on October 29, 1996. She gave testimony about the day she found out that a boy, whose head she had seen being hit against a rock, was actually her 12-year-old son. In the vehemence of her relived grief and anger, Mrs. Madlana both spoke about earlier ideas of revenge ("poison the white man's children") and about never wanting to forgive "if they don't come before the commission." At this point a commissioner, Mr. Lewin, intervenes, expressing that "we can all understand the pain and grief that you have and the anger you have." He continues as follows:

> What you have told us will never be forgotten. You have now told people in public, you have shared your grief and this is something that is actually very important that you do that. We will through our investigative unit follow up as closely as possible and when we find these people yes we will bring them to you, bring you together with them so that they too can feel what you feel.

Near the end of the hearing another commissioner expressed the TRC's wish that the perpetrators would "come before the people and tell the truth so that people like you can be able to forgive and reconcile." Thus, the somewhat unclear last line of Lewin's intervention has been replaced with a clear statement of the ultimate purpose of the hearings. More interestingly, however, the second commissioner seems to characterize Mrs. Madlane's anger and resistance to forgiveness as a sign of her temporary *inability* to overcome her compulsive passions. The case also appears as the last—and only— "negative" example in the chapter on forgiveness in the TRC's Final Report. It is prefaced with the words "that forgiveness is not cheap, and the journey towards overcoming deep feelings of anger and humiliation is a long one" (TRC Final Report 1998:380, para. 48).

In the next chapter I focus on the therapeutic perspective on resentment and unforgiveness. For now, let me just add an example of how being approached as someone in need of treatment can evoke resistance from a victim. It is taken from a victim hearing in Durban, Welkom, on October 9, 1996 (cited in Verdoolaege 2006):

> COMMISSIONER: Now, when you say, ever since this incident took place and you have this problematic relationship with white people, did you ever try to get any treatment or some counseling with regard to that?
>
> MR. MORAKE: No, I've never thought of getting any treatment because I feel that where they are, they are the ones who should be getting the treatment.

Real resistance to forgiveness does not spring up solely because it is emotionally difficult to overcome anger and vindictiveness. It could, for example, be grounded in completely sensible complaints about the lack of signs of remorse in the wrongdoer; resistance to state-sponsored forgiveness; refusals to forgive unilaterally (without or before any sign of remorse on behalf of the perpetrators), and the belief that the request for forgiveness came too late. The hearings and publications of the TRC did not seem to consider seriously any of these genuine concerns and objections, even though they all represent more than signs of the individuals' *inability* to overcome anger and vindictiveness. Consider two more statements from victims given in the HRV hearing in Johannesburg on October 21, 1996:

> According to me people should forgive each other, not the Government. The people who are affected who had the pain should be the ones who are talking about forgiveness, not the Government.
>
> I don't have the conciliation as they have taken them from my place to the place where they have killed them, I want them to go and fetch them where they've left them to bring them home so that we will be able to bury them peacefully and, they have killed our children so they want us to forgive them.

We are still less than halfway through the exploration of the question how anger, resentment, and the resistance to forgiveness were understood and treated in the South African context. Yet, already it is clear that claims like Ricoeur's—that "the commission certainly gave rise to a shared *katharsis*" (2004:484) —are misleading. Moreover, one should drop the notion that victims had unrestrained freedom of expression or that their testimony was not influenced by the commissioners. Although truth commissions provide a platform for victim testimony that is superior to that in a criminal trial (for a comprehensive comparative examination, see Aldana 2006), the absence of the harshness and demands of the adversarial context of criminal justice does not mean that victims testifying in truth and reconciliation commissions are simply left free to speak their truth. And even though in comparison with the proceedings of international criminal tribunals, anger (and emotion in general) was much more explicit and brought to the fore in the TRC (once named the "Kleenex commission"), it was done so only as something ideally to be overcome, perhaps "ventilated" but then transcended, and left behind on the journey toward reconciliation.[12] The TRC hearings were meant to help victims regain their dignity, but they were at the same time structured to promote national unity and reconciliation. In that process, the TRC failed to acknowledge the possible moral nature and legitimacy of the victims' and their relatives' resentment and resistance to the encouragement of forgiveness.

4

The Therapy of Anger

What Victims Feel and Want

C harles Villa-Vicencio, theologian and ordained Methodist minister, is former Director of Research for the TRC and the editor and author of several publications on the commission. His essay "Getting on With Life: A Move Towards Reconciliation" is generally marked by his insistence on realism and fairness. Against excessive expectations about the reconciliatory potential of the TRC, Charles Villa-Vicencio stresses that it was only given the task of *promoting* national unity and reconciliation. To counter exaggerated hopes about the cathartic benefits of truth telling, he underscores that *some* victims benefited from the experience. And as a corrective or supplement to a focus on forgiving and conciliatory victims, Villa-Vicencio emphasizes that forgiveness and reconciliation are not the first priority of *most* victims and survivors:

> Whatever the designs of the ruling elite and those most intimately involved in the TRC process, most victims and survivors experience deep resentment towards those responsible for their misery. Their primary objective is *rarely* reconciliation. They are (understandably) preoccupied with their own trauma and/or fired by the belief that revenge will bring relief. They want the perpetrator to be identified and, usually, punished (Villa-Vicencio 2000:200).

The "ruling elite" probably includes Desmond Tutu who (as we shall see in Chapter 5) tended to keep focus on forgiving victims.[1] By acknowledging that those who did not want to forgive constituted more than an insignificant minority, Villa-Vicencio provides a more realistic picture. All the same, one could have wished that the nuance of other aspects of the essay had been applied more richly to its treatment of resentment and unforgiving victims. Reflecting one of the trends we identified in hearings of the victims (Chapter 3), Villa-Vicencio lumps together a variety of emotions and attitudes. Although the excerpt above does not assert a necessary connection among the mentioned beliefs, emotions, and desires, neither does it do anything to suggest that resentment is not tied to traumatic self-preoccupation or irrational beliefs in revenge—or vice versa. To the contrary, it arguably sustains tendencies to equate resentment with psychological disturbance and demands for punishment with a desire for revenge. Yet, surely for some victims it is wrong to imply that their unforgiving or angry disposition is a symptom of trauma. And as we see in Part Two's examination of Jean Améry, the expression of deep resentments by some victims is not necessarily a sign of a refusal to reconcile.

Finally, some victims' demands for punishment are not testimony to a desire for revenge. Many victims are "fired" by the belief that *justice* will bring some measure of relief. "We took our plight to the TRC," a woman said, "and they told us to forgive and forget. How can we when justice against the perpetrators has not been done?" (Posel and Simpson 2002:132). In a similar vein, in the documentary *A Cry from the Grave*, a survivor of the Srebrenica massacre says: "I want these murderers to be arrested and punished. Otherwise, I will never find peace in my life." The hope of obtaining relief through genocide trials or punishment of the perpetrators is often not realized, yet what matters here is not the degree to which this hope is rationally justified. What matters is rather the need for a more nuanced and fair representation of victims who refuse to forgive or who call for justice and punishment. Villa-Vicencio's thoughts about recovery do not recognize the possibility that anger may be correlated with a passion for justice and that the state's fulfillment of its responsibility to prosecute and punish the perpetrators effectively is one way to help the survivors move on.

Getting on With Life

As stated in Chapter 1, the process of reconciliation is often thought to involve a transformation of emotions and attitudes. According to Villa-Vicencio, the legislation establishing the TRC challenged South Africans to *transcend* a variety of "negative" emotions—including resentment—in order to move ahead to a better future. In the process, "the victim is asked to give priority to his or her obligations as a *citizen* rather than a *violated person*" (2000:201; italics in original). Whether out of self-interest or political responsibility, the aggrieved survivor should not allow "past wrongdoing and resentment towards others to undermine the political process" toward coexistence (208). As Nelson Mandela has put it: "Personal bitterness is irrelevant. It is a luxury that we, as individuals and as a country, simply cannot afford" (cited in Graybill 2002:21).[2] Like Mandela, Villa-Vicencio seems to suggests that the self-interest of the aggrieved individual and what is necessary to promote reconciliation overlap. That is, trying to comply with the plea to transcend resentment does not only amount to contributing to the common good, but it is also the condition for getting on with one's life. In other words, nursing resentment, bitterness, and grievances is detrimental both to the nation and the individual. Resentment simply functions as the negative to be overcome, and victims who harbor resentment are destroying their life and jeopardizing the process of reconciliation.

Villa-Vicencio applies this perspective in his response to a remark made by an angry black South African woman named Kalu. Let us take a close look at her statement and at Villa-Vicencio's response. It is quoted extensively here because it illuminates the nature and limitations of Villa-Vicencio's perspective on anger, resentment, and the unforgiving victim.

> "What really makes me angry about the TRC and Tutu is that they are putting pressure on me to forgive. . . . I don't know if I will ever be able to forgive. I carry this ball of anger within me and I don't know where to begin dealing with it. The oppression was bad, but what is much worse, what makes me even angrier is that they are trying to dictate my forgiveness." Her words capture the pathos involved in the long and fragile journey towards reconciliation. No one has the right to prevail on Kalu to forgive. The question is whether victims and survivors can be enabled *to get on with the rest of their lives* in the sense of not allowing anger or self-pity to be the all-consuming dimension of their existence. It is a tall order. It involves taking responsibility for their own lives as well as the future direction of the nation. It involves becoming a *citizen* in the fullest sense of the word (Villa-Vicencio 2000:201f; italics in original).

As his essay continues, Villa-Vicencio refers to a victim who was able to move on through forgiveness and compassion. Yet, what is important, writes Villa-Vicencio, is not whether one forgives but that victims—"for their own sake" and in various ways—are enabled to deal "with the 'ball of anger' that prevents one from getting one with life" (2000:202).

Something is lost in the transition from Kalu's complaint to Villa-Vicencio's response. Kalu's anger is of course painful to her, it might be detrimental to her well-being, and it probably affects her social relationships. At the same time, it is more than a painful and unpleasant feeling, and its expression is not simply about venting pain and frustration. From what we hear, judging from the basis of Kalu's statement itself, her anger seems at root a moral response to a perceived wrong—the TRC's pressure on her to forgive. Indeed, she feels and has to deal with "a ball of anger." But she is angry because she believes that she has been violated by an institution that she had expected would treat her with dignity. Her anger appears to be exactly what the philosophers mentioned in Chapter 1, conceptualized as the moral emotions or reactive attitude of resentment. As emphasized in several philosophical accounts of resentment (but most strongly in Margaret Walker's [2006b] account), this emotion is not only or always from injuries to oneself. The resentful person is not necessarily preoccupied by his or her injury. That person—and prima facie that seems to be the case for Kalu—might as well be expressing a commitment to certain moral standards that should have been operating in a certain situation, but were breached. When this is true, it is wrong to represent or treat the holder of resentment as someone preoccupied with his or her own trauma or suffering. Moreover, to the extent that the expression of resentment seeks a response from offenders or others, that response has to do with a reassurance that the moral standards are still in place or at least that others are willing to engage in a dialogue about those norms at stake (cf. Walker 2006b). For example, Kalu's anger is about the breach embodied in the TRC's pressure on victims to forgive; its appropriate response would address this cause and object of her anger.

Writing that no one has the right to prevail on Kalu to forgive, Villa-Vicencio seems to take her anger seriously. Indeed, later in the essay he emphasizes that it is "never the right of the state, any state body or any individual to demand that any victim forgive or be reconciled" (207). Yet, according to Villa-Vicencio, the real question is whether people like Kalu "can be enabled *to get on with the rest of their lives* in the sense of not allowing anger or self-pity to be the all-consuming dimension of their existence" (201f; italics in original). Thus, Villa-Vicencio suggests a shift of focus from the moral issue (the alleged malpractice of the TRC) to the possibilities of relief from all-consuming anger and self-pity and from being unable to move on and pursue or engage in other aspects of life.

Villa-Vicencio thus adopts neither the posture of the moralist or minister. Victims and survivors "should" deal with their anger and get on with life for their own sake as well as for the sake of the nation. Mixing psychosocial and political considerations, Villa-Vicencio adopts the perspective of the psychotherapist and places the angry victim in the position of the patient. Like the therapist, Villa-Vicencio is concerned with enabling the victims or survivors to overcome the emotional and existential wounds arising after victimization. This perspective, as well as the desire to help victims get on with their lives, is evidently *not* problematic as such. To the contrary, there is a strong need for analysis and reflection about the possibilities and limits of given forms of psychotherapy or psychosocial rehabilitation after mass atrocities.[3] Nonetheless, I suggest that Villa-Vicencio's essay manifests certain tendencies found in the use of therapeutic language and approaches.

The Lures of the Therapeutic Perspective

The therapeutic approach can be problematic for several reasons. First, it *can* become blind or deaf to other perspectives. Approaching anger mainly or solely as a disturbance to be treated can undermine the kind of communication that can be the point of the expression of anger. The concern about persistent anger as having an adverse impact on health can diminish the power and relevance of the moral and political protest of which anger can be an integral part. Victims and survivors are concerned about more than the goals and values privileged in the therapeutic perspective. Some survivors might be fully aware that their preservation and expression of resentment are bad for their health, functioning, and ability to engage with other things than the atrocity of the past. Yet, they choose to hold on to their resentment because of a sense of moral duty to those who were murdered or as a protest in circumstances where the atrocity is followed by cheap reconciliation or the absence of punishment. When the therapeutic concern with victims' ability to get on with their lives becomes blind or deaf to such aspects and reasons for continued resentment, it can add insult to injury.

Second, therapeutic and psychological language tends to *pathologize.* The emotions or passions treated as pathology are deviant and excessive; they are causes of malfunctioning and suffering. When given free rein, there is a risk that the therapeutic perspective neglects tempered and rational, or disruptive but justifiable, instances of emotional response. As Lawrence Langer puts it in his essay, "Memory and Justice After the Holocaust and Apartheid" (2006:87), "Holocaust survivors may continue to despise those who betrayed, brutalized, or murdered their kind, but anyone who hears their testimony (or knows them personally) will instantly recognize that such feelings, while (understandably) affecting their outlook, have not succeeded in poisoning their lives." Likewise, even though Kalu speaks of a "ball of anger," it does not suggest that she is *overcome* by anger or self-pity. Villa-Vicencio's emphasis on the pathological extreme is in accordance with tendencies identified in the previous chapter on the hearings and in the advocacy of forgiveness more generally. But in relation to victims in general, as well as to Kalu in particular, the lack of a distinction between pathological extremes and more viable modalities of coping is a misrepresentation. More than that, the role of anger in relation to psychological coping or recovery is ambiguous: "The individual who forgives for psychological or spiritual reasons 'lets go' of useful anger and has less psychic energy to put forward toward obtaining justice. Although anger can be self-destructive and paralyzing, it can also motivate and engage victims in struggles for justice" (Lamb 2006:55).

Indeed, several psychologists have argued that the experience and expression of anger—up to a certain point—are part of a process of recovery. There are even reasons to believe that it is counterproductive to the goal of recovery to urge victims of extreme wrongdoing to transcend anger in order to forgive. The first step toward recovery may, on the contrary, be to *raise* anger in the victim.[4] "It has to be acknowledged," as Graeme Simpson has noted in relation to the TRC, "that expressions of anger and the desire for revenge (rather than forgiveness) on the part of the victims, may in fact be more functional to the sort of substantive recovery best characterized by the shift in identity from 'victim' to 'survivor'" (quoted in Graybill 2002:50). Psychologist Judith L. Herman even talks about the "fantasy of forgiveness," a fantasy that can develop into a kind of "cruel torture, because it remains out of reach for most ordinary human beings" (Herman 1992:190). According to Herman, the promotion of forgiveness as a road to mental and physical recovery "often becomes a formidable impediment to mourning" (190) and thus to the much talked-about "healing."[5]

Third, in the excerpt above, Villa-Vicencio writes that dealing with the "ball of anger" or the task of getting on with life requires that victims take "responsibility for their own lives as well as the future direction of the nation. It involves becoming a *citizen* in the fullest sense of the word" (2000:202). Is Villa-Vicencio alleging that victims like Kalu are indulging in victimhood and that they neglect the proper concerns and duties of a citizen? The passage seems to play on widespread notions of victimized people. As Arne Johan Vetlesen has put it,

We hear a lot about the dangerousness of victims, about their self-righteousness, their unreadiness and inability to focus on anyone else than themselves; about their predilection for viewing themselves as always passive, always suffering, always downtrodden, and so for denying their agency and share of responsibility for things that come to pass (Vetlesen 2006:43).

The pitfalls of victimhood are real, but it seems grossly reductive and unfair to press all resentful and unforgiving victims into this mold. Of course, if one has already accepted the notion of a victim as one enthralled by all-consuming anger and self-pity, then the appeal to assume responsibility makes sense. In that case, to harbor anger or resentment becomes a sign of a *personal* failure or obstinacy on behalf of the "self-pitying" victim.

Let me finish this chapter by returning to Villa-Vicencio's reassurance that no one has the right to demand that victims forgive or to "prevail" on Kalu to forgive. At first glance, this statement seems to validate Kalu's anger. And yet, the reassurance that he offers is not likely to guarantee that the offense against which Kalu's anger is directed will not be repeated. That is, if the "pressure" she protests equals the trends that were identified in Chapter 3 on the hearings, then it is not a question about explicit demands or imperatives. Villa-Vicencio's reassurance that forgiveness can never be demanded does not imply that it should not be encouraged and advocated. Indeed, the essay ends by stating that forgiveness is "a coveted ideal to be gently pursued. It cannot be imposed" (209). More generally, proponents of the value of forgiveness in restorative justice in general, or in the TRC in particular, often stress that forgiveness can and should never be demanded or imposed. This is however— unwittingly or not—a kind of smoke screen, because the real issue, in terms of victims' complaints about the proceedings, is precisely the use of subtle and covert pressures: what is not demanded directly but is clearly expected and ways of speaking and examples that are provided or ignored or forgotten.

5
Desmond Tutu on Anger

Those Who Will Not Forgive

The life and works of Desmond Tutu are truly impressive: he is a famous apartheid opponent and Nobel Peace Prize laureate, Archbishop Emeritus, the chairperson and most prominent spokesperson of the TRC, a "moral voice" of the world. In relation to his involvement with the TRC, Tutu has been traveling the world, giving talks about his experiences and lessons learned. A story that Tutu apparently loves to tell and retell is one about his encounters with the grievously wronged yet forgiving victims who appeared before the commission. During the hearings, in his books, and in speeches, Tutu has expressed repeatedly how he rejoiced and was thrilled by those who were ready and willing to forgive the perpetrators. They are praised for their generosity, their overcoming of resentment and vindictiveness, and their contribution to the making of a new South Africa. Indeed, on several occasions, Tutu has urged his audiences to regard concrete expressions of forgiveness or the overcoming of anger as the result of holy or divine intervention: "Many times I have said, 'Really, the only appropriate response is for us to take off our shoes, because we are standing on holy ground'" (Tutu 2002:xii).[1]

This chapter focuses not on Tutu's praise of forgiveness but rather on how he understands and represents victims expressing anger, resentment and an unwillingness to forgive:

Of course there were those who said they would not forgive. That demonstrated for me the important point that forgiveness could not be taken for granted; it was neither cheap nor easy. As it happens, these were the exceptions. Far more frequently what we encountered was deeply moving and humbling (1999:271).

Elsewhere, Tutu writes that those who were not "ready," as he puts it, to forgive demonstrated that "forgiveness is not facile or cheap. It is a costly business that makes those who are willing to forgive even more extraordinary" (Tutu 1998:267). In both instances, Tutu does not dwell on the negative, but quickly returns to his appraisal of the forgiving victims. His encounter with the unforgiving victims or relatives, whom Tutu obviously does not find to be so deeply moving, does not prompt him to discuss whether it may sometimes be legitimate *not* to forgive or whether victims considering whether to forgive may be caught in a tension between two sets of genuine values.

Tutu often recognizes how difficult it may be to forgive. If he did not, expressing amazement and exhilaration in the face of the declarations of willingness to forgive would have been completely inexplicable. Yet, he does not acknowledge that the difficulty with forgiving may involve any real moral problems or dilemmas. Instead, he considers that overcoming anger, resentment, or desires for revenge is psychologically difficult because these emotions and attitudes may exercise a strong hold on the victim. The victim might not be able or ready to forgive, but to forgive is absolutely good and beneficial. It is a kind of generosity that seems to be "costly" only in a superficial sense. Nowhere does Tutu seriously discuss the possibility that the preservation of resentment or refusing to forgive might be justifiable on moral grounds.

In *Getting Even: Forgiveness and Its Limits* (2003), Jeffrie Murphy frames a more probing and balanced discussion of resentment and forgiveness with the following question: "Suppose that I am a victim of *evil*—of violent crime, state torture, or other serious wrongdoing. What kind of victim should I try to be—a vindictive victim perhaps seeking vengeance or a forgiving victim perhaps seeking reconciliation?" (Murphy 2003:3; italics in original).

According to Murphy, these two responses pose a "deep tension between competing values" (2003:4). Thus, Murphy sees the difficulty of forgiving as *more* than a question about how to overcome strong but essentially amoral or even evil passions and compulsions. Indeed, overcoming resentment and forgiving may compromise "values of genuine importance" (Murphy 2003:115). It is this kind of acknowledgment and the discussion following from it that I find missing in Tutu's talk of those who forgive and those who do not.

The fact that Tutu acted as the chair of a state institution gives rise to several questions concerning the political and ethical legitimacy of the *public* promotion of forgiveness. That is, most liberals will be at odds with the advocacy of forgiveness in the socio-political realm: as a matter of an infringement of the public-private distinction (i.e., how to feel and whether to forgive or not ought to remain a private or personal decision) or as a question of the boundaries of public reason (i.e., the public encouragement of forgiveness imposed a particular Christian valuation of forgiving). Much has been written about these issues of legitimacy and on whether it is possible to establish a strictly political concept of forgiveness.[2] However, in this chapter I am rather concerned with Tutu's understanding of anger, resentment, and the unforgiving victim. Suffice it to say, that I join the argument of Elizabeth Kiss that, even if one grants that its public promotion of forgiveness and reconciliation was democratically legitimate, the TRC ought to have been obliged to acknowledge the legitimacy of anger and demands for retributive justice, just as a government should acknowledge the legitimacy of conscientious objections to its efforts to mobilize its citizens to participate in a—for the sake of argument—just war (Kiss 2003:85).

Resentment: A Legitimate Moral Sentiment?

Philosopher David Heyd has suggested that Desmond Tutu *does* acknowledge resentment as a moral sentiment; that is, he considers it morally legitimate on the individual level. According to Heyd,

> Tutu admits that reconciliation means renouncing a legitimate moral sentiment…. Even if on the personal level, resentment and vengeance are understandable, on the social and political level they are suicidal and in the name of collective survival should be overcome. This does not mean that Tutu wishes to completely relinquish the individual's perspective. For example, he acknowledges the freedom of the victim to refuse to forgive the wrongdoer (Heyd 2004:194).

The question is what this acknowledgment of the individual's perspective and of the victim's freedom to refuse to forgive is meant to imply. I am not convinced that it implies recognition of the moral legitimacy of resentment. Yet, Heyd's (in itself sensible) characterization of Tutu can be supported by pointing to a large number of statements in which Tutu stresses how exhilarated he is by "the magnanimity of those who should *by rights* be consumed by bitterness and a lust for revenge; who instead have time after time shown an astonishing magnanimity and willingness to forgive" (TRC Final Report 1998, vol. I, ch. 1, para. 71; italics added).[3] As Tutu describes bitterness and the lust for revenge as something the victims are entitled to "by rights," such statements seem to suggest that he recognizes the moral standing of the reactive attitudes. Yet, in my opinion, it is not possible to construe Tutu's position on resentment and forgiveness in accordance with the conventional notion of what is moral and righteous versus what is supererogatory or good beyond duty. If Tutu really acknowledges resentment as a legitimate moral sentiment, it seems strange that he consistently identifies the attitudes that are the victims' "by rights" with "bitterness and a lust for revenge." One must wonder why it is so hard to find utterances acknowledging anecdotes of righteous resentment or justified unforgiveness. However, what undermines Heyd's interpretation are not simply such tendencies to focus on emotional excess. If one contextualizes the "by rights" statements in Tutu's wider ethical and theological thinking, one conclusion becomes clear: no one who cares about virtue, God, or humanity—as conceived by Tutu—would ever retain anger or resentment. Let me try to show why this is the case.

Tutu's statements about the "remarkable generosity of spirit" of those victims who showed themselves willing to forgive (instead of being by rights filled with bitterness) are typically introduced as the second half of a broader statement about his confrontation with evil and goodness during his work as the chairman of the TRC. In several contexts, Tutu begins by explaining how devastating the confrontation with human depravity and evil was. However, he always adds that "paradoxically one comes away from it exhilarated by the revelation of the goodness of people" (Tutu 2002:xi) and that the reason why the confrontation with the evil of the perpetrators does not leave the witnessing commissioner devastated is the generosity of the forgiving victims:

> Mercifully, wonderfully, that [i.e. the reality of evil] was only one side of the picture. . . . Gloriously, there was another side that would be revealed as well. It was the side that showed people who by rights should have been filled with bitterness. . . . Instead they were to demonstrate a remarkable generosity of spirit . . . in their willingness to forgive (Tutu 1999:144).

The significance of the forgiving victims is not limited to the hope and exhilaration they engender in fellow human beings. In Tutu's theological perspective, the magnanimity of the deeply injured and yet forgiving survivors is further contextualized in his speculation about God's attitude to His creation. Again, it is the forgiving victims who, according to Tutu, reassure the otherwise skeptical God that His creation is good and worthy of existence:

> There may indeed have been moments when God may have regretted creating us. But I am certain there have been many more times when God has looked and seen all these wonderful people who have shone in the dark night of evil and torture and abuses and suffering; shone as they demonstrated their nobility of spirit, their magnanimity as

they have been ready to forgive, and so they have dispelled the murkiness. . . . It has filled people with new hope that despair, darkness, anger and resentment and hatred would not have the last word (Tutu 1999:158).

The passage exemplifies the rhetoric of an either/or choice between forgiveness and resentment (along with a variety of negative alternatives); in other words, the notion that there can no future without forgiveness. Clearly, nothing in this passage suggests Tutu's acknowledgment of resentment as a legitimate moral sentiment on any level. The passage also illustrates the most characteristic feature of religious discourse: its appeal to divine authority.[4] It is not just Desmond Tutu who marvels at the displays of forgiveness; God Himself is exhilarated. Therefore, it is no wonder that Tutu repeatedly insists that expressions of forgiveness or overcoming of anger and bitterness should be responded to as something holy. By implication, to refuse to forgive or to preserve anger or resentment seems equal to being part of the scheme of things that nearly brought God to despair about His Creation. Some theologians would probably balk at the ease with which Tutu aligns God with his own opinions. I am more concerned about the pressure that this kind of religious discourse might place on victims or relatives considering whether to forgive or to seek other varieties of vindication.

Anger, *Ubuntu,* and Social Harmony

Why is Tutu *so* unhappy about not just revenge but also anger and resentment expressed by unforgiving victims? The answer has to do with the alleged force of the notion of *ubuntu* in the African worldview.[5] According to Tutu, *ubuntu* speaks to the essence of two aspects of being human. It is a term of high praise as it refers to a kind of perfection of human virtue. The person whose character is impregnated with *ubuntu* is disposed to be generous, self-assured, hospitable, compassionate, open, sharing, caring about others—and, of course, forgiving (cf. Tutu 1999:31). At the same time, Tutu also uses *ubuntu* to designate an African insight into a fundamental feature of the human condition: its *interdependency.* The self-assurance and humaneness of the person who has *ubuntu* come from knowing that "we belong in a bundle of life" and that the fate of each one of us is inextricably intertwined with our relationships to others. Tutu addresses the question of how anger and resentment then enter the picture:

My humanity is caught up in your humanity, and when your humanity is enhanced—whether I like it or not—my humanity is enhanced as well. Likewise, when you are dehumanized, inexorably, I am dehumanized as well.

So there is a deep yearning in African society for communal peace and harmony. It is for us the *summum bonum*, the greatest good. For in it, we find the sustenance that enables us to be truly human. Anything that erodes this central good is inimical to all, and nothing is more destructive than resentment and anger and revenge.

In a way, therefore, to forgive is the best form of self-interest, because I'm also releasing myself from the bonds that hold me captive, and it is important that I do all I can to restore relationship [sic]. Because without relationship [sic], I am nothing, I will shrivel (*U.S. Catholic* 2000).[6]

This statement is clear evidence that Tutu does *not* acknowledge resentment as a legitimate moral sentiment on any level. But the mere lack of acknowledgment does not capture the radical nature of Tutu's approach to anger. He denounces anger, resentment, and revenge in the strongest possible terms by stating, "*Nothing* is more destructive than revenge and anger and resentment." Even if this statement may mean that a number of other things might be equally destructive, the rhetorical emphasis on the angry reactive attitudes does pinpoint them as particularly deserving of disapproval. However, does Tutu really say that anger and resentment are more blameworthy or as destructive as cruelty and malice or even indifference in the face of evil? Even if victims' anger, resentment, and revenge are posited to be the main causes of genocidal violence and societal destruction—and according to Walker (2006a), who discusses the notion of cycles of violence, one should not make that causal connection—it is difficult to subscribe to any position that implies that victims' resentment constitutes a greater personal vice and a more noteworthy threat to human coexistence than the indifference, hatred, or malice of those who intentionally inflict grave suffering in the first place.

Yet, perhaps Tutu only means that nothing is more destructive than anger *among possible responses to being wronged*; thus, his claim that any other attitude or response—but forgiveness in particular—is preferable. This interpretation only works if one accepts two untenable assumptions: first, that forgiveness is *always* morally, psychologically, and socially preferable to resentment, and second, that resentment has absolutely no constructive or positive role to play in the maintenance of social harmony and human relationships. The distance between this claim and the philosophical approaches outlined in Chapter 1 could not be greater. No trace is left of the widely shared position that justified anger, resentment, and indignation function as "a weapon, put into our hands by nature, against injury, injustice, and cruelty" (Butler 1897:121). The same goes with regard to Strawson's point that being susceptible to resentment is a fundamental aspect of what it means to be involved—as a fellow human being—in interpersonal relationships. Yet, if these less radical approaches were sound (and I think that they are), the very idea of making an enemy of anger (and resentment and revenge) in general appears fundamentally misguided and potentially harmful.

Now, let us return to the question with which this section began. *Why* is Tutu so radically against anger, resentment, and revenge—urging anyone to avoid them "like the plague" (Tutu 1999:31, cf. note 5). The answer: anger, resentment, and revenge undermine communal peace and social harmony. The problem with this reasoning is not just the already mentioned point that, in fact, resentment has a more constructive role to play in relation to the upholding of social relations. More fundamentally, the problem lies with Tutu's highly positive valuation of an apolitical and amoral notion of friction-less social harmony. We live in a social and historical reality where intentional wrongdoing is part of the game. One may agree with Tutu that resentment does, indeed, disrupt "social harmony,"[7] but disagree with his absolute appreciation of such harmony. As David C. Crocker (2000) has underscored, dissent or moral outrage may be justified even though it disrupts friendliness and social harmony. The idea that harmony is the greatest good of all is, in my opinion, an idealization that minimizes the space for legitimate conflict and contestation and that hardly fits a society striving to develop a pluralist liberal democracy. It seems incompatible with the very human rights culture that the TRC was presumed to help foster. One of the important functions that resentment can serve is to point to the reality of existing conflict and discord. In the face of hasty and hollow conciliatoriness, resentment, even bitterness, may be preserved exactly to unearth an existing conflict; we return to this possibility in Part Two.

But why elevate social harmony to the status of *summum bonum* in the first place? Because, and we are still trying to follow Tutu's line of reasoning, without social harmony, the individual will shrivel: being truly human is only possible in the context of harmonious relationships—one cannot dehumanize the other without dehumanizing oneself. Forgiveness, on the one hand, restores relationships, social harmony, and thus also the sustenance that enables us—the victim no less than the perpetrator—to be truly human. Anger, resentment, and revenge, on the other hand, erode social harmony and thus also our possibility of being truly human. However, even if one grants that we cannot flourish outside of human relationships, it does not seem to follow that each and every specific relationship to a specific group or individual should be restored. The person who does not forgive those who wronged his or her next of kin is not likely to shrivel in existential desolation. Most people thrive on a whole host of relationships, and with regard to a given perpetrator the only relationship they have might be the one between victim and perpetrator of a given crime. Not all relationships are worthy of restoration, and maintaining networks of humane relationships is hardly possible on the basis of an attitude that makes a hegemony of harmony. Anger and resentment certainly disrupt social harmony, but Tutu seems to suggest that being angry, resentful, or vindictive is incompatible with having *ubuntu* or with the *ubuntu* understanding of human interdependence. Whether directly or indirectly, Tutu claims that negative attitudes and emotions are detrimental to being "truly human." But this is only so if one accepts the question-begging assumption that all-consuming bitterness, malicious hatred, and excessive vengefulness capture all there is to say about resentment. Anger *can* dehumanize, but this does not justify the wholesale dismissal of anger and resentment.

It is clear by now that Tutu cannot be said to hold the view that resentment is a legitimate moral sentiment. Insofar as he has shown concern about the "others" —the unforgiving or unreconcilable victims—he has used them to amplify the praiseworthiness of the forgivers. When talking about the alternative to forgiveness, he has consistently chosen to focus on possessive bitterness, the lust for revenge, hatred, and the like. Additionally, resentment is opposed to the kind of response to evil that pleases God and to the kind of human attitude (*ubuntu*) that marks the humane person; in this last respect, resentment destroys the highest good.

At this point one might argue that my critique has treated and criticized a piece of rhetoric as if it were a carefully elaborated philosophical argument. This is partly true, but the reason why such scrutiny is relevant and legitimate is because Tutu's speeches and opinions are regularly met with high praise and acclamation around the world. When I told a Scottish minister that I was writing a critique of Tutu's discourse on resentment and forgiveness, he responded that he would never criticize Tutu because he has done so much good for the world. Yet, all of Tutu's good works do not justify refraining from a necessary critique of his thinking.

Desmond Tutu's statements on anger and resentment should not be interpreted as representing *the* Christian—or even Anglican—position on those emotions. First, New Testament sources on the attitudes of Jesus present quite an ambiguous message. As William Harris has put it, "a gospel of forgiveness and pity was bound to be tendentially against extreme forms of anger" (2001:396), but the message one receives from the Gospels depends in large part on what one wants to hear. Jesus rages with wrath on several occasions. For example in Matthew 23:33 he snaps, "You snakes, you vipers' brood, how can you escape being condemned to hell?" In addition there is, for example, Augustine who seriously considered whether angels could feel anger and who did not disapprove of anger when it was aimed at correcting the sinner (cf. Harris 2001:391–99, Murphy 2003). Within Tutu's own Anglican tradition, one finds the already mentioned Bishop Joseph Butler and his famous sermon "Upon Resentment" from 1726. In 1946 Reinhold Niebuhr wrote a remarkably interesting and, even more remarkably, mostly unnoticed essay on "Anger and Forgiveness." Like Butler, Niebuhr uses Paul's admonition, "Be ye angry and sin not," as a point of departure for a nuanced reflection on the moral aspects of anger. Expressing the sense of ambiguity that informs the essay as a whole, Niebuhr remarks that "only a perversely detached person can view the commitment of a wrong without anger.... Yet anger is also the root of much evil" (Niebuhr 1946:26). In current Christian theology, Nigel Biggar (2001) has presented similarly complex perspectives on anger.

The precursors of Tutu's stance toward anger echoes are probably to be found among the Stoic thinkers. Absolutistic disapprovals of anger can for example be found in the writings of Cicero, Seneca, Musonius Rufus, and Epictetus (cf. Harris 2001).[8] Although it would be a mistake to treat Tutu's statements on anger as on a par with much more elaborate philosophical works, the parallels are easy to identify: a condemnation of anger as the worst of vices and the cause of error and lack of insight and the notion that the good and wise person will not be angry or that he or she will quench quickly the first impulse to anger. Still, Tutu adds his own twist to the Stoic condemnation of anger with his particular emphasis on communal peace and social harmony. Moreover, his "therapy" of anger does not rely on attempts to undermine ascriptions of responsibility and intentional wrongdoing and thus undermine the notions about deservedness that sustain resentment and retribution. Tutu shows no disinclination to talk about "the depth of depravity and evil" (Tutu 1998:266) or to explain how his task as commissioner forced him to look "into the abyss of human evil" (Tutu 1999a:xi). He has even explained how the commissioners' confrontation with massive horrors made them understand how it is possible to describe the perpetrators of such evils as inhuman monsters. Nonetheless, what "filled all *decent* people with a sense of outrage and revulsion" (1999:125; italics added) was the horrible *deeds*. "We had," writes Tutu, "to distinguish between . . . the sinner and the sin, to hate and condemn the sin while being filled with compassion for the sinner" (1999: 83). It is hard to reconcile this last statement with Tutu's plea to shun anger like the plague. This statement could have been the start of a reconsideration of the moral value of emotions that undermine social harmony, but it remains an anomaly in an otherwise consistent depreciation of the anger and resentment. Now, how does the denouncement of anger, resentment, and revenge influence the advocacy of forgiveness?

Boosterism of Forgiveness

Notions of overcoming resentment or justified anger are central or constitutive of many conceptions of forgiveness.[9] Ironically, however, resentment or righteous anger can be caused by imprudence in the manner in which forgiveness is advocated. Instead of facilitating the overcoming of resentment, the advocacy of forgiveness can create new and justified resentments among victims as well as observers. As we have seen in the previous chapters, resentment could be caused by victims' experience of being pressured or expected to forgive unpunished perpetrators of gross human rights violations. Another cause of resentment in victims and others is the pathologization or condemnation of anger in the advocacy of forgiveness. Victim advocates argued that the TRC should not only have recognized and legitimated the anger of victims and their family members but also "provided space for people to express feelings of sadness and rage" (Chapman 2001:269). In short, under certain circumstance, "third-party" advocacy of forgiveness can wrong the victims and be a cause of a new layer of resentment. It is not simply a matter of adding *insult* to injury. As Margaret Walker writes, "To coerce in any way a person already harmed or disrespected by a wrong into relinquishing her own need to grieve, reproach, and make demands may itself be harmful or disrespectful" (2006b: 179).

As mentioned in Chapter 1, I am convinced that there is a need for ethical reflection on the pitfalls of advocating or encouraging others to forgive. Assumptions that forgiveness is absolutely morally superior to resentment, or that the willingness or granting of forgiveness is always admirable, support what Jeffrie Murphy has called the "boosterism of forgiveness" (Lamb and Murphy 2002:ix). This boosterism occurs when forgiveness is recommended, praised, or encouraged in "overly sentimental and enthusiastic" ways and when it is presented as a "universal prescription" or with a haste that fails to appreciate the moral legitimacy of resentment (Lamb and Murphy 2002:ix). Dietrich Bonhoeffer's concept of "cheap grace" (Bonhoeffer 1963) is also relevant here, but given its context in Christian theological discussions about Christian life, I prefer a concept with a wider scope and with a clearer focus on the features of the public promotion of forgiveness after mass atrocities. Hence, the use of the concept of boosterism and the opportunity to speak of the "boosters of forgiveness." In this section I apply some of the nuances central to the philosophical discussion of forgiveness to the TRC boosterism of forgiveness, as expressed primarily but certainly not exclusively through the language of Desmond Tutu. I also reconstruct this boosterism from an analysis of the trends in the TRC hearings.

Taking an overall view of the philosophical literature on forgiveness, it is possible to distinguish between two fields of inquiry and discussion.[10] The first domain of discussion concerns the question of what it means to forgive. In this context, forgiving is typically characterized as an act or performance, and it is delimited through comparison with a variety of other speech acts or changes of behavior and attitude. The list of such acts includes forgetting, excusing, justifying, understanding, condoning, according mercy, and reconciling. The second domain of discussion is not about what distinguishes forgiving from nonforgiving; instead, it is about several distinctions that set apart different conceptions of forgiveness. Some accounts of forgiveness subscribe to the indispensability of perpetrator repentance; others assert that unconditional or unilateral forgiveness is possible and admirable when it happens. Some argue that only the direct victim of wrongdoing can forgive, whereas others think that forgiveness "by proxy" is possible and legitimate. (In theological discussions, one may argue whether clergy or God can or should forgive perpetrators for their sins against other human beings). Some are convinced that forgiveness has a legitimate and highly valuable role to play in politics and public affairs. Others restrict forgiveness to the private or religious realm, arguing that the real article will self-destruct if used as a reconciliation instrument or as something to be exchanged in a public institution. Finally, whereas some think that it makes sense to speak of the unforgivable as a limit to the powers of forgiveness, others argue that there is no such thing or that forgiveness is exactly meant to forgive the unforgivable.[11]

Now, the point behind this all too brief recapitulation is to establish a distinction between two dimensions along which forgiveness advocacy can vary. In relation to the first domain, forgiving can be advocated or debated with stringent precision, or it can blur into or be mixed with other speech acts or behaviors, such as excusing, forgetting, and the like. In relation to the second domain, the advocate of forgiveness can take a more or less restrictive stance. Roughly speaking, those who advocate what I call "forgiveness minimalism" would confine forgiveness exclusively to the direct victims, would accept the idea of the unforgivable in some instances, and would insist that forgiveness becomes problematic in various ways if advocated or granted irrespective of perpetrator repentance. Those who advocate "forgiveness maximalism" would allow various kinds of forgiveness "by proxy," would rule out the idea of the unforgivable (or perhaps insist that this is what forgiveness forgives), and would praise unconditional forgiveness as especially admirable. Thus, a concept or discourse of forgiveness can (a) be more or less blurred and (b) be placed on a continuum between minimalism and maximalism.[12] The more blurred and the less minimalist the concept of forgiveness, the greater the danger that the advocacy of forgiveness can take forms that are harmful or disrespectful to victims who retain resentment or refuse to forgive.

The TRC discourse was both blurred and maximalist—and thus a preeminent example of forgiveness boosterism. It was blurred, for example, because the willingness to forgive was thought to require not only the overcoming of desires for vengeance or revenge but also an acceptance of amnesty or the abandonment of a demand for legal retribution. According to the minimal definition of forgiveness, the person who has forgiven or who is willing to forgive will certainly not desire the satisfaction of the vindictive emotions. Yet, one may demand punishment for other reasons, such as for retributive and utilitarian reasons. It is therefore possible to be willing to forgive and overcome resentment *and* to insist that the criminals should be punished (Murphy 2003:17). Blurring of the concepts of forgiving and reconciling also occurred in the TRC hearings.[13] This was problematic because some victims may have wished to forgive in some sense without necessarily restoring or establishing a relationship with the offender and others might have been willing to reconcile without being willing to forgive. The kind of reconciliation desired by those who advocate reconciliation without forgiveness was probably different from the kind of reconciliation pictured by those who tied it to a process of confession, forgiveness, and repentance. The former type of reconciliation might be restricted to a willingness to share a state and respect the law in order to coexist in peace.[14]

TRC discourses on forgiveness constituted a form of maximalism for several reasons. First, although Tutu observed that apology and repentance were very important, he also encouraged and admired unconditional or unilateral forgiveness. In a statement to an HRV hearing in Johannesburg on April 29, 1996, he stressed that "forgiveness ultimately is to say you [the victim] give people the chance to change. You open a door for someone to move from a dark past to a new and enlightened present and future." In this way, Tutu tried to encourage the victims to take "the first step": to articulate a willingness to forgive *before* even knowing whom to forgive and before knowing anything about the perpetrators' present attitude to their past criminal records. This concept of so-called unilateral or unconditional forgiveness is a genuinely controversial concept of forgiveness. As Tutu puts it, it might be "Christ-like": "Jesus did not wait until those who were nailing him to the cross had asked for forgiveness. He was ready, as they drove the nails, to pray to his Father to forgive them"(1999:272). Tutu completes that last sentence by adding, "and he [Jesus] even provided an excuse for what they were doing" (272).[15] Jesus of course said that those who drove in the nails did not know what they were doing. The question is whether the simultaneous praying for forgiveness and the provision of an excuse for those who do evil is another form of blurring the concept of forgiveness. At least the moral and conceptual difference between forgiving and excusing someone should be recognized.

The concept of unilateral forgiveness might also be harmful to a more fragile and merely human victim whose publicly expressed willingness to forgive may be met by a lying, self-excusing, or unrepentant perpetrator. Tutu has argued that a notion of forgiveness that is dependent on the culprit's confession or repentance would be unjust to the victims by locking them into victimhood (1999:Chapter 11). This line of thinking is based on the untenable presumption that the only way in which victims of wrongdoing may deal with their anger or resentment is by forgiving those who harmed them. Therapists advocating forgiveness emphasize this point too, but, as noted by Norvin Richards, the considerations urged on the victim (to reframe his or her view of the wrongdoer) "are at least as well suited to function as excuses as they are to be taken as reasons to forgive" (Richards 2002:83). This blurring is conceptually and ethically problematic because forgiving and excusing are based on antagonistic assumptions about the responsibility and blameworthiness of the wrongdoer and send different messages: "You are responsible for what you did, but I forgive you" versus "I see that you must be excused from responsibility." Forgiving implies an acknowledgment of responsibility that might get lost when it is confused with excusing, which is one reason why the use of a blurred concept of forgiveness as part of a transitional justice process can be problematic.

The second reason why the TRC forgiveness discourse can be seen as a form of maximalism concerns the use of forgiveness in the public and sociopolitical realm. That the officials of a public—and allegedly secular—institution engaged in praising some individuals' willingness to forgive is controversial. Was it legitimate to make it a regular practice to ask the victims or the bereaved whether they could forgive, how they felt about the eventual granting of amnesty, and the like? Should a public and presumably secular institution make it its business to try to heal and to evaluate emotional stances of its citizens at all? And should a public institution that must deal with citizens of all faiths promote an unmistakably Christian notion of forgiveness? Probably not, argues Stuart Wilson; but "victims should be able to expect their emotions not to be treated as public property" (S. Wilson 2001:47).

In discussions of forgiveness concerning the Holocaust, a central issue is who has the right or the standing to forgive: only the direct victims or also their relatives or descendants or members of the persecuted group in general. The discourse of forgiveness that took place in the context of the TRC adopts a maximalist concept of forgiveness because often forgiveness was sought from the relatives of the (dead) victims.

The Holocaust-focused discussion of forgiveness also raises the question whether some deeds and some evildoers are unforgivable (Garrard and Scarre 2003, Lang 1999, Wiesenthal 1998). Tutu did not accept any limitations on forgiveness. In a memorable interview with Danish television, Tutu even left space for the idea of an Adolf Hitler in Heaven.

Let me give an example of the effect that an apparent lack of limits on forgiveness has on its value. (The lack of acknowledgment of the possibility that there may be such a thing as hasty or harmful forgiving may be seen as the flip side of the lack of acknowledgment of the possible legitimacy and worthiness of resentment). In speeches and writings, Tutu has repeatedly cited this example of testimony from a Mrs. Savage:

> A white woman is a victim of a hand-grenade attack by one of the liberation movements. A lot of her friends are killed. And she ends up having to have open-heart surgery, and she goes into the ICU. She

comes to the Truth and Reconciliation Commission to tell her story. And she tells her story. And she says, "You know, when I came out of hospital, my children had to bathe me, had to clothe me, had to feed me. And I can't walk through the security checkpoint at an airport— I've still got shrapnel inside me—so, all kinds of alarms go off when I walk through." Do you know what she said? She said, of this experience that left her in this condition? It has—can you credit it? —she says, "It has enriched my life." She says, "I'd like to meet the perpetrator, I'd like to meet him in a spirit of forgiveness. I would like to forgive him." Which is extraordinary. But then, she goes on to say, she goes on to say—can you believe it? —she goes on to say, "I hope he forgives me."[16]

Tutu holds forth this case as an example that "ought to leave people quite speechless at the wonder of it all" (1999:147). Tutu is exhilarated not just by the woman's evaluation of her suffering and her willingness to forgive and reconcile before confronting the offender but also by her hope that *she* will be forgiven. Is resentment so immoral or harmful and forgiveness so noble and valuable that it is always and unconditionally good and praiseworthy to overcome resentment? What I find missing are considerations of the possibility of excessive forgiving and deficient resentment. The hope that one will be forgiven is at least conventionally the prerogative of the sinner or, more broadly, the person who, intentionally and responsibly, has done wrong to another. When victims of terrorism hope that those who dropped the bomb can forgive them, perhaps one should consider what damage a too strong appreciation of forgiveness can do to people's sense of responsibility and culpability.

Reading the transcripts of the actual hearing, one finds that Mrs. Savage also made a long statement about all the pain and misery that the attack on her brought on her entire family. This part of her statement never figures in Tutu's uses of her case: it makes his appreciation of the victim's having been enriched by suffering somewhat suspect by bringing to attention the useless suffering that the same incident inflicted on other persons. Let me close this chapter with the continuation of Mrs. Savage's testimony:

Look I suppose that is something that I did omit. The bomb blast took its toll on my family. I believe I'm a very strong person; I did have a complete breakdown after six months. My daughter also had a breakdown; she was, well all the children tried to be mother, father, sister, brother, husband, everything to me, they really carried me, they picked me up and carried me. My son has had his problems as well, I think psychologically, it affected my family in terms of them just being able to believe that it could actually happen to me. . . . I think of all the

people affected by the bomb blast, it affected my dad the worst. He just
went into a very deep depression and he died about six months ago.
When I was ill he just used to sit next my bed and cry and say, "You
know, I can't believe this." I feel bad because you know I'm not the
only victim, but that is how it affected us, and then my mum, she
couldn't carry on without him and she died two months later.
Basically it just broke his heart (HRV hearing, April 17, 1996).[17]

6

Layers and Remainders

Nested Resentments

When we want to determine whether resentment is justified, we commonly try to find out what it is about and to assess whether a wrong or an injury that is worth becoming angry about has occurred. Trying to understand and judge the anger and resentment of victims and survivors in the aftermath of mass atrocities is a complex undertaking, in part because it seems that one has to keep in focus several "layers" or a history, rather than a single event, of compounded violations. In the case of the victims and survivors appearing before the HRV Committee of the TRC, there were first (at the bottom) the original violations: the tortures, rapes, and humiliations forming the substance of a survivor's resentful and unreconciled memory. Then there was the governmentally sanctioned amnesty policy that obliterated the right of the victims or their relatives to seek redress in courts of law, both criminal and civil. Even if one assumes that amnesty was a precondition for a peaceful transition to democracy, the suspension of the right to legal redress could reasonably be felt like a sacrifice of justice. Third, victims and relatives could be legitimately angry because they were faced with a powerful public celebration of forgiveness and restorative justice, one that often discouraged and diminished their righteous resentment or indignation occasioned by the original offenses and the amnesty policy.

To the extent that the victim's resentments are not split neatly and packaged according to the different violations, one has to deal with *nested* or *compounded* resentments. It is as important to pay attention to the differences among the sources of the victim's nested resentments as it is to keep in mind their interconnections. Without keeping those interconnections in focus, attention to victims' resentments in a postatrocity context risks focusing too narrowly on the immediate postatrocity causes: the amnesty policy and a sense of being pressured to forgive or forget. To the degree that the victim's response to various postatrocity policies or attitudes is seen as related only to the "darker" complex of original atrocities and their related emotional responses (outrage, horror, consternation, fear) and remainders (shame, guilt, distrust, and the like), this narrow focus leads in turn to a truncated understanding. Without a focus on the differences among the layers of resentment, one's understanding is equally impaired. For example, the distinction between the second and third layer of violation brings to attention the significance that both *attitudes* and policies or actual forms of repair can carry for the victims. That is, it matters not only whether the perpetrators are punished or whether reparations are offered, but also whether a given policy is presented as an agonizing compromise or as a morally superior approach. To illustrate the importance of attitudes, let us consider a judgment of the Constitutional Court of South Africa and the philosophical concept of *moral remainders*.

Acknowledging Remainders

As explained in the beginning of Part One, this book addresses not the amnesty policy itself, but rather the manner in which prominent proponents of and within the TRC characterized those who were unwilling to support it. This section presents an example of an institutional response to the amnesty policy that differed greatly from that adopted by the TRC. The response of the Constitutional Court of South Africa to a lawsuit brought by the Azanian Peoples' Organisation and by a small group of relatives of well-known anti-apartheid activists exemplifies a kind of reasoning and advocacy that neither celebrated forgiveness nor vilified resentment and desires for retribution. One of the plaintiffs, Ntsiki Biko, was the widow of Steven Biko who was killed by five policemen in 1977, and she expressed the gist of the lawsuit in this statement: "We all want reconciliation, but it must come with something. It must come with justice" (Hesse and Post 1999:14).

The applicants submitted that the South African Parliament had no constitutional power to authorize the TRC's Amnesty Committee to indemnify any wrongdoer from criminal or civil liability arising from the perpetration of the gross human rights violations described in the legislation authorizing the

TRC. Interestingly, although the Constitutional Court concluded that the South African constitution did permit the amnesty policy and it articulated the arguments why this policy was substantially justifiable in the actual context, the Court's judgment is also one of the most succinct statements about the values and principles that the amnesty policy obliterated:

> The effect of an amnesty undoubtedly impacts upon very fundamental human rights. All persons are entitled to the protection of the law against unlawful invasions of their right to life, their right to respect for and protection of dignity and their right not to be subject to torture of any kind. When those rights are invaded those aggrieved by such invasion have the right to obtain redress in the ordinary courts of law and those guilty of perpetrating such violations are answerable before such courts, both civilly and criminally. An amnesty to the wrongdoer effectively obliterates such rights (Constitutional Court of South Africa 1996, Sec. 9, p. 11).

This awareness of the amnesty policy's costs in terms of the victim's loss of rights suffuses the entire judgment, delivered by Justice Ismail Mahomed. The judgment affirms the policy, but not without expressing an understanding of the applicants' resentment of it. Consider, for example, the Court's comment on the applicants' resistance to following the advice of their lawyer to drop parts of their suit, and note, in relation to the words about the desire for punishment, its divergence from Desmond Tutu's repeated reference to the utterly destructive "lust for revenge":

> I understand perfectly well why the applicants would want to insist that those wrongdoers who abused their authority and wrongfully murdered, maimed or tortured very much loved members of their families who had, in their view, been engaged in a noble struggle to confront the inhumanity of apartheid, should vigorously be prosecuted and effectively punished for their callous and inhuman conduct in violation of the criminal law. I can therefore also understand why they are emotionally unable to identify themselves with the consequences of the legal concession made by Mr. Soggot and if that concession was wrong in law I would have no hesitation whatsoever in rejecting it (1996, Sec. 16. p. 16).

The Court's defense of the amnesty provision starts with this concession: "every decent human being must feel grave discomfort" by the prospects that perpetrators of "evil acts" will be protected by amnesty (Sec. 17, p. 17). And yet, it sees the act establishing amnesty as justifiable because it seems the most promising way in which to balance justice for the victims of past crimes while advancing the transition to a future when the people of South Africa may enjoy "some of the human rights so unfairly denied to the generations which preceded them" (Sec. 50). Furthermore, according to the Court, criminal prosecutions would only have kept intact "the abstract right" to such prosecutions of the wrongdoers, keeping the victims substantially ignorant about what happened, thus perpetuating their "legitimate sense of resentment and grief" (Sec. 17). The TRC amnesty could, on the other hand, help the "dependents of the tortured and the wounded, the maimed and the dead discover what did in truth happen to their loved ones" (Sec. 17).

This is not the place for a full analysis and discussion of the Court's judgment. I set it forth here as an example of a more balanced and dilemma-sensitive approach to the policy of "amnesty for truth." The Court's reasoning is interesting because of its recognition that the transition was not resolvable without *moral remainders*[1]: the "imbalances, debts, or unexpiated wrongs that remain even after we have done what can be done to put things right" (Card 2002:169). In *Love's Knowledge* (1992), Martha Nussbaum asks what kinds of emotional and practical moral recognition are appropriate for agents who, facing a dilemma, are forced to choose between two or more morally deficient actions (1992:63). As Nussbaum writes (referring to the blame that the chorus directed toward Agamemnon in Aeschylus's *The Orestia*), negligence of the losses, regrets, or compromises that may be involved even when we act for the best may amount to "grave moral deficiency" (64). It matters deeply whether the policy that might justifiably be preferred is treated and advocated simply as the winning or superior alternative or, as Nussbaum puts it, "as a course of action that overrides a genuine moral value" (65). According to Nussbaum, the virtuous political leader will acknowledge and even focus on such dilemmas, "because to do so reaffirms and strengthens attachment to the values in question, in such a way that one will be less likely to violate them in other circumstances" (66). Moral remainders come to the fore precisely in the acknowledgment of the moral costs or dilemmas intrinsic to the political solution in a given conflict.

Since introduced by Bernard Williams in 1973, the concept of "moral remainder" has gained widespread usage in moral philosophy. It has been used to refer to the unexpiated wrongs (the things not made right) themselves as well as to the emotional residues inherent in the responses to such wrongs—regret, remorse, resentment, shame, guilt, and the like (cf. Card 2002:169). That is, although the acknowledgment of the moral remainder might be expressed in the form of certain emotional residues (shame, regret, resentment, guilt, gratitude), in the context of responses to political mass violence certain political statements might matter as much or more than the emotional issue. For example, whether a political leader actually feels remorse or not may be less significant than whether he changes the public record by uttering (under the right circumstances) a public apology or a balanced explanation of why he chose a given solution. What primarily matters here is the moral significance that is tied to the acknowledgment of moral remainders. In line with Nussbaum's discussion of the virtuous political leader, Claudia Card argues that the expression of moral remainders offers a "limited redemption in that they reveal our appreciation that all has not been made right, or that not all is as it should be (or would be, ideally) between us" (Card 2002:169). The moral remainder is particularly relevant in the aftermath of atrocities in relation to which any response is somehow inadequate. As Card puts it, "Remainders are rectificatory feelings regarding what otherwise proves unrectifiable by our actions" (169).

Stuart Wilson calls for recognition of a moral remainder in his critique of the "Myth of Restorative Justice" (2001). In line with the ruling of the Constitutional Court, Wilson grants that prosecutions might have been ineffective and risky and that revealing the truth and creating political stability are genuinely valuable outcomes. Wilson suggests that we should think of the TRC as the response to a situation in which "whatever is done, one faces regret about not having been able to meet the important moral requirements of the path not taken. This regret is called 'moral remainder'" (2001:555). In my opinion, the judgment of the Constitutional Court offers an interesting example of how the acknowledgment of moral remainder can unfold in the context of transitional justice.

Transition to Part Two

As we move from Part One to Part Two, we change both time and location, shifting from postapartheid South Africa to postwar Germany. More important, the transition to Part Two involves a shift of perspective from that of the advocate of forgiveness and reconciliation to that of the resentful and unforgiving victim. One of the shortcomings of most discussions of resentment and forgiveness after mass atrocities is the lack of voice given to the first-person victim perspective—in particular, the lack of attention to the challenging voice of resistance. Granted, victim statements of resistance and refusals to forgive are often integrated into papers and debates, but they mainly appear simply as illustrations of the lines of the argument formulated and discussed by and among practitioners and academics. One of Part Two's aims is to take seriously in a completely different way the victim's perspective. The examination of the reflections of Jean Améry represents a "window" to the first-person perspective (or the perspective of one of those to whom the advocacy of forgiveness or the characterization of resentment matters the most) and not only a thought-provoking and intuitively implausible position. The most profound value of Améry's essays has to do with the quality of his reflections. We gain access not only to opinions or claims and desires but also to a range of philosophical reflections on concrete experience.

II

Jean Améry on Resentment and Reconciliation

The time is out of joint: O, cursed spite,/That ever I was born to set it right!

SHAKESPEARE, HAMLET

7

Contextualizing *"Ressentiments"*

From South Africa to Postwar Germany

Three decades before the TRC in South Africa initiated its proceedings, Jean Améry struggled to gainsay contemporary assumptions that victims opposing forgiveness and pleas to forget or "move on" had to be possessed by hatred, the lust for revenge, or a subjective and pathological inability to get on with life. Yet, differences between postapartheid South Africa and postwar Germany abound, and leaping from one context to the other can be a precarious exercise. World War II and the crimes of the Holocaust cannot be equated with the human rights violations of the apartheid regime.[1] Neither can the situation of a surviving Nazi victim living in Central Europe be equated with that of apartheid victims in South Africa. For example, in South Africa there was the determination to face the truth of the past, and victims were not hoped or expected simply to forget or to recover through the sheer passing of time. Jean Améry, to the contrary, was struggling against appeals to forget or to simply look ahead. Nonetheless, I would like to show that Améry's reflections offer a moral perspective on resentment and reconciliation that could both challenge and enrich current discussions (and not just debates on the TRC) about the moral sources of resistance to forgiveness and reconciliation.

Jean Améry published his most influential essay collection in 1966 under the German title, *Jenseits von Schuld und Sühne* (in English: *Beyond*

Guilt and Atonement). These essays were not published in an English-language version until 1980 when they appeared under the title *At the Mind's Limits* (using the title of the first essay to name the entire collection). Particularly interesting in this context is his essay originally entitled "*Ressentiments*" (in the 1980 translation, "Resentments"). In the following I refer to the English translation (Améry 1999), but given the significance of the original terms, I consistently emend the translation and use a direct translation of the 1966 German title as well as the French noun used by Améry.

The essay in question contains a meditation in the course of which the prolonged and at first glance shameful and semi-conscious *ressentiment* harbored by the Nazi victim comes to be posited as the affective aspect of an unyielding allegiance to certain genuinely moral demands. The "man of *ressentiment*" is commonly imagined as an unforgiving and irreconcilable, ignoble, and vengeful character. At first glance Améry seems to confirm this picture as he addresses the advocacy of forgiveness and reconciliation only to express his antipathy to its pathetic, hollow, and thoughtless aspects. However, Améry's attempt to rehabilitate a special kind of *ressentiment* is connected to a notion of reconciliation or re-creation of human community; this connection alone makes the effort to read the essay worthwhile. Through his account both of *ressentiment* and his notion of reconciliation, Améry carves out a position on forgiveness that continues to surprise, provoke, and inspire. Therefore, *Beyond Guilt and Atonement* contributes to a more nuanced understanding of unforgiving victims and their negative emotions.

Beyond Guilt and Atonement was an intervention in a particular time and context. Its essays were not written for the unsituated philosophical reader, but for Améry's German contemporaries. In fact, they were originally written to be broadcast in 1964–65 on the Radio of South Germany (*Süddeutscher Rundfunk*), and given that the audience was familiar with his subject and its controversial nature, much is assumed or only alluded to.[2] Therefore, this chapter sets the scene for the analysis of the essay by providing a short introduction to the works and life of Améry, a presentation of the book in which the essay was placed, and a brief overview of the historical context in which it must be situated. Additionally, as the final preparatory step before we can get on with the examination of the essay, I explain my approach to the essay and indicate how I hope to add other readings of it.

Jean Améry: Life and Works

The works of Jean Améry have long been appreciated by survivors as well as scholars of the Holocaust. His defiant and counterintuitive positions have been recognized for their extraordinary provocative qualities by such eminent figures as Theodor W. Adorno; see the commentary to *Werke* in (see the commentary to *Werke* in Améry 2002b), Imre Kertész (1996), and Primo Levi (1988). Health care professionals working with the rehabilitation of torture victims often quote Améry's essay on the nature of torture and its indelible effects on the victim. Still, Améry is far from the mainstream avenues of philosophical thinking in general and the philosophy of forgiveness and reconciliation in particular. Although his writings are known by writers on resentment and many scholars of transitional justice, the value of his perspective on victims' responses to atrocity has not been recognized sufficiently.

Jean Améry was born in Austria as Hans Maier in 1912.[3] His father was an assimilated Jew, his mother a Catholic.[4] With the passing of the Nuremberg Laws in 1935, his Jewish ancestry, until then not recognized by Améry, became fatal—both politically and existentially fatal. In December 1938, Améry fled with his Jewish wife to Antwerpen in neutral Belgium. Améry describes the last part of the flight as follows:

> The road led through the wintry night in the Eifel, on smugglers' routes to Belgium, whose custom officials and policemen would have refused us a legal crossing of the border, for we were coming into the country as refugees, without passport and visa, without any valid national identity. . . . After we had arrived so "safely" in Antwerp and had confirmed this in a cable to the members of our family who had remained at home, we exchanged the rest of our money, altogether fifteen marks and fifty pfennigs, if I recall correctly. That was the wealth with which we were to begin a new life, as it is said. The old one had forsaken us. For always? For always. But that I only know now, almost twenty-seven years later (Améry 1999:41).[5]

In May 1940, the Wehrmacht of the Third Reich occupied Belgium. In the very same month, Améry was deported as an "enemy alien" to an internment camp (Saint-Cyprien). He soon escaped, jumping from a running train but was recaptured and taken to Gurs, a large camp in southern France near the Spanish border. In July 1941, Améry succeeded in escaping once again and returned, through Paris, to his wife, who had been hiding in Brussels. Once in Brussels, he joined a German-speaking organization in the Belgian resistance movement. However, in July 1943, Améry was caught and tortured by the Gestapo. Soon identified as a Jew, he was sent to several concentration and extermination camps, including Auschwitz. Améry arrived in Auschwitz on January 17, 1944 along with 655 other persons, of whom 417 were immediately killed. In a posthumously published manuscript that has not been translated from German—"On the Psychology of the German People" (in Améry

2002)—Améry describes an incident from the scene of arrival in Auschwitz. The manuscript was signed Hanns Mayer and finished as early as in June 1945:

> Concentration camp Auschwitz, January 1944:
> Following the arrival of a transport of several hundred Jews, men, women and children, they are divided in the usual manner by the SS people. First the men capable of work are separated from the women, children and the very old, and finally this second group is also broken up by taking the children from their mothers. . . . One woman, whose searching eyes have been looking for her own child in vain among the huddled, quietly crying children, suddenly breaks away from her companions, her hair in disarray, gesticulating tragically, screaming for her child and already obviously displaying the first signs of derangement. . . . She then comes to an SS man on guard duty. "My child," she says, "have you seen my child anywhere?" "It's a child you want, is it?" the SS man replies with perfect calm, "wait here . . ." And he slowly approaches the group of little ones, who are now instinctively crying a little louder in fear. He bends down and seizes a boy of about four by the foot. He lifts him up, swings him round a few times through the air, and finally hurls him with all his might against the desperately searching mother, so that she falls to the ground at the force of the impact, uttering a scream that is just as inhuman as the eyes of the SS man (Améry 2002:2:507, trans. Catherine Schwerin).

In contrast to some optimistic attempts to prove that the human spirit survives any ordeal, Améry wrote of his experience that "the word always dies where the claim of some reality is total" (Améry 1999:20):

> "The wall stands speechless and cold, the flags clank in the wind," I muttered to myself in mechanical association. Then I repeated the stanza somewhat louder, listened to the words, tried to track the rhythm, and expected that the emotional and mental response that for years this Hölderlin poem had awakened in me would emerge. But nothing happened. The poem could no longer transcend reality. There it was and all that remained was objective statement: such and such, and the Kapo roars "left," and the soup was watery, and the flags are clanking in the wind (Améry 1999:7).[6]

In 1945, British troops liberated Bergen-Belsen, the last of the camps to which Améry was deported. Améry returned—as one of the 615 survivors of the 25,437 Jews deported from Belgium—to Brussels and learned that his wife had died: "the only person," as Améry writes, "for whose sake I had held on to life for two years" (1999:43). Améry settled in Brussels, and in 1955 he began publishing under the French anagram of his name; Hans Maier (or Mayer) became Jean Améry. He wrote several novels and philosophical papers, and for various European newspapers and journals, he wrote a large number of journalistic articles and brief biographies.[7] Traveling through Germany and other Central European countries, he became a well-known essayist and public intellectual and earned important literary prizes.

However, Améry did not begin writing his most well-known essays on torture, exile, and the victim's condition until the Auschwitz trial was held in Frankfurt in 1963–65; that is, until the passing of two decades of silence about "the time that was impossible to lose" (1999:xiii).[8] In these essays, as in most of his important works, Améry uses his own life and experiences as the object of literary experimentation and philosophical elucidation. What accounts for the forceful tone and appeal of Améry's writings is not only the serious and probing nature of his topics and thought but also the authentic combination of the concrete with the philosophical and the common with the personal. Améry's objective is to "proceed from the concrete event, but never become lost in it" (Améry 1999:xi).

Among his later writings are several works on suicide, and the closeness between life and works is, sadly, also evident here (Améry 1967, 1977). In 1974, Améry attempted suicide, and four years later, on October 17, 1978, he succeeded. At age sixty-six, he took his own life in a hotel room in Salzburg.

Beyond Guilt and Atonement

It is not easy to categorize *Beyond Guilt and Atonement*, but its proper place is no doubt among the extraordinary works that make up the most challenging segment of Holocaust literature. In quality and complexity, it can be compared to the writings of Primo Levi, Charlotte Delbo, Jorge Semprun, or Imre Kertész. Like the works of all of these authors, it is a book to which one can return repeatedly and through which one is challenged to see the world from an unfamiliar perspective. In the preface to the first edition, Améry stresses that the book is not a documentary work, but rather an examination or a phenomenological description of the existence of the victim (1999:xiii):

"What occupies me, and what I am qualified to speak about, is the victims of this [i.e. the Third] Reich. I don't want to erect a monument to them, for to be a victim alone is not an honor. I only wanted to describe their condition" (ix).

Based on his personal experience, Améry tries to articulate philosophically the experiences and postwar situation or the *conditio inhumana* of the victims of the Third Reich" (vii). In comparison with the postwar literature on

Auschwitz available in 1966, *Beyond Guilt and Atonement* added what W.G. Sebald has called an authentic voice to a literary scene that was still dominated by "a generalized dramatic and poetic tone [that] often obstructed closer understanding of those terrible events" (Sebald 2003:146). The essays are testimony of a commitment to phenomenological reflection that is strictly tied to a concrete and experienced reality (see Gerhard Scheit's commentary in *Werke*, Améry 2002: 655ff). Améry wants to "become clear" about the nature of his predicament, and his writings give testimony of a constant struggle with the inadequacies of conventional (pre-Auschwitz) vocabularies to describe the radical nature of the destruction inflicted on the victims. Throughout his essays Améry seeks to conceptualize as precisely as possible the particular nature of his—the victim's—experiences, condition, and emotions. One repeatedly finds negative statements asserting that a given aspect of the Nazi survivor's condition is not captured by this or that concept or notion: the *ressentiment* of the survivor is not like the *ressentiment* characterized by Nietzsche; the homesickness of the person expelled from the Third Reich is not like the condition known from sentimental folk songs and poems. Améry constantly picks up well-known concepts and notions in order to turn and toss them around until they fit the case at hand more precisely, until the inability to penetrate the specifics of the situation is lessened. In this way, Améry's essays express a determined and deliberate wish to avoid false abstractions or a careless reliance on inadequate concepts.[9]

In his famous article, "The Essay as Form," Theodor W. Adorno writes that the essay pays for its "affinity with open intellectual experience by the lack of security, a lack which the norm of established thought fears like death" (2000:101). The essay form reflects a childish freedom: "It does not begin with Adam and Eve but with what it wants to discuss; it says what is at issue and stops where it feels itself complete—not where nothing is left to say" (93). Améry's essays generally have several of the characteristics lauded by Adorno: they are explicitly tentative and do not aspire to say either every or the last word about their topic; they do not unfold a clearly and systematically structured argument; and they blend autobiography, introspection, and literature with conceptual analysis and reflection. As Adorno puts it, the form of the essay "testifies to the non-identity that it has to express," and it is thus well suited to the struggle to capture what escapes our given concepts and understanding. Thus, to express the special kind of unsettling illumination sought by Améry, the genre of the essay is the ideal form.

Améry first considered "*Ressentiments*" as the title for the series of radio lectures he read on South German radio, which indicates the importance of the particular essay that came to bear this title (it was first entitled "The Germans"). The two titles—*Beyond Guilt and Atonement*, which was ultimately selected, and "*Ressentiments*"—both allude to the works of Friedrich

Nietzsche, the author of *Beyond Good and Evil* and the most influential source of modern understandings of *ressentiment*. Yet, what does the word "beyond" signify in Améry's title? He is emphatic that his intention is first and foremost to describe the existential condition of the victim: "much will be said about guilt and also about atonement.... Still, I believe that the findings of this study lie beyond the question of guilt and atonement. I described the state of someone who was overcome, that is all" (1999:xiv). The concept of "description" can easily give the wrong impression of the nature of the book. In this case, the description is in itself an achievement because it articulates a range of experiences that are often and, perhaps too quickly, said to be "unspeakable." The "description . . . that is all" phrase might also suggest that Améry would adopt a third-person observation position vis-à-vis his own experiences. But this is not the case:

> If in the first line of the Auschwitz essay I had still believed that I could remain circumspect and face the reader with refined objectivity, I now saw that this was simply impossible. Where the word "I" was to have been avoided completely, it proved to be the single useful starting point. I had planned a contemplative, essayistic study. What resulted was a personal confession refracted through meditation (1999: xiii).[10]

Beyond Guilt and Atonement includes five interrelated essays on Auschwitz, torture, homelessness, *ressentiment*, and the "necessity and impossibility of being a Jew." Taken together, these essays offer an account of the fragility of the intersubjective or social conditions on which the life and dignity of the individual are premised. Améry examines the things that are lost, including basic assumptions about dignity, identity, home, and trust in the world and other human beings. As he put it, the essays describe the state of one who was overcome. The latter phrase also is part of the subtitle of the book. In German it reads *Bewältigungsversuche eines Überwältigten*, which means something like attempts to overcome—or to manage—by one who was overcome. The English translation refrains from even trying to capture the allusive play at words with the German term *Vergangenheitsbewältigung*, a catchword for the activity of managing or overcoming the Nazi past. Instead it bears the subtitle: *Contemplations by a Survivor on Auschwitz and its Realities*. It is not surprising that a new subtitle is invented for the English-language edition. The German is not easy to translate, but more important, the connotations that are functional in the German context are inevitably lost in any English translation.

Yet, writing in German that the essays represent an attempt of "one who was overcome" to manage or overcome, Améry indicates two things. First, the book will present to its readers a victim's perspective on how to "manage" the past. This concept was in itself extraordinary. Whereas the Holocaust and the experiences and perspective of its victims have today become part of popular culture, one needs to consider that Améry wrote at a time when the particular features of Nazi genocide were still only dawning on the world (i.e., as something distinct and as an independent crime that was more than a side effect of Nazi warfare) and when the status of its victims was gradually changing from offensive ascriptions of vengefulness or shame to dubious notions of moral insight and accomplishment. Second, the word *Versuche* (attempts) can be seen as a subtle critical comment on the concept of *Vergangenheitsbewältigung* itself, insofar as that concept implies a notion that the past can be overcome. More concretely, highlighting the essays as "attempts" may be seen as a corrective to facile contemporary beliefs that the Nazi past could and had already been overcome and therefore left behind or neutralized in "the cold storage of history" (xi).[11]

Indeed, Améry's essays are true to the meaning of the French "*essais*" (i.e., to experiment, to try). They do not settle the case, but try to unearth the past and the problems hidden beneath facile appeals to look to the future or to forgive and forget. In the preface, Améry even warns us that "to the extent that the reader would venture to join me at all he will have no choice but to accompany me, in the same tempo, through the darkness that I illuminated step by step. In the process, he will come upon contradictions in which I myself got caught up" (xiv). A neat and clear presentation would be a kind of distortion. Given the radical nature of the experiences explored in *Beyond Guilt and Atonement* as a whole, the process of striving for enlightenment and articulation has to be conscious of its own limitations. The third preface, written in 1976, provides the following condensed programmatic statement:

> I had no clarity when I was writing this little book, I do not have it today, and I hope that I never will. Clarification would amount to disposal, settlement of the case, which can then be placed in the files of history. My book is meant to aid in preventing precisely this. For nothing is resolved, no conflict is settled, no remembering has become mere memory. . . . Emotions? For all I care, yes. Where is it decreed that enlightenment must be free of emotion? To me the opposite seems to be true. Enlightenment can properly fulfill its task only if it sets to work with passion (Améry 1999:xi)

Germany 1945–65

Today, in light of the German memory culture of recent decades, *Vergangenheitsbewältigung* has nearly come to be a term of appreciation. It has come to signify a serious and thorough relationship to the past, a conscientious social performance, and a consciousness of historical responsibility and the duty to remember.[12] However, in the first decades following 1945, this meaning was not associated with the use of this term and of related terms like *Vergangenheitspolitik* (politics of the past) or *Aufarbeitung der Vergangenheit* (working through the past). "Coming to terms with the past" connoted something very different in the first years following the defeat/liberation. As Theodor W. Adorno emphasized in 1959, contemporary discourse did not imply a serious working through of the past; notice, that he also anticipates the *ressentiment* that comes to be the concern of Améry:

> It suggests, rather, wishing to turn the page and, if possible, wiping it from memory. The attitude that it would be proper for everything to be forgiven and forgotten by those who were wronged is expressed by the party that committed the injustice. In a scholarly controversy I once wrote that in the hangman's house one shouldn't speak of the noose; otherwise, you wind up with *ressentiment*. . . . One wants to get free of the past: rightly so, since one cannot live in its shadow. . . . But wrongly so, since the past one wishes to evade is still so intensely alive (Adorno 1986:115).

In line with Adorno, leading historians on the history of postwar Germany and the political and cultural responses to the National Socialist past, such as Jeffrey Herf (1997) and Norbert Frei (2002), have shown how the criminal trials and political expurgations administered by the Allies immediately after the war were soon followed by amnesty laws and the release from jail, reintegration, and rehabilitation of civil servants, lawyers, and others professionals and groups. Konrad Adenauer was the leader of the postwar Christian Democratic Party and chancellor of the Federal Republic of Germany from 1949 to 1963. His government's policies of amnesty and reintegration reflected, according to these historians, a massive popular wish to "let bygones be bygones" or to move on with a *tabula rasa* (a clean slate) that would leave behind painful questions about guilt and responsibility. As Frei puts it, the Germans in general seem to have felt that they had "atoned enough through aerial bombardment, flight and expulsion" (2002:6).[13] In a 1949 poll of German citizens conducted by the office of the American High Commissioner of Germany, 59 percent of respondents thought that National Socialism had been "a good idea badly carried out." Nationwide surveys conducted 1951–52 showed that an average of 41 percent of the respondents saw more good than evil in Nazi ideas (cf. Herf 1997: 274). These are just some of the polling data indicating that Adenauer was in tune with majority sentiments when he, in his first *Regierungserklärung* (governmental policy statement)[14] as chancellor of the Federal Republic of Germany, criticized the de-Nazification process and promised to examine the question of amnesty. It was, according to Adenauer, simply not believable that anti-Semitism could still exist in Germany.[15] The primary critics of Adenauer's politics of amnesty and integration and those who expressed the majority opinion's preference for forgetting the past were leading voices of the Social Democrat opposition (see Herf 1997 on opposition leaders, Kurt Schumacher, Ernst Reuter, and Carlo Schmid). Thus, the seriousness that characterizes today's public German memory culture is the result not of a linear development, but rather of a contested debate that was for decades fought by a minority.

How then to characterize German society's attitude to the Holocaust at the time when Améry authored his essays? The president of West Germany from 1959 to 1969, Heinrich Lübke, said in an early speech to the Society for Christian-Jewish Cooperation: "We hope that the Jews will not leave the good-will present in our contribution to restitution unanswered. It would be unfruitful, and over time would be paralyzing, if we did not feel that trust grows on the other side as well" (quoted in Herf 1997:332). As Herf comments, "Lübke articulated the impatience of those in West Germany who had heard enough talk about the Nazi past, who did not want to be burdened by the actions of a 'small minority,' and who wanted the West German President to focus less on what the Nazis had done to others and more on the victimization of Germans by the Nazis and by the Allies" (Herf 1997:332).

Given the political use of the discourse of forgiveness in the South African TRC, one might wonder whether or how Nazi victims were encouraged to forgive in postwar Germany. This is not the place for anything remotely like a comparative examination, yet it makes sense to underscore the salient differences as well as similarities between the two. For example, most South African churches were critical of the apartheid regime. In Germany, to the contrary— and as argued by German postwar historian, Norbert Frei—the churches (in comparison with other societal actors) were particularly "unscrupulous" in their agitation against de-Nazification and in their more or less blanket defense of the old and corrupted elites (Frei 2000:164). Closer to our focus, Katharina von Kellenbach has argued that the churches mainly used their "moral capital to mobilize nationally and internationally on behalf of forgiveness for the perpetrators" (Kellenbach 2001a: 657). In addition, the role of the victims in the two contexts was worlds apart. In South Africa, the victims were typically at center stage. In postwar Germany, considering examples of postwar German pastoral care of Nazi perpetrators, as well as the pleas directed from church representatives to the Allied powers, one is effectively reminded that the transaction of forgiveness did not necessarily involve the victim at all (cf. Krondorfer et al. 2006). Yet, even though the advocacy of forgiveness (by Christian actors) in the two contexts was partly motivated by very different and more or less legitimate considerations, there are also similarities to consider; for example, the denunciation of punishment, the belief that restorative justice is morally superior to retributive or criminal justice, and—most important here—the tendency to frame unforgiving victims as harbingers of hate and revenge:

> In Germany, immediately after the war, both Protestant and Roman Catholic churches used their moral capital to mobilize nationally and internationally on behalf of forgiveness for the perpetrators . . . The Clemency Board of the US Military government received thousands of letters from laity and clergy, who used Christian arguments in their denunciation of Allied punishment for the perpetrators. . . . Christian attitudes of mercy and forgiveness were presented as superior to "Jewish" calls for justice and judicial prosecution of perpetrators. The Jewish survivors' refusal to forgive was seen as a hateful attitude rooted in revenge rather than a form of necessary justice (Kellenbach 2001a:657).[16]

Decades would pass before the genocidal crimes of the National Socialist regime became recognized as what Améry called "the darkest and at the same time most characteristic deeds of the Third Reich" (1999: xiv).[17] In an essay from 1950, "The Aftermath of Nazi Rule: Report from Germany" (reprinted in Arendt 1994), Hannah Arendt takes note of a certain "lack of response" that seemed to be evident everywhere: "This general lack of emotion, at any rate this apparent heartlessness, sometimes covered with cheap sentimentality, is only the most conspicuous outward symptom of a deep-rooted, stubborn, and at times vicious refusal to face and come to terms with what really happened" (Arendt 1994:259).[18] Like Arendt, Améry and several other Jewish survivors who returned to Germany in the first decade after the war registered this tendency to move on "as if nothing has happened." This lack of response was, according to Arendt, not a harmless and to-be-expected phenomenon, but the second moral collapse occasioned by the catastrophe. With similar gravity, the writer Ralph Giordano characterizes the postwar repression and denial as the Germans' *second* great guilt or fault (Giordano 2000: 246–66). Even though it is debatable whether the failure to respond appropriately can be seen in such negative terms, Arendt and Giordano are correct in emphasizing the great moral significance of the ways in which postwar societies deal with their pasts.

The mid-sixties were a time of change. The shift of generations, the trial of Eichmann in Jerusalem (1961), and the so-called Auschwitz trial in Frankfurt (1963–65) were "stations" on the path to our present focus on the Holocaust. The trial in Frankfurt was the largest, longest, and most important German Nazi trial. One of its main actors, Fritz Bauer, hoped it would serve as a national didactic exercise that would not only result in the conviction of a handful of individual defendants but would also teach the nation about its past. For many reasons, this goal proved more difficult to reach than expected. As Devin Pendas (2006) has explained in a comprehensive contextual and historical analysis of the trial, achieving the aim of recovering the truth about the past was significantly hindered by the use of a criminal law that relied on assumptions about individual agency that were completely inadequate to the reality of state-organized mass murder. Also, although the trial *was* a significant step in the German process of developing a responsible confrontation with the Nazi past, the impact of the trial on majority opinion was not as "transformative" as one would have wished. Here is a passage from Hannah Arendt's comments on German public opinion at the time of the trial (written in 1966):

> It [i.e. the majority opinion] was manifest in the behavior of the defendants—in their laughing, smiling, smirking impertinence toward prosecution and witnesses, their lack of respect for the court, their "disdainful and threatening" glances toward the public in rare instances where gasps of horror were heard. . . . It was manifest in the behavior of the lawyers who kept reminding the judges that they must pay no attention to "what one will think of us in the outside world," implying over and over again that not a German desire for justice but the world opinion influenced by the victims' desire for "retribution" and "vengeance" was the true cause of their clients' present trouble (Arendt 2003:228).

To enter the German public scene in the 1960s, speaking as Améry did as a resentful and demanding Jewish victim, must have required a considerable amount of integrity and determination. Indeed, *Beyond Guilt and Atonement* was written and published as a revolt against what a German historian has called "the continuous silencing, covering up and glossing over of the past" by the societal elites (judges, clerics, doctors, journalists, officers, civil servants etc.) who were complicit in the injustices of the past and unwilling to be held accountable" (Fischer 2003:11).[19] Améry does not address *Beyond Guilt and Atonement* to other victims: "They know what it is all about" (xiv). Instead, and in accordance with the original presentation of the essays to the listeners of South German Radio, the work is addressed to contemporary Germans:

> To the Germans, however, who in their overwhelming majority do not, or no longer, feel affected by the darkest and at the same time most characteristic deeds of the Third Reich, I would like to relate a

few things here that until now have perhaps not been revealed to them (Améry 1999:xiv).

Thus, Améry's struggle is a fight against what he calls "hollow, thoughtless, utterly false conciliatoriness" (ix) or "the pathos of forgiveness and reconciliation" (65). From his draft for the blurb on the book jacket (Améry 2002:623) to the first edition to the last preface written for its reissue in 1977, Améry emphasized that what the postwar situation of evasion or forgetfulness made necessary (on behalf of the victims) was not conciliatoriness, but a frankness that could unearth unacknowledged past and glossed-over tensions:

> For nothing is resolved, no conflict is settled, no remembering has become mere memory. What happened, happened. But *that* it happened cannot be so easily accepted. I rebel: against my past, against history, and against a present that places the incomprehensible in the cold storage of history (xi).

In spite of Améry's repeated assertions that all he can and wants to do is to "describe," *Beyond Guilt and Atonement* is also a moral-political (re)action, an attempt to provoke a revolution in the German memory culture. As such it is also a highly polemical and often sarcastic piece of criticism. "Sarcasm" comes from the Greek *sarcazein*, meaning literally "to tear flesh" and figuratively "to speak bitterly." This is indeed what Améry does in his polemic on contemporary attitudes toward the past. Above, I quoted Améry's decree that enlightenment had to "set to work *with* passion" (xi). In the essay on *ressentiment*, he defies repeatedly the classical prescription to proceed *sine ira et studio* (i.e., without anger and bias). *"Ressentiments"* is, as Primo Levi wrote, "a long, anguish-filled essay" (Levi 1988:138), but Levi did not appreciate the point that the *ressentiments* under examination "must necessarily form part of their analysis" (Améry 1999:72).

Améry reckoned that the majority of Germans would not welcome his refusal of forgiveness, his critique of contemporary notions of reconciliation, and his unwillingness to stop holding them responsible for the past. Yet, although he did not have much faith in the generation of the perpetrators, accomplices, and bystanders, his works are permeated with a sometimes very worn-out hope that it is possible to come to an understanding (*"Verständigung"*) with the new German generations (see his 1978 interview with Ingo Hermann in Hermann 1992:82). However, Améry also knew that many young Germans were "sick and tired of hearing again and again that our fathers killed six million Jews" (Améry 1999:75), and he acknowledges a need to explain why they in any sense should feel responsible for the Nazi past. In the preface to the German *Taschenbuch* edition from 1970, Améry's concern about the attitudes of German youth to the Nazi past moves to the forefront. He begins the preface referring to a number of interviews (from 1968) with German youth concerning statutory limitations for Nazi crimes. As representative of the majority of respondents, he quotes the following opinion of a young girl: "I am for stopping it at last, for how far shall that go anyway? Up to the third and fourth generation? New generations grow up, and I think one should let bygones be bygones" (Améry 2002a:626). Améry's response finely articulates the purpose of his undertaking:

> I write these lines hoping that my essays will reach the youth for which the past of the Third Reich is wiped out or at least 'worthy' of being wiped out. . . . It is not the law that should last "up to the third and fourth generation," as the student meant, but recollection. One should not and must not "let bygones be bygones," because otherwise the past could rise from the ashes and become a new present. The German people and the young Germans of today will guard themselves against the danger of a new Nazism most effectively through understanding and digesting the old Nazism (Améry 2002:626–28).

What motivates and sustains Améry's unyielding resistance to forgetfulness is the cautious hope expressed in the final line of the original preface, which I believe is the most important passage in *Beyond Guilt and Atonement*: "Finally, I sometimes hope that this study has met its aims; then it could concern all those who wish to live together as fellow human beings" (1999: xiv).

It is important to remember this sentence, and we return to it toward the end of the book. It is a key to Améry's attempt to show that the resistance to forgiveness or the expression of resentment can be consistent with a striving for reconciliation and a mutual recognition of humanity; that is, exactly what was excluded from the TRC process in South Africa.

Reading "Ressentiments"

In "*Ressentiments,*" Améry does not proceed in a systematic, balanced, or procedurally clear fashion. He mingles arguments and explanations with scorn, polemic, and touching but also obscure passages. As he cautions in the preface to *Beyond Guilt and Atonement*, the reader must accompany him "through the darkness" and "in the process, he will come upon contradictions in which I myself got caught up" (1999: xiv). Thus, in the essay on *ressentiment*, the topic and the aim of the examination seem to change with the course of the reflections, and he uses central concepts equivocally. In the manner of narratives rather than of conventional philosophical argument, the essay embodies a story to be told and a meaning to be revealed through the time of the telling. Given the complex but often condensed form of the essay, it is not surprising that different readers have found the essay inspiring or provoking in different ways and have used it to argue different points. Yet, even if one pays proper heed to the way in which the essay invites different interpretations, the tensions among them are remarkable. Thus, according to one interpretation, "Resistance *quand même* . . . is the essence of Améry's philosophy" (Sebald 2003: 155f); in another that Améry's was "a morality . . . of despair and resignation," that resentment ought to be preserved indefinitely, and that reconciliation must be refused (Heyd 2004:196). Yet, according to another reader, Améry wants to be released from his emotional predicament and is driven by a profound desire for reconciliation (Chaumont 1990).

In the following chapters, I provide a close and comprehensive examination of Améry's essay. Yet why this exceedingly thorough and lengthy reading? First, because of the current or instrumental value of the thought in the essay: Améry's counterintuitive defense of *ressentiment* and critique of the "pathos of forgiveness and reconciliation" provide a valuable victim perspective on how individuals and groups may deal with an atrocious past and its legacy. It is, additionally, a most interesting contribution to the philosophical exploration of the moral nature and social function of resentment and other emotions. A second reason for the lengthy analysis is to bring out for examination the ambiguities, tensions, and odd statements inherent in the essay. "*Ressentiments*" is a challenge to the interpreter. Its topic and problem seem to change with the course of the reflections, the key concepts are used equivocally, and it is written with an irony and tone that call for cautious exegesis. I have spent a great deal of intellectual energy trying to sort out the tensions of the text and to find out where they could be alleviated and where not. After reaching a certain point of frustration, I decided that the only way to distinguish among what was pure inconsistency, what was necessary ambiguity, and what perhaps, deep down, was a coherent point of view, was to analyze the essay from beginning to end—page by page. Thus, I decided to provide the close reading not because of some allegiance to the pleasures of exegesis, but from the belief that I could only arrive at a more comprehensive understanding of the essay and of the relative standing of divergent interpretations by trying to gather in one reading all the important dimensions of the text.

The thorough reading has, thirdly, been motivated by my observation that the ambiguities of the essay have not been sufficiently recognized and discussed by Améry's readers. I analyze both the essay's most enigmatic and apparently self-explanatory passages while not explaining away the genuine puzzles and ambiguities of the reasoning under scrutiny. In line with this approach I minimize the use of paraphrasing, which may cover up problems, and instead opt for the combination of sometimes rather lengthy quotations and subsequent comments.

Finally, although my examination follows the essay from beginning to end, it is not a hermetic analysis of Améry's essay only. As my analysis proceeds, I reconstruct the full conceptual scope and value of the ideas and claims that are formulated more tersely by Améry. Furthermore, I relate his ideas and claims to those of other contemporary thinkers. For example, in relation to Améry's thoughts on historical responsibility, I consider the ideas of Jürgen Habermas. With respect to Améry's remarks on the victim's desire to undo the past, I analyze relevant passages from the works of Paul Ricoeur. In this way, the reading of the essay not only narrows down to the tiniest detail on a given page but opens up the horizon to the general themes in question. I only realized, rather late in my analysis, that the essay touches on most of the central questions that would be raised, say, in a conference on how to deal with past political violence: the tension between the demands and rights of individuals versus considerations of the common good; between backward- and forward-looking perspectives; between the language of healing and reconciliation and the discourse of moral dignity and mutual respect; the limits of the striving for closure; the question of guilt and responsibility; and, of course, the moral nature and value of the victim's refusal to forgive and the preservation of *ressentiment*. All the same, the following is primarily a detailed reading of one text; the essay is the "spine" of the forthcoming reflections.

The essay *"Ressentiments"* has been the subject of philosophical examination, but in all cases the readings and discussions have been kept within the confines of a single paper, and often Améry has only been used to illustrate a point made by the author. In Chapter 13, I focus on relevant parts of the critical reception, primarily David Heyd's "Ressentiment and Reconciliation: Alternative Responses to Historical Evil" (Heyd 2004) and Jean-Michel Chaumont's "Geschichtliche Verantwortung und menschliche Würde bei Jean Améry" (1990; "Historical Responsibility and Human Dignity in Jean Améry"). To be able to engage in a more substantial discussion of the reception of Améry's work, I have chosen to postpone the examination of critical interpretations until the completion of the present analysis. More than that, I want to use a split in his critical reception to raise a question about certain shortcomings in our understanding of victims' possibilities of response. However, I do refer to these works when relevant.

Let me now indicate how I position my reading. The essay may be likened to one of the reversible pictures where one can "flip" between one of two possible perceptions: Heyd (and others) tend to the one side, Chaumont (and others) to the other. The former portrays Améry's *ressentiment* as an unforgiving remembrance in response to the inexpiable horror of the Nazi past.

Insofar as reconciliation comes into the picture, it is as something to be refused. Instead, *ressentiment* is to be preserved indefinitely. The other perspective emphasizes the way in which Améry presents his *ressentiments* as a result of the faulty German *Vergangenheitsbewältigung*. In this interpretation, another Améry appears. He is a writer driven by a desire for redemption and reconciliation and a survivor who feels abandoned by his contemporaries. In this perspective, *ressentiment* is not as much about the atrocious past as about the indifferent present. The split in the reception reflects, I think, a fundamental ambiguity in the essay. In this book, I would like to present a reading that cuts across the split without losing sight of unavoidable ambiguities. But more about this is found in Chapter 13, "A Multifarious Reception." (If you want to read about the reception of the essay before engaging with the analysis, then read Chapter 13 first and then go back to Chapter 8).

Now, let us begin with the beginning and follow Améry through his meditations in the essay. In so far as one gets lost in the reading, there is an overview of the essay as a whole in Appendix I.

8
Opening Moves

Sometimes it happens that in the summer I travel through a thriving land. It is hardly necessary to tell of the model cleanliness of its large cities, of its idyllic towns and villages, to point out the quality of the good to be bought there, the unfailing perfection of its handicrafts, or the impressive combination of cosmopolitan modernity and wistful historical consciousness that is evidenced everywhere. All this has long been legendary and is a delight to the world. . . . I feel uncomfortable in this peaceful, lovely land, inhabited by hardworking, efficient, and modern people. The reader has already guessed why: I belong to that fortunately slowly disappearing species of those who by general agreement are called the victims of Nazism.

(AMÉRY 1999: 62–63)

Thus, Améry opens the essay on his *ressentiments* by placing himself in the position of the deviant and distrustful victim. The country he travels is "a delight to the world"; it "offers the world an example not only of economic prosperity but also of democratic stability and political moderation" (1999: 62). And then there is this lonely "I" who cannot join the popular perspective and whose memories of the Nazi past of the country and its inhabitants make him unable to travel the present without ruminating about its relationship to and possibly hidden affinity with the past. Different attitudes to the past and to the passing of time become central themes in the essay, but they are indicated already on the opening pages: the rehabilitation of Germany "has long since been legendary," "for years this situation has been considered exemplary," and "as has long been proved, its happy people want no part of national demagogues and agitators" (62–63). It remains to be said that Améry has not "moved on" along with the rest of the world. Fossilized like the wife of Lot, he lives with the catastrophe in sight, unable to join the call to look but to the future.[1] However, there is no open hostility toward him; indeed Améry adds that he is always received with extreme politeness. Yet, he cannot "judge how deep their apparent urbanity goes" (62–63); he cannot go along with the satisfaction and assurance with which the world looks on postwar Germany, but is persistently plagued by deep-seated distrust.[2]

At the end of the essay, we will know more about the whole situation, but let me state here that Améry's reflections on his *ressentiments* only strengthen the gloominess of the opening pages. Near the end of the essay Améry refers again to his travels in Germany: "I travel through the thriving land." But then he adds, "and I feel less and less comfortable as I do. . . . Fateful land, where some stand eternally in the light and others eternally in the darkness" (80). Travels connote change and the encounter with the new and the different, but in the end Améry's voyages in Germany mainly remind him of the atrocious past. Indeed, the last time Améry makes use of the travel picture, he slips from the present journeys and back into the memory of the transports in evacuation trains leading from Auschwitz to Buchenwald to Bergen-Belsen. It is as if the distance between the past and the present had been obliterated. Améry recalls the faces of the Germans from within cattle cars and evacuation trains, and he remembers "faces of stone. A proud people" (80). Thinking of his German contemporaries at the time of the writing, Améry finds "the old pride, and on our side it is the old helplessness. Woe to the conquered" (81). Given such a pessimistic perspective, it is no wonder that Améry pleads repeatedly with the reader not to "put down the book" in spite of the unpleasant nature of the exploration.

Now, let us focus on what happens between the beginning and the end of this uncovering of impending bitterness and loneliness. The essay might be said to lead nowhere, but this does not mean that the protest and vision revealed along the way are any less worthy of consideration.

From Clarification to Justification

The passage quoted above continues with the following declaration of purpose:

> The people of whom I am speaking and whom I am addressing here show muted understanding for my retrospective grudge. But I myself do not entirely understand this grudge, not yet; and that is what I would like to become clear about in this essay. I would be thankful to the reader if he were willing to follow me, even if in the hour before us he more than once feels the wish to put down the book. I speak as a victim and examine my *ressentiments* (Améry 1999: 63).

This is a fairly clear declaration of a point of view (the victim's), an address (the German people), a subject matter (his retrospective grudge or *ressentiment*), a problem (lack of understanding), and a task (clarification).

The reader who has followed Améry through his confessions and meditations of the preceding essays knows to distance the victim perspective adopted by Améry from sometimes morally ambiguous endorsements of a victim identity. Améry far from indulges or exploits his ordeals as a victim. "To be a victim alone," states Améry "is not an honor" (ix). In the opening essay on the intellectual in Auschwitz he ends with the following statement:

> We did not become wiser in Auschwitz. . . . We did not become "deeper," if that calamitous depth is at all a definable intellectual quantity. It goes without saying, I believe, that in Auschwitz we did not become better, more human, more humane, and more mature ethically. You do not observe dehumanized man committing his deeds and misdeeds without having your notions of inherent human dignity placed in doubt (19–20).

"Speaking as a victim" means trying to bring out for examination the inhuman condition of the Nazi victim. It also means trying to infuse the public debate with an unpopular and unpleasant perspective. Yet, most fundamentally, speaking out as a victim, Améry appeals to a concept of human dignity and to a vision of coexistence that goes beyond any narrow concerns about his own victimization. Concerning the *address*, it is from the outset plain that the essay is first and foremost addressed to Améry's contemporary Germans, but it only becomes clear much later why Améry is so insistent that they should follow him through his, as he warns, unpleasant and, it appears, fruitless exploration of the retrospective grudge he harbors against them. Améry expects the German readers of his essay to become disgusted, offended, or impatient by the essay. And yet, the essay is compelling because of his hope that, nonetheless, the ideal reader, for whom the book would be a cause of a change of attitude, actually exists. "Tact," writes Améry, "is something good and important [but] it is not suited for the radical analysis that *together* we are striving for here" (63, italics added). Interestingly, for Améry, the preservation of *ressentiment* goes together with an endeavor to overcome the divide between the group of victims and the group whose members planned, committed, or tolerated the crimes of the past. Consider Améry's original suggestion for a blurb to *Beyond Guilt and Atonement*: "Not a vague pathos of reconciliation comes across with his considerations but that radical sincerity which alone can clear the way for a future dialogue" (Améry 2002b:623, trans. Claudia Welz).[3]

The essay's declared *task* is to "examine" or "become clear" about the nature and value of the given retrospective grudge. This aim might be "tactless," but in comparison with what is to come, it is relatively uncontroversial. Given the use of concepts like understanding, analysis, and clarification, nothing is indicated about whether the psychic state under examination will be repudiated or endorsed. The *problem* is simply one of understanding.

However, one page after he declares his wish for clarification and analysis, the nature of the task is radicalized as Améry (as if by caprice) reformulates the project. Now, he wants to *justify ressentiment*. The modification of the project occurs within three sentences, the third of which provides the change:

> What matters to me is the *description* of the subjective state of the victim. What I can contribute is the *analysis* of the *ressentiments*, gained from introspection. My personal task is to *justify* a psychic condition that has been condemned by moralists and psychologists alike. The former regard it as a taint, the latter as a kind of sickness (64, italics added).

A justification of *ressentiment*? Améry himself adds that "a less rewarding business of confession cannot be imagined" (64). This is not an understatement.

The two concepts chosen to announce the *subject matter* require more detailed consideration. Apparently adopting the perspective of those who prefer to "move on," Améry categorizes his attitude toward his German contemporaries both as a grudge and as an instance of *ressentiment*. Améry seems to use the two terms interchangeably (in the closing line of the essay he uses "grudge" again), but what is the relationship between holding a grudge and harboring *ressentiment*? Max Scheler argues that the German word "*Groll*" (grudge) covers a basic component of the meaning of the vernacular French use of the noun "*ressentiment*." In "*ressentiment*" (according to Scheler), a particular negative or hostile emotional reaction to someone or something is repeatedly relived; through this "repeated experiencing and reliving of a particular emotional response" (Scheler 1998:25), the emotion in question might become a deep-seated character trait of the person: a gloomy and engrained hostility—perhaps, one may add, generalized and directed toward all sorts of things or persons. Scheler suggests that the meaning of the German word "*Groll*" overlaps with the French "*ressentiment*" in the following way:

> "Rancor" [in the translation, "Grollen" has been translated as "rancor"] is just such a suppressed wrath, independent of the ego's activity, which moves obscurely through the mind. It finally takes shape through the repeated reliving of intentionalities of hatred or other hostile emotions. In itself it does not contain a specific hostile intention, but it nourishes any number of such intentions (Scheler 1998:25).

"*Ressentiment*" is a more theorized and complex condition than "the grudging," and given the prominence of the Nietzschean picture of the man of *ressentiment*, the degrading and pathological connotations are probably exaggerated when a person is considered a *Ressentimentträger* (a person who harbors *ressentiment*). Whereas the harboring of *ressentiment* is commonly seen as essentially tied to envy, spite and a thwarted desire for revenge, holding a grudge is less tied to specific base and loathsome emotions or character states. Perhaps we can find the clue to the question why Améry drifts from grudge to *ressentiment* and vice versa if we notice what the two emotional conditions have in common. Holding a grudge and *ressentiment* share a gloomy aspect and the way in which they may consolidate as a character trait of the person. Yet more important, in this context, is the sense that they can both be characterized as a particular kind of emotionally inflected *memory*. Grudges can, as Solomon Schimmel puts it, "be 'banked' for decades" (2002:36), and the same can of course be said about the memories of offense nurtured by the "man of *ressentiment*." As Scheler writes,

> The continual reliving of the emotion [. . .] is not a mere intellectual recollection of the emotion and of the events to which it responded— it is a re-experiencing of the emotion itself, a renewal of the original feeling (1998:25).

In both grudging and in *ressentiment*, the negative emotional reaction to a wrong—whether real, exaggerated, or imagined—is remembered vividly. Drawing on Scheler, I suggest that neither *ressentiment* nor grudging is accurately seen as involving a single, specific emotion.[4]

Rather, a range of emotions are involved, and to say that someone nurses a grudge or harbors *ressentiment* does not *a priori* identify which emotions or intentions the particular person keeps processing. According to Scheler, the emotions and affects "primarily concerned" are revenge, hatred, malice, envy, the impulse to detract, and spite (cf. Scheler 1992:117). These are evidently all emotions and cravings with which none of us would like to be identified, but the question is whether Scheler's list exhausts the spectrum of emotions that can be processed in *ressentiment*.

To say that someone is "nursing a grudge" or is "possessed by *ressentiment*" is normally to express blame or condemnation.[5] Such blame may of course be premised on a variety of assumptions: that the offense responded to is conjured up or wildly exaggerated, that it is wrong or harmful (e.g., relationship-destructive or unhealthy) to dwell on the irrevocable past, that the motives or character states involved are loathsome and destructive, and so forth.[6] Key to the assignment of blame is the temporal excess associated with both phenomena. One aspect of normative assessments of anger or resentment is tied to intuitions about the length of time the virtuous agent ought to be angry. As Aristotle wrote, the bad-tempered man is known not only by his failure to be angry at the right things with the proper level of intensity, but also by his inability to let go of anger when the right length of time has been reached (cf. *The Nichomachean Ethics*, 1125b30–1126b10). The person who is nursing a grudge or who is possessed by *ressentiment* might have "begun" with an anger or indignation that was appropriate and legitimate and only with the passing of time has it slipped into *ressentiment* or an embittered anger. Philip Fisher emphasizes the extent to which our understanding of passions like anger and grief is marked by notions of their "appropriate duration" (2002:87). The interesting point is that time can determine not only the propriety of an emotional experience but also its identity:

> In *Hamlet* the prince's sullen gloominess protests against the casual brevity of the period of mourning allowed for his father. How could the joys and passions of his mother's new marriage take place so quickly after the sudden death of his father? What is mourning if it is too quickly ended? Finding in your own heart that it takes time to mourn, you realize that there is a duration of mourning, and that duration, in each case, is of its essence. Too-quickly-ended mourning is not mourning at all but perfunctory gestures of mourning. This is Hamlet's accusation against his mother and her new husband (Fisher 2002:87).

The role of time with respect to grief is as relevant in the case of anger, indignation, and resentment. Keeping alive an attitude of hostility to another for a long time may reflect an inability or unwillingness to "let go" in due time.

However, another key assumption underlying the moral chastisement of the grudge holder and the man of *ressentiment* is that they (secretly) cherish their memories of offense, their resentment, and pain:

> If one is justified in continually holding resentment, then not forgiving does not constitute holding a grudge; whereas if one is not justified, then to continue harboring resentment does constitute holding a grudge. . . . *The grudge holder delights in taking pleasure in his resentment and wants there to be nothing that would give him a reason to be less resentful*; whereas having good reasons not to forgive is perfectly compatible with wishing that the person would come to be worthy of forgiveness. It seems clear, then, that harboring a grudge surely veers in the direction of being a vice (Thomas 2003:205, italics added).

The suspicion, or presumption, that cases of relentless resentment can be explained (and chastised) as the expression of victims' unhealthy and disgraceful delight in their victim identity is ready at hand when the anger of people who have been wronged in the past exceeds ordinary notions of appropriate duration. The question is to what extent Améry's *ressentiment*/grudge differs from the popular as well as philosophical picture of a loathsome and poisoning attitude.

Still, given the conventional understanding of *ressentiment*, an intent to analyze and examine it sounds reasonable, but a justificatory project seems not only unrewarding but also self-defeating. An endeavor to justify a condition associated with self-poisoning, value delusion, repression, and emotions like vindictiveness, hatred, malice, spite, and envy? One wonders what explains this sudden, premature rush to justification. Possibly, Améry means "justify" in the sense of providing an explanation why such *ressentiments* should be seen as permissible, or maybe he really wants to justify himself; showing that his being in the grip of *ressentiment* should not be used to blame him. Why does Améry want to or think he needs to *justify ressentiment*? It would have made more sense, if he had instead announced the inapplicability of the concept to victims in his position. The beginning of an answer why he justifies *ressentiment* lies in the lines that follow his last quoted passage: "I must acknowledge it [i.e. *ressentiment*], bear the social taint, and first accept the sickness as an integrating part of my personality and then legitimize it. A less rewarding business of confession cannot be imagined" (Améry 1999:64).[7] A confession is conventionally understood as an interpersonal or public acknowledgment of sin or guilt; it is something a sinner or a blameworthy or criminal person does. To confess is an ambivalent act: *what* one confesses (what one has done, what one has been) is something blameworthy, and thus the confession reveals the guilt or shame of the confessor. At the same time, the very *act* of confessing is commonly lauded in religious as well as political and legal settings. It brings moral credit to confessors who feel remorse and thus distance the present self from the culpable act or character confessed. Combined with repentance, confession may pave the way to forgiveness and sometimes even bring a measure of moral admiration of the confessing person. Améry's repeated statements about a need to confess mock, I think, conventional opinion that his persistent refusal to forgive and forget would be deemed an appropriate occasion for a confession. What he offers instead is a "mock confession." He writes that he must confess to his *ressentiments*, but *not* to distance himself from them morally and most certainly not in the hope that he will be pardoned by the Germans for the obstinacy of his grudge. Not even, one could add (therapeutically speaking), as his first acknowledgment of the need for his sickness to be treated.

Still, why does Améry assume the epithet "*ressentiment*" at all? Why "must" he accept and bear the taint? Améry may cling to the past and he may be mistrusting and ruminative, but where is the hypersensitivity to petty

injuries and the frustrated vindictiveness, envy, malice, and spite so characteristic of our picture of the man of *ressentiment*? Indeed, given the gloomy
aspect of *ressentiment* and the conventional picture of the man of *ressentiment*, genuine *ressentiment* seems nearly incompatible with the awareness that
one is possessed by it. Améry explains his "methodology"—the dialectic of
acceptance and revolt (cf. "first accept the sickness . . . then legitimize it")—
more thoroughly in the last essay in *Beyond Guilt and Atonement*. Primo Levi
thought that Améry's approach was "paradoxical and contradictionary" (Levi
1988:129), but this might be a misjudgment. Améry's strategy stems from the
persecuted victim's experience of the inescapable significance of the given
social reality. Referring to the conditions of protest during the years of persecution, Améry argues that it would have been senseless to attempt a protest
against a social body that deprived the victims of all rights, dignity and, ultimately, life on the grounds of one's self-understanding":

> The merely individual, subjective claim ("I am a human being and as
> such I have my dignity, no matter what you do or say!") is an empty
> academic game, or madness. Still, the degraded person, threatened
> with death, is able ... to convince society of his dignity by taking his
> fate upon himself and at the same time rising in revolt against it"
> (89).[8]

The revolt against degrading/annihilatory social conditions and construc-
tions—*Entwürdigung*—has to begin in "the unqualified recognition that the
verdict of the social group is a given reality" (89).[9] When Améry, in relation to
his *ressentiment*, writes that he must confess to it, accept the stigma, and then
legitimize it, he is practicing the same fundamental approach as exemplified
in the final essay. Thus, when Améry writes that he must "first accept," one
must be sure to grasp what he does accept and what he does not accept. He
accepts that *ressentiment* from a psychological perspective is seen as a sickness,
but to the extent that he wants to legitimize it, he seems to defy what might be
called a therapeutic blindness to an allegedly legitimate moral perspective on
the condition. Furthermore he acknowledges that his confession will bring
him moral blame from the society he wants to address. He simply does not
accept the moral authority of the "verdict."

The whole project makes most sense, I think, as a response to the reality
of the presumptuous, contemporary social judgment of the Nazi victim's
unyielding distrust and refusal to accept the call to forgive and/or forget. In
other words, Améry embarks on the project to justify *ressentiment* primarily
because of his experience or expectation that this was how the resistance to the
call to forgive and forget would be classified by the majority of the Germans
whom he wished to address. (This rationale, by the way, does not exclude that

the motivation could also in part derive from his own sense or suspicion that he genuinely was trapped in something like *ressentiment*).

Were unforgiving and irreconcilable survivors judged as *"Ressentiment-trägern"* (harborers of *ressentiment*)? Did Améry respond to a real contemporary social mood? In 1948, Adorno wrote that "it was already considered a form of boring *ressentiment* to remind people of the extermination of the Jews" (cited in Claussen 1998:198). But I have not been able to find any systematic historical investigation of this question. The already given overview of the historical context of *Beyond Guilt and Atonement* seems, however, to indicate at least the rationality of the expectation that victims adopting the position of Améry had to contest judgments that they were simply possessed by something like a grudge, *ressentiment*, revenge, or the like.[10]

In an impassioned response to French debates regarding statutory limitations on Nazi war crimes that occurred around 1965,[11] Vladimir Jankélévitch rages against the characterization of unforgiving survivors as spiteful: "Let the others, those who are not concerned, not blame us if we dwell indefinitely on the litanies of bitterness. . . . When six million human beings are murdered in the name of principles, is it not to be expected that survivors will speak of it for awhile, that they must irritate and tire others?" (Jankélévitch 1996:569). Jankélévitch argues that the only thing one could "do" in relation to the atrocious past was to "feel, inexhaustibly" (572). This translation cannot capture what Jankélévitch actually writes in the original French text (i.e., "*ressentir, inépuisablement*"; Jankélévitch 1986:62). Envisaging that advocates of statutory limitations will try to diminish the duty to remember by characterizing it as an expression of *ressentiment* and an "inability to settle the past" (572), Jankélévitch retorts vehemently:

> The sentiment we experience is not called rancor but horror—insurmountable horror over what happened, horror of the fanatics who perpetrated this thing, of the passive who accepted it, and the indifferent who have already forgotten it. This is our "*ressentiment.*" For "*ressentiment*" can also be the renewed and intensely lived feeling of the inexpiable thing; it protests against a moral amnesty that is nothing but shameful amnesia; it maintains the sacred flame of disquiet and faith to invisible things (Jankélévitch 1996:572, translation emended).[12]

The simultaneous appearance of a defense of a special kind of "*ressentiment*" (with or without quotation marks) in the essays of Améry and Jankélévitch may at least testify to the reality of a sense, among some victims and survivors, that they were seen as "*Ressentimentträger*" by those who wished for statutory limitations, forgetting, forgiving, and reconciliation. Améry wanted to change the status quo and challenge given notions of acceptable ways of responding to the past. Even if the label of *"Ressentimentträger"* was not popularly used to silence or blame survivors who kept talking about the past or who claimed restitution of their property, such victims were resented by many Germans during the first postwar decades. Thus, it might not be historically accurate to explain Améry's decision to defend *ressentiment* as a response to the public use of the term. Instead, one may say that Améry responded to a *Zeitgeist*.

Reimagining *Ressentiment*

Améry writes that *ressentiment* has been "condemned by moralists and psychologists alike. The former regard it as a taint, the latter as a kind of sickness" (64). A little further on, he is more specific about the perspectives in opposition to which he has to argue his case. On the moralist side, Améry places Nietzsche and quotes a famous passage from the *Genealogy of Morals*:

> *Ressentiment* defines such creatures who are denied genuine reaction, that of the deed, and who compensate for it through an imaginary revenge. . . . The resentful person is neither sincere, nor naïve, nor honest and forthright with himself. His soul squints . . . (cited in Améry 1999:67).

Améry acknowledges the "general agreement that the final say on *ressentiment* is that of Friedrich Nietzsche" (67), but against academic consensus and against Nietzsche, Améry invokes the authority of the eyewitness to an unprecedented catastrophe:

> Thus spake the man who dreamed of the synthesis of the brute with the superman. He must be answered by those who witnessed the union of the brute with the subhuman; they were present when a certain humankind joyously celebrated a festival of cruelty, as Nietzsche himself expressed it (68).[13]

The *Genealogy's* picture of the man of *ressentiment* as a merely reactive being[14]; as driven by gloomy envy, spite, and vengefulness[15]; and as marked by deceitfulness[16] is indeed part of what Améry wants to gainsay. How he does so, we discover along the way through the essay. At this point, the essay simply slips into the other (psychological) perspective to be contested, as Améry wonders: "But am I attempting this rejoinder in full command of my mental powers?" (68):

Mistrustingly, I examine myself. It could be that I am sick, for after observing us victims, objective scientific method, in its lovely detachment has already come up with the concept of the "concentration camp syndrome." ... It is said that we are "warped." That causes me to recall fleetingly the way my arms were twisted high behind my back when they tortured me. But it also sets me the task of defining anew our warped state, namely as a form of the human condition that morally as well as historically is of a higher order than healthy straightness. I must delimit our *ressentiment* on two sides and shield them against two explications: that of Nietzsche, who morally condemned *ressentiment*, and that of modern psychology, which is able to picture it only as a disturbing conflict" (68).

Thus, on the basis of two short identifications of the relevant opposing perspectives, Améry arrives at the final formulation of his task. Even later, Améry also talks about "the special kind of *ressentiments*, of which neither Nietzsche nor Max Scheler... was able to have any notion" (71). This final qualification of the nature of the task is an important change from the earlier declared intention simply to justify *ressentiment*. Granted the reality of a different kind of *ressentiment*, the possibility arises that it could be of a legitimate kind—one that could bring if not moral credit then at least not moral blame to its holder. The project becomes less absurd and more philosophically interesting insofar as it promises to challenge the hegemony of Nietzsche's notion of *ressentiment*. Even today, Nietzsche's picture of *ressentiment* is often seen as adequate and final. The moral and conceptually "revolutionary" question raised by Améry is, then, whether the perspective suggested by Nietzsche was adequate. Maybe there is a need for conceptual innovation. However, if the notion of a different kind is to make sense, it still needs to share some of the basic elements conventionally attributed to *ressentiment*. This should caution against hasty exhilaration about the moral value of any kind of *ressentiment*. Also worth keeping in mind is the polemical nature of Améry's use and defense of the term. The reason why he fights under the banner of *ressentiment* is not a free-standing attraction to this concept, but a sense that a Nietzschean and psychological understanding of the term captures the social judgment of him and his kind.

Améry does not (and at this point I guess nobody will be surprised) proceed to expound his nonstandard variety of *ressentiment* systematically, nor does he deal with the two rivaling explications in a remotely structured fashion. He does not, for example, explicitly articulate what differentiates the alleged "special kind" of *ressentiment* under consideration from Nietzsche's and Scheler's accounts. Rather, he demonstrates and asserts his position, and the other explications and perspectives are polemically attacked along the way.

Améry's contestation of Nietzsche's and Scheler's accounts of *ressentiment* is not in any sense comparable to a genuine theoretical or scholarly discussion of their theories. To avoid getting sidestepped in lengthy analyses of the works of Nietzsche and Scheler, I only take into consideration passages and parts of Nietzsche's and Scheler's writings on *ressentiment* when it appears to me necessary in order to deal with Améry's reasoning.

When Améry claims that modern psychology is only able to picture *ressentiment* as a disturbing conflict or a kind of sickness (as he put it in the second declaration of purpose; cf. Améry 1999:64), has he got a point? His problem with contemporary psychological perspectives on *ressentiment* and the concentration camp survivor has three aspects, and I address all three of them here.

The most straightforward problem arises, as Améry feels a need to convince those he addresses that he is not delirious, psychotic, or "mentally distorted" (68). In other words, that his reasoning is not only frank but sound, and that his *ressentiment* responds to an objective or "precisely reflected reality" (96).[17] "I," writes Améry, "am not "traumatized," but rather my spiritual and psychic condition corresponds completely to reality"(99).[18] Améry wants to address the Germans. Being labeled as "traumatized" or "mentally deranged" would of course all too easily exempt them from any responsibility to listen. They could, so to say, leave him to the psychotherapist.

Second comes the most important problem with the psychological perspective; that is, its alleged blindness to *ressentiment* as more than a sickness or pathology to be treated, a blindness that Améry connects to a value horizon that privileges "healthy straightness." As Jenny Edkins has shown, "the diagnosis and treatment of trauma survivors can serve to discipline their memories and render them politically powerless" (Edkins 2003:52). Referring to Kali Tal's *Worlds of Hurt: Reading the Literature of Trauma* (1996), Edkins writes about the medicalization and pathologization that can take place "when survivors are treated as victims of an illness—posttraumatic stress syndrome. They are treated by various forms of psychiatric and medical practice, the aim being rehabilitation and the resumption of normal life. The testimony is seen as a product of the illness, a symptom, and its political value destroyed" (190).[19] Not all psychologists studying trauma, however, are insensitive to the limits of therapeutic language, practice, and values. In her preface to the anthology *Trauma: Explorations in Memory*, psychologist Cathy Caruth (1995:vii–viii) claims that the *unique* contribution of the essays in the volume is "to ask how we can listen to trauma beyond its pathology for the truth that it tells us." Thus, although I tend to find Améry's critique of the pathologizing nature of the psychological perspective to be unnecessarily polemical, there is no doubt that he responds to a genuine problem. It equals that of Kalu in South Africa (cf. the chapters in Part One on the TRC) and other victims whose decision to voice a moral protest in spite of the pain involved are met with therapeutic counsels to let go.

To counter the reductive approach, Améry invokes a notion of a form of the human condition that is of a higher order than healthy straightness. He does not deny that the harboring of *ressentiment* is detrimental to the well-being of its holder, and as we proceed, the agonizing aspects of the state to be justified appear with stronger force. Améry's position should not be conflated with any kind of bravado about suffering. He simply appeals to a sense that there is something humanely unworthy about the therapeutic blindness to, or suspension of, a moral stance due to concerns about matters of health.[20]

The third aspect of Améry's contestation of the psychological perspective on (the man of) *ressentiment* has to do with the "lovely detachment" of modern scientific psychology. What disturbs Améry is probably best explained by the way in which the psychological or therapeutic perspective can turn the other person into an object to be dealt with or treated. I have already mentioned Peter F. Strawson and his well-known article on "Freedom and Resentment." It provides an enlightening perspective on the logic of Améry's determination to stand by his *ressentiment* and his disparagement of an objective attitude. Strawson contrasts two opposing but not mutually exclusive sets of attitudes: the attitude of involvement or participation in a human relationship, on the one hand, and the objective attitude on the other. Strawson's distinction is extraordinarily pertinent to an articulation of what is at stake in Améry's essay:

> To adopt the objective attitude to another human being is to see him, perhaps, as an object of social policy; as a subject for what, in a wide range of sense, might be called treatment; as something certainly to be taken into account, perhaps precautionary account of; to be managed or handled or cured or trained. . . . The objective attitude may be emotionally toned in many ways, but not in all ways. It may include repulsion or fear, it may include pity or even love, though not all kinds of love. But it cannot include the range of reactive feelings and attitudes which belong to involvement or participation with others in interpersonal human relationships; it cannot include resentment, gratitude, forgiveness, anger. . . . If your attitude towards someone is wholly objective, then though you may fight him, even negotiate with him, you cannot reason with him (Strawson 1974:9).

Améry's animosity toward the "lovely detachment" (68) of objective scientific method must be understood both on the basis of his past experiences and in relation to his hopes. As the object of the Nazi politics of extermination,

Améry had perhaps experienced a most hyperbolic instantiation of the objective attitude. He knew what it meant to be seen and treated as an object.[21] This is not to imply that there is no gap between the Nazi dehumanization of Jews and other groups and the objective attitude adopted by health care professionals. The point is rather that the objective attitude, in whatever guise, is the contrary to what *Beyond Guilt and Atonement* aimed to promote. Améry's hopes that the book "could concern all those who wish to live together as human beings" (xiv). His wish for the restoration of a society where Jews and Germans could live together as human beings requires that the Germans "feel affected" by the darkest deeds of the Third Reich. In other words, the key to conflict resolution is not detachment and objectivity, but participation and affectivity in a sense to be delimited more clearly throughout the rest of the essay.

The Origins of Améry's *Ressentiments*

Améry opens his argument for the case for *ressentiment* with a retrospective narrative account that explains why *ressentiment* has become the "existential determinant" (64) of people like himself.[22] As already mentioned, unlike resentment, *ressentiment* is not an immediate response to something or someone. It is rather an attitude or a trait and the result of an extended process; as Améry puts it at this point: "the result of a long personal and historical development" (64). The account of this development begins on the day Améry leaves the last of his concentration camps in 1945 and ends in the "present." It can be split into two parts, both of which vividly illustrate the way in which resentment can fester, when implied expectations that responsibilities will be assumed are not met by the relevant parties.

Améry opens the retrospective account stating that *ressentiments* "were by no means evident on the day I left the last of my concentrations camps" (64). More than that, the first couple of years of the postwar period gave "no reason, hardly a real possibility, for *ressentiment* to form" (65). In those years, Améry instead felt that there was "mutual understanding between me and the rest of the world" (64).

> Those who had tortured me and turned me into a bug . . . were themselves an abomination to the victorious camp. Not only National Socialism, *Germany* was the object of a general feeling that before our eyes crystallized from hate into contempt. It would be an outright distortion of the truth if I did not confess here without any concealment that this was fine with me (64f; italics in original).

The contempt and abhorrence shown by the Allies—in part related to the horrors of the concentration and extermination camps and before the onset of

Cold War politics—provide Améry with a sense of reassurance and renewed trust. Later, he refers to "the brief global hour in which I was able to believe that from the bottom up everything was transformed. . . . I could believe that the deprivation of dignity that we had experienced had been a historical error" (91).[23] The abhorrence of the world "balanced" memories of the absence of expressions of abhorrence on the faces of the German bystanders. The targeting of Germany matched experiences of German mass complicity.[24] The importance of "third-party" expressions of strong reprobation cannot be underestimated when one is dealing with responses to state-sponsored mass crime.

To understand the victim's need for public acknowledgment of the horrible nature of what was done by the Nazis, one needs to keep in mind the devastating experience of silence or the absence of outrage to persecution and atrocity not only among the bystanders but also among the victims themselves. In the first essay of *Beyond Guilt and Atonement*, Améry tries to account for the way in which the prolonged exposure to the monstrous and inescapable reality of the "SS state" could bring its victims to a collapse of moral resistance and outrage. Resignation is, according to Améry, only a waystation in the destruction of the victim's moral resistance to the reality of dehumanization and extermination. Next follows a more devastating temptation:

> Were not those who were preparing to destroy him in the right owing to the undeniable fact that they were the stronger ones? . . . A Germany existed that drove Jews and political opponents to their death, since it believed that only this way could it become a full reality. And what of it? Greek civilization was built on slavery and an Athenian army had run wild on the Island of Melos as had the SS in Ukraine. . . . Against the horrors there wasn't much to say. . . . That is the way history was and that is the way it is. One had fallen under its wheel and doffed one's cap when a murderer came along (Améry 1999: 11f).

In circumstances where, as Martha Nussbaum writes, "evil prevails," the expression of anger or outrage may restore a sense of "moral order and humane concern"(Nussbaum 1994:404). Nussbaum recounts a story told by Elie Wiesel:

> Wiesel was a child in one of the Nazi death camps. On the day the Allied forces arrived, the first member of the liberating army he saw a very large black officer. Walking into the camp and seeing what was there to be seen, this man began to curse, shouting at the top of his

voice. As the child Wiesel watched, he went on shouting and cursing for a very long time. And the child Wiesel thought, watching him, now humanity has come back. Now with that anger, humanity has come back (Nussbaum 1994:403).

We return now to the question also broached in Part One: what is the relation between anger and humanity? As Nussbaum comments, "by his anger the soldier aligned himself with Wiesel and his fragile humanity. . . . His outrage expressed the judgment that things need not be this way, that one must expect better of human beings" (1994:416). According to Améry, the abhorrence shown by the Allies momentarily felt like a restoration of a moral order in which another human being is someone from whom help and concern can be expected. Today, international criminal law recognizes the importance to the victims of the authoritative or public expression of abhorrence, although this expression is carefully targeted at the criminal acts and atrocities as such. The Victims Trust Fond of the International Criminal Court, for example, finds trials attractive because they "can express the community's abhorrence of the atrocities committed."[25] The ICTY has likewise declared that it sees "public reprobation and stigmatization by the international community, which would thereby express its indignation over heinous crimes and denounce perpetrators," as an essential function of punishment (cited in Amann 2002:123). Yet, while anger and outrage in the face of horrible violence are seen as not only justified but also as an expression of moral care and solidarity, it is often thought to be morally wrong to abhor the criminal, especially when one extends the blame and abhorrence to entire groups.

Améry admits to both of the prima facie forms of blameworthy excess. Did Améry indulge in something malicious and degrading when he felt vindicated by abhorrence? Abhorrence and contempt tend to block compassion, which is often considered a reason for condemnation. Améry confirms this fear when he admits that he wanted no part of expressing any compassion for the vanquished and when he seems to loathe Jews "who in this hour were trembling with the pathos of forgiveness and reconciliation" (65). On the other hand, would it not be morally odious to expect the recently released survivor of torture and extermination to feel compassion for his tormentors? As should already be clear, Améry's endeavor in 1966 is not to call for a renewal of contempt and abhorrence. Yet, Améry aside, the question about the moral propriety of emotions and attitudes like abhorrence or disgust in the face of atrocious evils is challenging. In *Negative Dialectics* (1973), Adorno claims that *"Ekel"* (revulsion, abhorrence, disgust), felt in response to the horror of the death camps, is the emotional ground of a new categorical imperative (that is, in relation to the "old" concept formulated by Immanuel Kant).

Another particularly relevant emotional state is *horror* or the sense of something as morally horrible. In both cases, these states are either seldom considered or are usually denounced as morally dubious. Yet, this is not the place for further elaborations on this topic.[26]

The second part of the narrative is focused on the postwar developments that provide the grounds for Améry's *ressentiments*. As the Cold War began, the Allies' plans with Germany "had nothing, but absolutely nothing more to do with potato fields"(66),[27] Germany was soon accepted in the UN, and it was "dispassionately reckoned with in the power game" (66); the world forgot and forgave (cf. 75). In line with the earlier noted observations of Arendt and Adorno, Herf and Frei, Améry finds that the German voicing of contrition is replaced all too hastily with a belief that the past was overcome:

> The Germans saw themselves absolutely as victims. . . . Thus, as can all too easily be understood, they were not inclined to do more than to take the past of the Third Reich and, in their own way, to "overcome" it.[28]... In those days, at the same time as the Germans were conquering the world markets for their industrial products and were busy at home—not without a certain equanimity—with overcoming, our *ressentiments* increased; or perhaps I must restrain myself and say only that my *ressentiments* increased. . . . Suddenly there was good reason for *ressentiment* (66).

The cause and object of the *ressentiment* of which Améry here speaks are clearly the policies and attitudes that became dominant during the first two decades after the war: the evasion and neutralization of the past and the belief that it had been sufficiently atoned for, "overcome," or "made good again" because of monetary compensations and the highly selective trials of the top Nazis. Améry testifies to an increasing sense of resentment and indignation, but what facilitates his slipping into *ressentiment* proper? Here Améry's account concurs with Scheler's understanding of the social conditions explaining the formation of *ressentiment*. For *ressentiment* to fester, the person who thinks himself wronged has to be burdened with some sense of powerlessness, social disregard, or marginalization; he must feel a premonition that his protest will not be acknowledged or that the moral standing of his stance is not recognized. Améry concurs with this picture, as his account includes a story of marginalization, demonizing, and powerless righteousness:

> Jewish-born men of the same stamp as Gabriel Marcel showed themselves most eager to reassure their German contemporaries and fellow human beings. Only totally obstinate, morally condemnable hate,

already censured by history, they said, clings to a past that was clearly nothing other than an operational mishap of German history and in which the broad masses of the German people had no part. But to my own distress, I belonged to that disapproving minority with its hard feelings. Stubbornly, I held against Germany its twelve years under Hitler. I bore this grudge into the industrial paradise of the new Europe and into the majestic halls of the West. . . . I attracted the disapproving attention no less of my former fellows in battle and suffering, who were now gushing over about reconciliation, than of my enemies, who had just been converted to tolerance (67).

Clearly, Améry presents to us a *ressentiment* resulting from the failure of a state and a society to reassure its victims that the past has been acknowledged and that the appropriate responsibilities have been assumed. However, the reader of *Beyond Guilt and Atonement* as a whole might at this point recall the ending lines of the earlier essay on torture. They appear as the conclusion of an entire paragraph emphasizing the indelible effects of torture: the survivor of torture can no longer feel at home in the world, the shame of destruction cannot be erased, trust cannot be regained, and the experience of fellow man as a torturer ("anti-man") remains in the victim as "accumulated horror": "It is *fear* that henceforth reigns over him. Fear—and also what is called *ressentiment*. They remain, and have scarcely a chance to concentrate into a seething, purifying thirst for revenge" (1999:40). This statement seems to suggest that *ressentiment* was already present at the time of torture and captivity in the Nazi camps. Maybe the absence of *ressentiment* in the immediate postwar period should be understood as a momentary preemption of *ressentiment* due to the elation of liberation.[29] Taking into consideration the conditions under which the Nazi victims were persecuted, captivated, and murdered, the notion of a *ressentiment* bred by the original horrors certainly is plausible. If the formation of *ressentiment* is premised on the powerless victim's inability or fear of trying to "act out" an angry response to perceived wrongs, then the conditions imposed on the Nazi victim seem prone to the fostering of an intense, indeed indelible kind of *ressentiment*. Genocide survivors' testimonies of the horrors they suffered and witnessed are suffused with the moral pain felt by victims hiding or numbing the outrage they probably normally would have experienced and acted on as they faced threats and lethal assaults on their children, spouses, and others. One of the most succinct descriptions of this *ressentiment*-inducing agony and of the "shame of destruction" mentioned by Améry in the torture essay can be found in Primo Levi's *If This Is a Man* (originally published in Italy in 1947). Levi recounts the public hanging of a man who had been in contact with the little group of men who "had found the strength to act, to mature the fruits of their hatred" in an attempt of rebellion in Birkenau:

> Everyone heard the cry of the doomed man, it pierced through the old thick barriers of inertia and submissiveness, it struck the living core of man in each of us: "Kameraden, ich bin der Letze!" ('Comrades, I am the last one!'). I wish I could say that from the midst of us, an abject flock, a voice rose, a murmur, a sign of assent. But nothing happened. We remained standing, bent and grey, our heads dropped, and we did not uncover our heads until the German ordered us to do so. The trap door opened, the body wriggled horribly; the band began playing again and we were once more lined up and filed past the quivering body of the dying man. . . . To destroy a man is difficult, almost as difficult as to create one: it has not been easy, nor quick, but you Germans have succeeded. Here we are, docile under your gaze; from our side you have nothing more to fear; no acts of violence, no words of defiance, not even a look of judgment (Levi 1987:135–36).

Psychologists have also studied the effects of long-standing captivity and humiliation. Consider Judith Lewis Herman's assessment of the impact of unexpressed rage:

> During captivity, the victim cannot express her humiliated rage at the perpetrator, for to do so would jeopardize her survival. Even after release, the former prisoner may continue to fear retribution and may be slow to express rage against her captor. Moreover, she is left with a burden of unexpressed rage against all those who remained indifferent to her fate and who failed to help her (Herman 1992:94f).

Against this background, the idea of a *ressentiment* caused by the conditions of the original torture, humiliations, and horrors of the camps is entirely plausible. The problem is that the idea is hard to reconcile with Améry's explanation that *ressentiment* was not present in the immediate postwar years, but rather was occasioned by the postwar *Vergangenheitsbewältigung*. Was *ressentiment* maintained since the years of torture and degradation, or is it the result of a development starting some years after 1945? Was it perhaps only displaced as long as Améry felt the world concurred with his resentful perspective? Probably, one should take note of Améry's use of the plural form (*ressentiments*) and opt for a stance that allows his *ressentiments* to be compounded of both histories of violations.

Reforming *Ressentiment*

The retrospective narrative closes with this statement: "I preserved my *ressentiments*. And since I neither can nor want to get rid of them, I must live with them and am obliged to clarify them for those against whom they are directed" (Améry 1999: 67). In this way we are brought back to the beginning of the essay, even though we now know more about the nature of Améry's *ressentiments* and about the present situation and its prehistory. Améry *will* not get rid of his *ressentiments*. They are not just something with which he suffers, but somehow he embraces and grants them the character of a deliberate personal response. The moral anatomy of this "appropriation" is revealed only slowly, but if it is in accordance with the earlier strategy of acceptance and revolt, then we can anticipate that its endorsement will be ambiguous in the sense that it will at the same time amount to a revolt against "being-in-*ressentiment*." Insofar as this expectation is correct and we are dealing with the possibility of a special kind of *ressentiment*, we should be attentive to the ways in which the condition under exploration is like or unlike *ressentiment*, as it has been understood conventionally. Contrary to the hidden and gloomy nature of *ressentiment*, as ordinarily conceived, the special kind brought forth by Améry is articulated publicly. However, in accordance with the conventional notion of the "man of *ressentiment*," Améry is in a weak social position and without much hope that his call will be heeded. The poisoning effect of *ressentiment* is often thought to be tied to both of these aspects. Thus even though Améry articulates his *ressentiments* publicly, it is not surprising that his predicament only seems to worsen the more he thinks about it.

Like resentment and indignation, *ressentiment* is certainly a reactive attitude, but can it, like resentment, be a *moral* reactive attitude? This possibility is what has been refused traditionally. Whether a reactive emotion or attitude can be distinguished as moral or not, at least in part depends on the kind of belief that gives rise to it and the kind of concepts required for its explanation. It is, in other words, its cognitive or propositional content that delimits the moral emotion and explains why one is in the emotional state. According to this perspective, moral resentment stems from being treated unfairly; it arises from the belief that a moral wrong or injury has been done or that an important norm or expectation has been violated. According to Richard J. Wallace, what distinguishes *ressentiment* from resentment (a distinction that does not exclude the possibility that resentment may creep into *ressentiment*) is their different propositional contents: "*ressentiment* is essentially about one's lack of some value or good, whereas resentment is about the breach of demands" (Wallace 1994:247). Now, considering Améry's explanation why he is in the state of *ressentiment*, it seems clear that he invokes an explanation that implicitly makes the case that a legitimate expectation of a response that would address the outrage of what had happened has been violated. *Ressentiment* is triggered or caused by a belief that the given attitudes to the past and to how it should be dealt with constitute a moral injury—a second wrong done to the victims.

In consideration of what one may call the propositional distinction stipulated by Wallace, it is tempting to say that Améry is really speaking about resentment, perhaps bitter resentment, but not *ressentiment*. The attitude under examination is, roughly speaking, *about* the breach of normative expectations of moral acknowledgment, not the "evaluative thought that one lacks some characteristic that one values and wants very much to possess" (Wallace 1994:247). It would, at this point, be premature to reach any final judgment on this issue. Suffice it to say that I think there are reasons to recognize what Améry conceptualizes as *ressentiment* as something "monstrous"—a special kind indeed. But the question whether it will in the end be most appropriate to say "of *ressentiment*" or "of resentment" must be left open here. What remains certain, is that it is *about* moral wrongdoing, and in this respect, I cannot see why the *ressentiment* in question should not be admitted to the more honorable category of moral attitudes.

Of course, if one thinks that only reactive attitudes focused on the wrongs done to others may count as moral, then resentment about being wronged oneself will not qualify as a moral emotion. This notion is regularly reflected in the popular opinion that *indignation* is honorable and moral, whereas resentment is suspicious and self-centered. Yet, on the basis of any minimal notion of equal moral standing, it seems morally peculiar if a wrong done to another should count, whereas a wrong done to oneself should not. If it is moral to experience and express indignation when another is wronged, why should it not be so when the same wrong involves the agent who is subject to the emotion? (cf. Wallace 1994:35). One might object that the reasons why *ressentiment* has been banned from the company of the moral attitudes are not primarily related to the question of its cause. Indeed, *ressentiment* might have "begun" as moral resentment based on, for the sake of the argument, a completely appropriate belief that a moral injury has been done. What accounts for its bad reputation is rather the way in which the consciousness of the injury is processed, nursed, and exaggerated. Hence, even though it may be recognized that *ressentiment* is not necessarily a response to slights and conjured-up offenses, it is at this point difficult to see how *ressentiment* could be willingly retained.

Let me close this chapter by noting that Améry's attempt to justify *ressentiment* involves more precisely both an effort to rehabilitate *ressentiment* as such and a desire to vindicate the preservation of *ressentiment* in the particular socio-historical situation, the subject of his retrospective account. And insofar as one wants to discuss the moral standing of this particular instance, it is important to appreciate the degree to which the case for *ressentiment* is premised on the plausibility of the assessment of the concrete historical situation. Any reconstruction of Améry's position that forgets the contextual premises of his defense is hazardous (cf. Chapter 13).

9
Facing the Irreversible

> *There is no greater tormentor of the human breast than violent resentment which cannot be gratified.*
>
> (ADAM SMITH 1854/2000:174)

The *Zustand* Passage

The German term *"Zustand"* (condition, state) can be used when conducting a medical assessment of a patient's psychic and physical state. Améry uses this term in the following reflection on the nature of the existence determined by *ressentiment*, and he does not deny its life-damaging, unnatural, and irrational implications:

> [I]t did not escape me that *ressentiment* is not only an unnatural but also a logically inconsistent condition [*Zustand*]. It nails every one of us onto the cross of his ruined past. Absurdly, it demands that the irreversible be turned around, that the event be undone. *Ressentiment* blocks the exit to the genuine human dimension, the future. I know that the time-sense of the person trapped in *ressentiment* is twisted around, dis-ordered, if you wish, for it desires two impossible things: regression into the past and nullification of what happened. But more on this later. In any event, for this reason the man of *ressentiment* cannot join in the unisonous peace chorus all around him, which cheerfully proposes: not backward let us look but forward, to a better, common future! (68f/128).

This is one of the most cryptic and significant parts of the essay (let me refer to it as the *Zustand* passage). It does not set out the moral reasons why Améry does not *want* to get rid of his *ressentiments*. Neither does it provide the moral defense of the earlier claim that the harboring of *ressentiment* can be the reflex action of a more dignified or humane mode of being than the striving for healthy straightness. On the contrary, this passage reinforces the skeptic's thought that one really must be deluded not to want to get rid of *ressentiment*. In *The Periodic Table*, Primo Levi writes that, after his release from Auschwitz, he "became a man again, a person like everyone else, neither debased nor a saint: one of those people who form a family and look to the future rather than the past" (cited in Clendinnen 1999:51). And then there is Améry's man of *ressentiment*, nailed to a past that most other people were eager to forget. In this way, the excerpt really is an account of the *Zustand* of a "survivor" written twenty years, not to forget, after the liberation.

The *Zustand* passage accentuates the role of *ressentiment* as a violent occupation of the will and the time-sense of the person: *ressentiment nails* the victim to the past, *blocks* the exit to the future, and *twists* or *dis-orders* the time-sense of the person *trapped* in it. Améry's account resounds like the way in which Seneca gives to anger the overwhelming force of a rash and vehement passion: "when once the mind has been aroused and shaken, it becomes the slave of the disturbing agent" (Seneca 1970:125). Yet, it may seem odd to compare *ressentiment* to a passion. *Ressentiment* is not rash, but sluggish; it is a mood or a low-energy state in opposition to the vehement nature of violent rage, horror, or grief. More interestingly, the diminution over time that seems to be an essential feature of the passions contrasts with the excessive duration or endurance of emotions and memories taken into *ressentiment*. Yet, with respect to the force with which *ressentiment* dominates the will and the mind of the victim, Améry's account echoes Seneca's picture of anger's enslavement of the agent.[1] As the essay unfolds, the image of an alien force is replaced by the notion of an emotional ally sustaining the victim's moral revolt. Let us, however, not run ahead of the text.

The *Zustand* passage, as brief as it is, adds or touches on new and significant structural components of the condition to be explained. It is, furthermore, the closest we get to anything like an explicit conceptual delimitation of the victim's being-in-*ressentiment*. Whereas the earlier retrospective account is focused on the postwar causes that lead the victim into *ressentiment* (in other words, its etiology in particular postwar experiences), the present reflection purports to explain the victim's inability to "look but forward." Doing so, it also provides new hints as to the object and the peculiar desire inherent to the kind of *ressentiment* under inspection.

The *Zustand* passage has been quoted often, but to my knowledge its significance has only been seriously considered once, and no one has yet published a genuine analysis of its meaning.[2] Perhaps this is a wise decision because the only elements that one has to work with are the already quoted constellation of terse statements.

The Twisted Sense of Time

In *ressentiment*, the passing of time does not bring about healing or diminish anguish. The phrases used in the *Zustand* passage indicate precisely the way in which the twisted sense of time conflicts with the "natural" sense of time: whereas the person trapped in *ressentiment* desires "regression into the past" (68), the person with the natural sense of time is biased toward the future. As Améry writes: "What will be tomorrow is more valuable than what was yesterday. That is how the natural feeling for time will have it" (76).[3] Whereas the man of *ressentiment* demands an undoing of the past or that "the irreversible be turned around" (68), the person with the natural sense of time accepts that what has happened cannot be changed.

Améry ties the natural sense of time to biological and social time: wounds heal and societies move on. The concept of the natural sense of time includes the very common intuition that the passing of time brings with it a weakening of the legitimacy of resentment, criminal prosecution and punishment, claims for reparatory justice, remorse, and so forth. Yet, several writers have commented on the possibility that crimes against humanity are not covered by our ordinary ideas about the significance of the passing of time. Ruti Teitel, for example, observes that "the consequences of time here seem to go against our intuitions" (Teitel 2000:138).[4] Vladimir Jankélévitch expresses a similar point from an experiental perspective:

The time that dulls all things, the time that uses up sorrow as it erodes mountains, the time that favors pardon and forgetfulness, the time that consoles, settling and healing time, does not diminish the least the colossal slaughter; on the contrary, it never ceases to revive its horror. . . . Crimes against humanity are *imprescriptible*, that is, the penalties against them *cannot* lapse; time has no hold on them (Jankélévitch 1986: 556f).

The anguish and outrage of the memory of the person trapped in *ressentiment* do not fade away with the passing of time, just as the kind of memory theologically ascribed to the God of the Last Judgment does not lessen. Philip Fisher writes as follows:

The fading and final indifference that constitute an essential feature of the human experience of the passions in time is nonexistent within timeless eternity. The meaning of a Last Judgment within a philosophy of the passions lies in the fact that each and every act has to be seen to lie adjacent to the final moment of time, and to face judgment as though the "work of time" would never take place (Fisher 2002:105).

Like the memory of the God of the Last Judgment, the twisted time-sense and the memory of the person trapped in *ressentiment* keep alive the sense of the horror and shock of the past crimes. Given the proper context—widespread evasion, denial, and forgetfulness—the ability of *ressentiment* to harbor or preserve a vivid sense of what was violated can be said to be an aspect of its virtue.

At the same time, what Améry describes as the condition of the person trapped in *ressentiment* resembles in several ways what are seen today as defining elements of trauma. For example, Jenny Edkins writes that "trauma is that which refuses to take its place in history as done and finished with. It demands an acknowledgement of a different temporality, where past is produced by—or even takes place in—the present" (2003:59). The psychological concept of *hypermnesia* also seems to approximate the nature of the twisted time-sense of the person trapped in *ressentiment*. Hypermnesia, according to William Niederland, is the all too clear and strongly emotionally inflected memory of traumatic experiences of persecution and of the related shattering of the self (cf. Niederland 1980:230). In a description of a female Holocaust survivor suffering from hypermnesia (101), Niederland notes that, although she is oriented in time and space, her state of health is controlled by undigested memories of past horrors. She still sees how her bloodstained brother was led away; she hears the screaming of infants and clings to her beaten mother, and in a certain sense she is still staying with the dead and the dying of the concentration camp. She is, as Niederland notices, "well aware that all these events happened a long time ago, and yet she cannot get away from the memories and agonizing fantasies. In other words, she still lives in the concentration camp . . ." (Niederland 1980:101, trans. Claudia Welz).[5]

This is not the place to speculate whether this kind of traumatization was part of the *conditio inhumana* experienced by Améry. Moreover, I readily grant that many survivors of extreme atrocities suffer from comparable kinds of hypermnesia and that it is important to understand how to treat people suffering from such traumas. What matters here is what the therapeutical perspective tends to leave out of consideration; that is, the way in which the twisted sense of time can be grasped ethically and thus acquire a certain moral significance for the victim.

The Absurd Demand

As described above, the *Zustand* passage offers a rudimentary explanation why the "*ressentiment*-ful" victim is trapped, why he *cannot* join the plea to look but to the future, and why his sense of time is twisted around. It points to the compelling force of an absurd demand "that the irreversible be turned around, that the event be undone" (Améry 1999:68).

Emotions differ from one another both because of the beliefs they involve and the things they make one desire.[6] In our case, the specific kind of *ressentiment* in question seems to be distinguished by the demand that recurs repeatedly in the essay. Later, Améry reiterates the desire to "turn back time, to undo what had been done" (70) or "the genuinely humane and absurd demand that time be turned back . . . that irreversible processes be reversible" (77). The time-sense of the person trapped in *ressentiment* is twisted because of a desire for "two impossible things: regression into the past and nullification of what happened" (68).[7]

Trapped in *ressentiment*, the victim is possessed by a demand for something that simply cannot be delivered and a desire that it is impossible to satisfy. One cannot demand in relation to the past: the irreversible is what cannot be turned around, and the events of the past are what cannot be undone. The will's demand clashes with reality or more precisely the irreversibility of the past event. If a release from being-in-*ressentiment* is premised on a satisfaction of the absurd demand, then entrapment is chronic and inescapable. The *ressentiment*-ful victim is trapped by the very logic of his *ressentiment*; he cannot move on or join the plea to look to the future rather than the past, as long as the irreversible has not been turned around and the atrocious events of the ruined past have not been undone or overcome. Therefore, *ressentiment* persists because nothing anybody could do would be able to satisfy the demand or desire in question; nothing will undo or cancel out what happened. Therefore, trials, any kind of reparations including apologies, monuments, restitution of property, and memorial days—no response will be adequate except the strict undoing of the past events. Absurdly, *ressentiment* keeps demanding that impossibility.

Having been promised a rejoinder to Nietzsche, it is striking to notice that Améry's account of the condition of the person trapped in *ressentiment* is very close to an account of the predicament of the human will in Nietzsche's *Thus Spoke Zarathustra*:

> "It was"—that is what the will's teeth-gnashing and most lonely affliction is called. Powerless against that which has been done, the will is

an angry spectator of all things past. . . . It is sullenly wrathful that time does not run back; "That which was"—that is what the stone which it cannot roll away is called (Nietzsche 1891/1969:161).[8]

Before Améry and Scheler, Nietzsche had characterized *ressentiment* as an infliction of the memory. The memory of the man of *ressentiment* is, as Nietzsche wrote in *Ecce Homo*, "a festering wound" (1888/1979:45). However, the desire and predicament of Améry's man of *ressentiment* resemble Walter Benjamin's (1988) words about the angel of history, who wants to stay back and mend what has been broken. *Ressentiment* not just keeps the past alive. In the mind and will of the person trapped in it, it keeps the past *open* or *unfinished* insofar as the victim cannot accept that what happened, happened. This strange and intriguing thought can be approached from a variety of perspectives. Considering the state of the mind still shocked by the witnessing of a terrible crime, Philip Fisher writes, "The imagination returns again and again to the possibility that this did not have to happen to the victim, who still, for a time, retains the full human reality he or she had prior to the crime. The punishment, at first, is related in intensity to the imaginary possibility that we are undoing the damage to the victim as if by magic" (2002:106).

Ressentiment's modification of the "modality" of the past also brings to mind Jean-Paul Sartre's notion that the emotions are magical transformations of the world. Sartre sees the emotions as attempts to "live as though the relations between things and their potentialities were not governed by deterministic processes but by magic" (1977:63). According to Sartre, in the emotional experience the subject magically tries to escape an unbearable reality. Being unable to escape a danger by normal means, the person may faint in fear; that is, annihilate the dangerous world magically (66). Leaving aside the plausibility of Sartre's theory as a general theory of the emotions, the notion of the magical transformation of the world perhaps fits well with the consciousness of the person who apprehends the past in *ressentiment*. *Ressentiment* demands that the event must be undone. It surely cannot, but *ressentiment* seems to function *as if* the event was undoable, a task still to be done. Yet, in Améry's case the emotional condition hardly offers the person any kind of magical escape from unbearable reality. The demand for a strict undoing is seen more plausibly as a genuine moral comprehension of the limits of repair in the wake of radical evil. Hannah Arendt once wrote that "real evil is what causes us speechless horror, when all we can say is: 'This should never have happened'" (2003:75).

Actually, some of Arendt's reflections on the Holocaust come quite close to the themes under consideration here, particularly the unreconciled memory and the twisted sense of time:

We shall not be able to become reconciled to it, to come to terms with it, as we must with everything that is past. . . . Even the famous healing power of time has somehow failed us. On the contrary, this past has managed to grow worse as the years have gone by so that we are sometimes tempted to think, this will never be over as long as we are not all dead (Arendt 2003:55).

A tenor of defiance and revolt is more to the fore in Améry's writings, but the absurd demand delimiting Améry's *ressentiment* might be seen as the affective equivalent to a similar judgment that no response (punishment, reparation, or forgiveness) and no stretch of time could ever legitimate a belief that the evil past had been overcome. *Ressentiment* discloses to the victim possessed by it the depth of the damage done. It feeds a moral remainder that persists in spite of the passing of time—which indeed opposes the easy moving on with time. As Jankélévitch puts it, *ressentiment* can be "the renewed and intensely lived feeling of the inexpiable thing" (1996:572). Confronted with societal amnesia, the will to remember can be empowered by *ressentiment*. The wish and the demand inherent to the kind of *ressentiment* delimited by Améry are absurd or impossible. However, they protest against another kind of ethical impossibility: testimonies on the Holocaust often dwell on the "impossible" indifference with which people can witness other people being transported to death (cf. Geras 1999). Sometimes, the consternation is even extended to nature. Let me refer again to Jankélévitch: "Each spring the trees bloom at Auschwitz as they do everywhere, for the grass is not too disgusted to grow in those accursed fields" (Jankélévitch 1996:572). In this case, the reference to nature is often meant to emphasize that something else ought to have been expected from human beings; indeed, that it is "impossible" to accept that people can move on as if nothing had happened or as if what happened could be overcome simply through the passing of time. Paraphrasing a point captured by Arne Grøn, one can say that to move on is—in fact—possible, but ethically it is "impossible." To undo what has been done is in fact impossible, but wanting to do so saves the ethical possibility (Grøn 2006); that is, the possibility of relating with moral sensibility to what has been done.

But still, where does the absurd demand leave Améry's man of *ressentiment*? Paul Ricoeur has given the following advice to victims of crimes they consider to be inexpiable and unforgivable:

There is no better advice than to *wait for better times*. These times will see the first cathartic effect of the drawing-up of wrongs suffered by the injured, who will see the offender attain full understanding of the crimes that he or she has committed. There is a time for the unforgivable and a time for forgiveness. Forgiveness requires enduring patience" (Ricoeur 1996:11, italics added).

Améry's outlook is explicitly directed toward the social and historical—metaphysics or religion is not his concern, neither as a cause of distress or as a source of redemption. He could not accept the advice to wait for better times, not just because of the value he put on resistance but also because of the tone of faith professed in Ricoeur's advice ("will see"). Actually, Améry, at a certain point, wondered whether the essay with which we are concerned should have been entitled "Heillose Zeit"; that is, "Unholy Times" or "Dreadful Times" (Améry 2002:699, n. 29). Is there no redemption for Améry's man of *ressentiment*? Returning to Nietzsche's *Zarathustra*, we find a chapter entitled "On Redemption":

> To redeem the past and to transform every "It was" into an "I wanted it thus!" That alone do I call redemption! . . . All "It was" is a fragment, a riddle, a dreadful chance—until the creative will says to it: "But I willed it thus!" Until the creative will says to it: "But I will it thus! Thus shall I will it!" (Nietzsche 1891/1969:161).

Améry cannot accept this path of creative affirmation of the past; he cannot "will" the implied "eternal repetition" of Auschwitz (cf. Neiman 2002). The question is, however, whether Améry maintains a straightforward refusal to accept what happened. This question is gradually answered as we progress through the essay. What matters now is that Améry's rejoinder to Nietzsche mainly concerns the question of the proper moral response to the given predicament of the will. Nietzsche's search for redemption from the burden of the past is only one instance of an array of suggestions aimed to redeem us from the pain arising from the irreversible past: the idea of an *amor fati* can for example be supplemented by a Hegelian reconciliation with the cruelties of world history, and both can be set next to the current rhetoric of closure, healing, and moving on.[9]

Changing the Past—Or Its Significance to the Present?

One might object that the reading above interprets Améry's words about an impossible demand for a "regression" and an "undoing" of the past event all too literally. When, for example, Hannah Arendt writes that forgiving serves "to undo the deeds of the past" (Arendt 1989: 237), she does not grant the forgiver a superhuman power to suspend the "predicament of irreversibility."

More to the point, she does not even attribute the forgiver with a *desire* for this kind of absurd moral intervention in history. To undo, and to desire to undo, really means to release, or to desire to release, oneself and others from the effects or implications of the past event (e.g., from an entrapment in *ressentiment*, revenge, guilt, or shame). Paul Ricoeur makes a similar point when he asserts that the "poetic" power of forgiveness "consists in shattering the law of the irreversibility of time by changing the past, not as a record of all that has happened but in terms of its meaning for us today" (1996:10). What happened remains an indelible part of the past.

The "shattering" of irreversibility is actually only about the *significance* of the past event; the past stops "haunting" the present (cf. Ricoeur 1998:145, 155). Thus, philosophers have spoken figuratively about "shattering" or "undoing" the past. The question is whether Améry should be read as on a par with Arendt and Ricoeur, or whether he really means what he says when he talks about undoing the past. In correspondence to Arendt's and Ricoeur's talk of "undoing" and "chattering," a figurative interpretation of the *Zustand* passage would claim something like the following: when he wishes for a turning back of time and an undoing of what has been done, what Améry really wants is rather an overcoming of the negative *legacy* of the past for the present. In this case, what Améry craves for is not ontologically absurd or impossible. He just wants the past to become past.

The literal interpretation, however, fits the brief claims about the absurdity of the demand and the impossibility of the desire. This interpretation makes sense as an explanation of why the person is trapped and why he cannot get rid of his *ressentiments*. It also makes sense as the affective apprehension of an unforgivable and inexpiable crime and damage that cannot be made good again. It captures the moral impossibility of what happened. At the same time, the demand is absurd, and it is alluring to turn it into something that is possible and thus more reasonable. But what we are seeking here is the most accurate account of Améry's introspective self-examination, not the most rational reconstruction of his position. Moreover, it might be impossible to satisfy the wish/demand in question, but to desire that what happened had not happened is eminently human and testimony to a moral capability to revolt against what should never have been.

In my opinion, the *Zustand* passage calls for the literal or radical interpretation: the demand in question *is* absurd. The desire in question arguably is for an overcoming of the unbearable past. However, the crux of the matter is that a genuine reconciliation with the past—a reconciliation satisfying the terms set by the victim's *ressentiment*—would require an absurd and impossible undoing of the past. Thus, there can be no "disposal" of the past events, and this is why Améry persistently rebels against "[his] past, against history, and against a present that places the incomprehensible in the cold storage of history and thus falsifies it in a revolting way" (1999:xi).[10]

Ambiguities of *Ressentiment* and Reconciliation

The affinity between Améry's account of being-in-*ressentiment* and the problem of reconciliation with the past should make us pause. It means that attention in the essay has shifted from the initial focus on the animosity and mistrust permeating Améry's relationship to the Germans to its present focus on the *ressentiment*-ful victim's relationship to the past. Insofar as Améry's examination of his *ressentiments* revolves around the (im)possibility of reconciliation, the text has moved from the question of reconciliation *between* antagonistic groups to the question of reconciliation *with* past evils. As I show, one can only hope to provide a comprehensive interpretation of Améry's position, if one recognizes the way in which Améry's reflections move between these two dimensions—the social and the historical—of what *ressentiment* (or resentment) and reconciliation can be about.

"Emotion," writes Sartre, "returns to the object time after time and feeds upon it" (1977:57). Améry's *ressentiments* are first presented as a grudge against his contemporary Germans. The *ressentiment* in question is the result of the faulty and offensive forgetfulness and repression of the Nazi past following the years of persecution. In accordance with this analysis, one could naturally presume that Amery's *ressentiments* would be about the German postwar attitudes, and then the "event to be undone" would be the policy of premature rehabilitation and integration of war criminals, the offensive pleas for survivors to forgive and forget, and the like. But what constitutes the intentional object of *ressentiment*, as conceptualized in the *Zustand* passage? Surely, the "ruined past," the "event to be undone," or "what happened" refers to the original violations and injuries suffered and witnessed by Améry during the twelve years under Hitler. Yet, there is of course no reason why the *ressentiment* of the victim may not take several objects: Améry resents what happened, and he resents a variety of people and groups for having forgotten, forgiven, or accepted too hastily *that* it happened. As he puts it in the preface from 1976, he rebels not only against his past and against history, but also "against a present that places the incomprehensible in the cold storage of history" (xi). Thus, the intentional object of Améry's *ressentiments* encompasses both the postwar proceedings and the evils of the years of persecution, which is also clear from the range of examples to which he returns repeatedly. These range from a conversation with a South German businessman and other episodes from after the war to a host of episodes from the time between 1938 and 1945.

What matters here is avoiding the notion that Améry's *ressentiment* is *only* about either the original atrocities or about the ongoing lack of acknowledgment and accountability. The former interpretation loses sight of the ongoing, postwar problem with which Améry is trying to deal; it promotes the picture of a purely retrospective gaze and a *belated* response to past evil. The latter interpretation does not grasp the depth of the survivor's ordeal. At the same time, trying to capture the complex and compounded nature of Améry's *ressentiments* is far from easy, because his essay uses the same concept to address past and present issues and relations between groups as well as a certain relationship to the past. For example, later in the essay Améry "transposes" the talk of the absurd demand that the Nazi *past* must be undone to an ethical-political demand that the *Germans* undo this past by taking responsibility for it as an inalienable part of their history and national identity. Whereas the demand for an undoing of the past is absurd and impossible, the demand directed to the German society is only absurd because it is unrealistic (no nation-state had, at that time, turned a negative past into part of its historical national identity). This difference is what allows Améry to imagine a pacification of his *ressentiments* against the Germans; a pacification that cannot be envisaged at all in relation to the demand that the past as such should be undone.

Améry simply desires two different outcomes in the two different contexts. In relation to the Germans, he desires (*modus* Arendt and Ricoeur) an overcoming of the negative *significance* of the past for the present, but in relation to his past and in relation to the history shared by victims and perpetrators, Améry posits the much more radical demand that what happened had not happened. The complexity stems from the fact that he uses the same term (*ressentiment*, the absurd demand for the turning back of time) to cover the two different projects. The two dimensions are, furthermore, dialectically connected in the sense that the overcoming of the legacy of the past as concerns the present relationship between the resentful survivors and the Germans rests on whether the Germans will come to share with the survivors the impossible wish that what happened had not happened. Thus, the moral validity of the radical and absurd refusal to accept the past—the wish for the perfect undoing of what happened—is what inspires the making of the parallel, but less radical, demand directed toward the Germans.

As we shall see, the figurative interpretation of Améry's "undoing of the past" becomes attractive in those passages that address the conditions for an overcoming of tensions between Jews and Germans. However, this figurative interpretation remains a temptation that should be resisted, because it would remove the peculiar moral power and relevance from the entire undertaking. On the other hand, if one does not acknowledge that the absurd demand is also used as an ideal "yardstick" with which to put forth a demand that *can* be answered, then one places Améry in a too radical position.

This is a suitable place to reconsider the tension between the two pictures provided of the etiology of Améry's *ressentiments*. Has *ressentiment* remained as a legacy of the indelible effects of torture, or did it only begin to develop some time after Améry was liberated from the camps? If one considers only the essay on *ressentiment*, one gets the picture of a *ressentiment* that is the result of an offensive, premature "overcoming" of the politics of the past. Yet, although the *occasion* is the chain of wrongs done well after the end of the war, the object of the *ressentiment* includes the original atrocities that took place during the years of persecution. The postwar development constitutes a second injury through which the original terror and torture acquire a new and burdensome significance to the survivor. The *ressentiment* occasioned by the morally untenable postwar attitudes to the Nazi past reinforces indelible and painful memories of the original atrocities. This impact is important for more than exegetical reasons. It also exemplifies the profound importance to the victims of the moral repair to be performed in the wake of mass atrocity. When states turn their back on their victims, when societies proceed as if nothing extraordinary had happened, this inaction may not only breed resentment and indignation directed toward the neglect and offenses of impunity, forgetfulness, and the like. Worse than that, the second injury may deepen the trauma occasioned by the original horrors.

As indicated above, the ambiguity in the essay can also be approached through a focus on the issue of reconciliation. Reconciliation is often said to involve two or more parties; for example, Serbs, Croats, and Bosniaks; Hutus and Tutsis; Jews and Germans; black, white, and colored South Africans. The concept may indicate the process or the goal of coexistence or the "meeting of hearts and minds" itself. In this case, reconciliation is the overcoming, in some sense, of tensions and resentment between people (individuals and/or groups). But reconciliation can also be about the possibility of reconciling with one's past or a world in which such evil was possible. The former meaning of reconciliation—reconciliation between people—is most central in the present debates within the field of transitional justice. The latter meaning is, however, as old as theodicy and a prominent theme in the philosophy of history. Looking back at the *Zustand* passage in this light, one may say that it is concerned about the inability of the person trapped in *ressentiment* to reconcile with the past. The man of *ressentiment* cannot and will not accept that *it* happened. This is the problem of Benjamin's angel of history, Zarathrusta's disciples, Hegelian spectators to the shamble of history, and Ivan Karamazov. But, as suggested, the essay is also about the possible transformation of the relationship between victims and survivors, on the one hand, and perpetrators, bystanders, and their descendants on the other hand.

Therefore, one simply cannot give *one* answer to the question whether Améry wanted his *ressentiments* to be preserved infinitely or not or whether he refused or desired reconciliation. What is most significant here is the question of the relationship between the two discourses of reconciliation. Can one refuse to reconcile with the atrocities of the past and at the same time be willing to reconcile with the group by whom or in whose name the atrocities were committed? Can one reconcile with the past and resist reconciliation between people? Michael Ignatieff has asked whether there is a priority relationship between the two meanings of reconciliation, and it is interesting to compare his approach with Améry's point of view. First of all, Ignatieff emphasizes that one can have "coexistence without any heart-to-heart reconciliation at all" (2003:326). This is an important point, but what is more significant here is the related distinction between reconciliation between people and reconciliation with the world:

> Reconciliation of the second kind—being reconciled to the world as it is—contributes to the kind of cold coexistence achieved in post conflict situations. Reconciliation in the first sense—a meeting of hearts and minds—might be a distant, second-order consequence of reconciliation in the second sense—accepting the world as it is (Ignatieff 2003: 326).

Améry shares with Ignatieff the idea that coexistence and reconciliation in the first sense are the "second order." But in contrast to Ignatieff, we shall see how Améry argues that the path to coexistence between surviving Jews and the German people requires that the Germans come to share the victim's *unreconciled* relation to the world or, more precisely, to what happened in the past. In other words, Améry's original contribution to current thinking about reconciliation in part is the idea that a kind of reconciliation between peoples can build on a common refusal of reconciliation with the past.

10
Restoring Coexistence

Moral Conflict Resolution

The *Zustand* passage ends by noting the *ressentiment*-ful victim's inability to "join in the unisonous [sic] peace chorus all around him, which cheerfully proposes: not backward let us look but forward, to a better, common future!" (Améry 1999:69). The call to let bygones be bygones is just one of several forms of moving on that Améry refuses. Mentioning it brings Améry to comment on another proposal that both victims and torturers ought to "internalize" their suffering and guilt and "bear it in emotional asceticism" (69). Améry neither can nor wants to accept this call for a silent overcoming of the past:

> It is impossible for me to accept a parallelism that would have my path run beside that of the fellow who flogged me with a horse whip. I don't want to become the accomplice of my torturers; rather, I demand that the latter negate themselves and in the negation coordinate with me. The piles of corpses that lie between them and me cannot be removed in the process of internalization, so it seems to me, but on the contrary, through actualization, or, more strongly stated, by actively settling the unresolved conflict in the field of historical practice (69).

With this quote we move from the intrasubjective *Zustand* passage, with its focus on the "*ressentiment*-ful" person's relationship to his past/history, back to the intersubjective or social problem with which the essay opens; that is, the relationship or conflict between the resentful victim and the forgetful perpetrators.[1] In other words, we shift from a focus on the incomprehensible past to a concern about how to respond to a present conflict.

Améry's essay is permeated with conflicts and tensions between different perspectives on *ressentiment* and reconciliation, different senses of time, different attitudes to the Nazi past, and between conciliatory and resentful survivors. One conflict, however, appears as *the* acute moral, existential, and social problem to which the essay is most fundamentally trying to find a morally justifiable solution: that is the unresolved conflict between the victim and his torturers ("our problem" [69], as Améry asserts repeatedly). The excerpt cited above is intriguing reading. Having just examined the *Zustand* passage and the prospect of *ressentiment* "as an ongoing and self-perpetuating response to evil which cannot be undone" (Heyd 2004:196f), how can Améry talk about what would *settle* the conflict between him and his torturers? It would be nice and comfortable if one could say that Améry only thinks of *ressentiment* as the resistance to reconciliation with the past. But *ressentiment* is about more than what blocks a conciliatory or forgetful attitude to the past. At least in the beginning of the essay, *ressentiment* is presented as the key concept underlying the tension between Améry and the Germans. If this conflict came to be settled, would it not be logical to expect the holder of *ressentiment* to try to abandon this attitude; that is, if it does not extinguish itself in the face of the disappearance of the attitudes that made it appropriate? But what then about the notion of *ressentiment* as an *indelible* response to evil? Vladimir Jankélévitch's vehement defense of an indelible preservation of *ressentiment* is much more clear-cut than what we face in Améry's essay. Jankélévitch argues the case for the unending preservation of an angry and agonized memory of horror ("the inexpiable thing") because it is a moral debt owed to the dead of the past ("the past needs us"). Nothing—except their resurrection—could change the predicament and the duty to remember "because this agony will last until the end of the world" (Jankélévitch 1996:572). Améry is, however, not just concerned about the obligation to the dead victims and the urge to preserve a troubled memory of past events. He is as well trying to figure out the contours of a morally justifiable settlement of the conflict in question.

Then, how does Améry imagine the possibility of a settlement or resolution? The excerpt above opens with a legitimate refusal of a call for "internalization" that would simply silence the sufferer. Améry writes that he does not want to "become an accomplice of his torturers" and indeed accept both the proposal to "look but to the future" and the advocacy of an "internalization" that asks the victim to condone or acquiesce in evil and the status quo it has left behind (cf. Aurel Kolnai's [1973/74] "Forgiveness" on condoning).

Instead, Améry demands that the former perpetrators "negate themselves and in the negation coordinate with me" (69). What does this mean? Reconciliation and conflict resolution between antagonistic groups are often thought to imply some measure of compromise on both sides, as well as a readiness to empathize or see the conflict from the perspective of the other party.[2] Améry's demand, whatever the self-negation may actually imply, is to the contrary a unilateral demand that the torturer join his victim. This is probably not what mediators of conflict resolution or reconciliation would call a reasonable or viable strategy.

In the last part of the excerpt above, Améry indicates in highly abstract terms the way in which the conflict might be settled in a morally justifiable way. First, Améry calls for "actualization"; that is, the lingering conflict has to be unearthed or brought to the surface to be dealt with at all. The "twelve years that for us others really were a thousand" (78) should no longer be repressed or hushed up, but acclaimed as Germany's "negative possession" (78). What Améry calls "actualization" is from the perspective of the natural sense of time an unnecessary reopening of wounds that have—or should have—been healed by time. Second, Améry points to "the field of historical practice" as the public space in which the settlement of the lingering conflict might be possible.[3] Améry comes back later to the question what this actually means, and so do we in Chapter 11.

Still following the course of the essay we come to Améry's justification of the "unilateral" demand for coordination with the victim. But first we need to consider a short passage dealing with the objection that Améry is simply disguising a "barbaric, primitive lust for revenge in . . . high-brow terms" (69). The placement of this phrase seems strange, given the fact that we are not yet aware what Améry actually implies, when he asks for the perpetrators to "negate" themselves. The repeated reassurances that Améry does *not* crave revenge, probably say more about Améry's concern that his resistance to "the pathos of forgiveness and reconciliation" will be seen as placing him in the position of the seething avenger. In fact, "*Ressentiments*" can be seen as an attempt to undermine the vengeance or forgiveness dichotomy that we have already seen in action in the South African TRC. Améry later returns more substantially to the relationship between his position and a desire for revenge, and I postpone consideration of the issue until then. What is noteworthy here is merely that Améry rebuffs revenge by stating the impossibility of the thought that revenge would be able to resolve the "contradiction of [his] madly twisted time-sense" (1999:69).

What is interesting is not that revenge cannot repair a twisting that has already been defined as a desire for two *impossible* things: "regression into the past and nullification of what happened" (1999:68). No, what is remarkable is, first, the way in which the quote connects the *Zustand* passage and the present reflection on the terms of a settlement. This testifies to the already stated impossibility of a neat division between *ressentiment* as an enduring attitude toward the past and *ressentiment* as a "temporary" attitude of blame toward the Germans. Second, even though the rejection of revenge is compatible with a rejection of any resolution at all, the whole tenor of the passage indicates that there is something that will be able to resolve the conflict and the contradiction of the madly twisted time-sense. Again, is the *ressentiment* of which Améry speaks, and the condition in which he finds himself, indelible or not? Is it perhaps both things in different respects?

The deliberations justifying the "biased" demand that the perpetrators "negate themselves and in the negation coordinate with me" (69), open one of the most interesting parts of the essay. Améry is well aware that his openly professed *ressentiment* as well as his victim perspective on the controversy will be used to disqualify his deliberations about a settlement as irrational and biased. All the same, Améry claims to know that he is "captive of the *moral truth* of the conflict" (70). What is the moral truth of the conflict? As unhelpful as ever, Améry never provides an explicit answer. He speaks of the moral truth not only of the conflict, but also of the blows he received and of the crimes committed against him.

At this point in the essay, the essential claim is that the nature—its starting point, character, and eventual resolution—of the conflict is *moral*. At stake are neither colliding interests (e.g., in territory or stolen property) nor different accounts of the forensic or factual truth.[4] What matters to Améry and what the controversy, in his account, is first and foremost about, are moral acknowledgment or discernment and moral guilt and responsibility. To be more precise, what is at stake and in question are different attitudes or relations to the moral truth: the survivor is *captive* of the truth, the perpetrator has never faced it, and society does not care about it. Améry is concerned about the continued absence of an agonized acknowledgment by the torturers, their accomplices, and those who merely stood by silently of the moral quality and implications of the atrocities committed, supported, or tolerated by them in the Nazi past:

> The crimes of National Socialism had no moral quality for the doer, who always trusted in the norm system of his Führer and his Reich. The monster, who is not chained by his conscience to his deed, sees it from his viewpoint only as an objectification of his will, not as a moral event. The Flemish SS-man Wajs who . . . beat me on the head with a shovel handle whenever I didn't work fast enough, felt the tool to be emanations of his psycho-physical dynamics. Only I possessed, and still possess, the moral truth of the blows that even today roar in my skull (70).

Améry desires that "the crime become a moral reality for the criminal . . . that he be swept into the truth of his atrocity" (70). By using the term "sweep," however, the translators have softened the sentence. The word *"hingerissen"* is translated more accurately as either "tugged" or "torn into."[5] The violence of the verb seems deliberate, because we are here at the heart of the predicament haunting the post-Auschwitz existence of Améry: his conviction that the "moral truth" has not been acknowledged or is denied, evaded, and repressed by his torturers, their accomplices, and the silent bystanders.[6] It is the radical asymmetry between the victim's painful apprehension of the moral nature of what happened and the perpetrators' resistance to acknowledgment that justifies what I have called the *unilateral* demand that the perpetrator "coordinate with the victim" (69).

The *ressentiment* of the surviving victim in the face of collective neglect and forgetting is an essential part of Améry's picture of "the *conditio inhumana* of the victims of the Third Reich" (vii).[7] Améry's essay shows why and how the plight of the victim did not terminate with the liberation from the death camps. Améry points out not only that the wounds inflicted on the victims of persecution and the captivity in the camps could be beyond the limits of repair.[8] More than that, he attests to the injury and wrongs that can be done in so-called *post*conflict societies. Today, that misrecognition of others can do real harm is widely accepted, but this was not true when Améry was writing the essay. As Charles Taylor writes in his influential essay on "The Politics of Recognition," "Nonrecognition or misrecognition can inflict harm, can be a form of oppression, imprisoning someone in a false, distorted, and reduced mode of being" (Taylor 1994:25).

Améry admits, that "in deliberating our problem I am 'biased'" (69). His understated declaration that the problem—how to respond to the conflict in question—is "our problem" is not coincidental. Améry wants to engage the moral and critical faculties of his German respondents, to reveal to the unaffected that there is something with which they have forgotten to deal. Yet, even though Améry wants the Germans to recognize the existence of a shared problem, he completely dismisses demands for an *objective* approach to the controversy:

> It seems logically senseless to me to demand objectivity in the controversy with my torturers, with those who helped them, and with the others who stood by silently. The atrocity as atrocity has no objective character. Mass murder, torture, injury of every kind are objectively nothing but chains of physical events, describable in the formalized language of the natural sciences. They are facts within a physical system, not deeds within a moral system (70).

"Objectivity" is a notoriously slippery or polyvalent term. One meaning is an appreciation of an *impartial* perspective that accords equal weight to both sides to a conflict. In relation to Améry's mentioning of his "bias," one would naturally expect the objectivity in question to be objectivity-as-impartiality. Keeping in mind the unilateral (or anti-leveling) aspect of Améry's notion of the proper response to the controversy at hand, we have already established that Améry refuses the validity of this meaning of objectivity in the given "asymmetrical" case.[9] It is tempting to see the present dismissal of a demand for objectivity as an extra justification of the unilateral demand that the perpetrators and bystanders "negate" themselves and join the victims. In my opinion, however, the objective stance refused in the excerpt above is of another kind. The kind of objectivity at stake is wrong not only because of its false and offensive leveling of the victims and perpetrators. More than that, it is senseless, because once assumed, the atrocious moral nature of what happened would be lost from view. Améry thus argues against objectivity as a demand that the victim and the other involved parties adopt a dispassionate or personally and emotionally detached standpoint, and that they neutralize or internalize their "subjective" reactions to their deeds, experiences, suffering, and the like. This is akin to what Peter F. Strawson (1974) called "the objective attitude" and what is often thought to be central to natural scientists' stance toward the world.[10]

As the excerpt continues, Améry connects the embrace of the objective attitude with the relationship of the Nazi perpetrator toward his own deeds and the crimes of National Socialism more broadly. Indeed, the cultivation and admiration of callous murderers were part of the Nazi culture. It included the ability to objectify oneself and others, to view and treat the victims of the genocidal policy simply as objects, and to reduce oneself to an instrument implementing the will of the *Führer*. This numbing of emotional reaction and active concealment of the moral character of action are two of the prerequisites for the mass perpetration of genocide (cf. Bauman 1989:24). One of the most horrifying documents that illustrate that mass murder was seen with the objective attitude of the technician is a memo concerned with technical improvements made to the concentration camp gas vans that preceded the gas chambers as killing machines. The writer, Willy Just, refers to the human beings who were gassed in the vans as "cargo"—of which 97,000 pieces were "processed." He is not allowing the facts of what happened to disturb the challenge of finding a more efficient and cost-effective way of implementing mass murder:

A shorter fully loaded truck could operate much more quickly. A shortening of the rear compartment would not disadvantageously affect the weight balance, overloading the front axle, because actually a correction in the weight of the distribution takes place automatically through the fact that the cargo in the struggle toward the back door during the operation always is preponderantly located there (cited in Bauman 1989:197).[11]

The most profound reason why Améry protests vehemently against the demand for objectivity relates, however, to the role he has intended his *ressentiment* to play with regard to the actualization of the "forgotten" conflict. As Améry puts it, "My *ressentiments* are there in order that the crime become a moral reality for the criminal" (70). Améry brandishes his *ressentiment* as a "weapon"[12] against the injustice of forgetfulness and nonacknowledgment. The victim's vivid and emotionally inflected memories or *ressentiments* are not a hindrance to be set aside, but the very key to an actualization of the conflict. In other words, the victim's emotional apprehension and response to the past and to the controversy at hand are supposed to goad the responsible agents into acknowledging the moral truth of their atrocity.[13]

The attempt to reverse the belief that objectivity is preferable to subjectivity can even be said to characterize *Beyond Guilt and Atonement* as a whole. In the preface from 1966, Améry writes how he first believed that he would be able to face the reader with distant and "refined objectivity." He soon realized that the word "I" was the most useful starting point, and thus *Beyond Guilt and Atonement* became a "personal confession refracted through meditation" (xiii). In fact *Beyond Guilt and Atonement* is the most important instrument of Améry's attempt to actualize the conflict. Addressed to the Germans and written in the hope it would be of "concern to all those who wish to live together as fellow human beings" (xiv), *Beyond Guilt and Atonement* as a whole *is* Améry's intervention in the conflict; it *is* the public manifestation of his *ressentiments*.[14]

One might reasonably worry about the efficacy of Améry's project. Can the victim's *ressentiment* goad the unrepentant perpetrator into moral acknowledgment? Can the withholding and expression of resentment spur moral discernment among perpetrators? The prospects seem bleak, but even if the preservation of *ressentiment* is completely ineffective, it does not need to imply that the victim should let go of it; there might, as we shall come to see, be further moral reasons (connected with self-respect and his obligation toward the dead victims) why Améry does not want to get rid of his *ressentiment* in the face of the continued reality of nonacknowledgment.

Ressentiment and the Release From Abandonment

Why does Améry want the torturer and others to face the moral reality of their deeds? Why bother, at all, with their comprehension of the past—the very enterprise being a sure recipe for continued frustration? The answer to these questions is salient to an understanding of Améry's struggle and position and an important explanation for why he preserves his *ressentiments*:

> SS-man Wajs from Antwerp, a repeated murderer and an especially adroit torturer, paid with his life. What more can my foul thirst for revenge demand? But if I have searched my mind properly it is not a matter of revenge, nor one of atonement. The experience of persecution was, at the very bottom, that of an extreme loneliness. At stake for me is the release [Erlösung] from the abandonment [Verlassensein] that has persisted from that time until today (70/131).

Améry repeatedly denies being motivated by desires for revenge. He does, as he asserts, not live in the "bloody illusion" (69) that revenge could compensate for his suffering or resolve the twisting of his time-sense. The very idea of revenge appears to him nonsensical as a response to the Holocaust: no "sane person among us [would] ever venture the morally impossible thought that four to six million Germans should be forcibly taken to their death" (77).[15] Yet, Améry believes it would be impossible to provide an explanation that would refute the suspicion that he is "drowning the ugly reality of a malicious instinct in the verbal torrent of an unverifiable thesis" (69). It counts, however, in his favor that he did not refrain from expressing his support of revenge in the instances where he did find it admirable.[16] Atonement, on the other hand, is simply irrelevant to Améry; it has, he asserts, rather carelessly, "only theological meaning" (77).

At stake, then, is the release from the sense of abandonment that has persisted ever since. In *Beyond Guilt and Atonement*, the essay on torture first describes the victim's experience of persecution as an extreme loneliness. During torture, the victim loses what Améry calls "trust in the world" (28), especially the expectation that he will receive help and concern for his injuries (cf. 29). The experience of the other person—either the insensitive instrument of torture or the indifferent spectator of persecution—becomes, when no help can be expected and no act or resistance is possible, "an existential consummation of destruction" (28):

> If from the experience of torture any knowledge at all remains that goes beyond the plain nightmarish, it is that of a great amazement and a foreignness in the world that cannot be compensated by any sort of subsequent human communication. Amazed, the tortured person experienced that in this world there can be the other as absolute sovereign, and sovereignty revealed itself as the power to inflict suffering and to destroy. . . . Whoever has succumbed to torture can no longer

feel at home in the world. . . . That one's fellow man was experienced as the anti-man remains in the tortured person as accumulated horror. It blocks the view into a world in which the principle of hope rules (40).

The experience of loneliness is, however, as much about the indifference or passivity of the bystanders as it is about the torturers. As detailed by Norman Geras (1999), Holocaust testimonies and memoirs of victims are permeated with the feeling of being abandoned: friends close their doors, shades are drawn on the windows, and the overwhelming majority stand and watch in silence, fear, or pleasure, but in all cases in passivity (Geras 1999:4): "I know," says one of Saul Bellow's characters, "that humankind marks certain people for death. Against them shuts a door" (as cited in Geras 1994:6). The loneliness in question stems from the experienced indifference of the bystanders and the perpetrators to the suffering of the victim. "Mass destruction," writes Bauman, "was accompanied not by the uproar of emotions, but [by] the dead silence of unconcern" (1989:18). It is, likewise, the figure of the passive and perhaps indifferent bystander who constitutes the prime example in the memories expressed in Améry's essay on *ressentiment*. It is the loneliness of the person whose normative expectations of interhuman solidarity and care are most radically disrupted. When the reality of the injuries is repressed, when impunity and forgetfulness reign, and when the victims' protests are set aside as expressions of pathology or barbarity, *Verlassensein* or existence in abandonment is the fate of the victims. We return to the way in which different chronological and moral layers of violation can be nested within each other.

To recapitulate: Améry does not *want* to let go of his *ressentiments* because he wants to use them to goad the torturers to face the moral truth of their atrocity. Améry hopes that the moral "conversion" of the perpetrator would release the victim from an existence in abandonment. What does this release or redemption involve? How does Améry imagine its conditions of possibility?

When SS-man Wajs stood before the firing squad, he experienced the moral truth of his crimes. At that moment, he was with *me*—and I was no longer alone with the shovel handle. I would like to believe that at the instant of his execution he wanted exactly as much as I to turn back time, to undo what had been done. When they led him to the place of execution, the anti-man had once again become a fellow man (70).

The passage connects several threads: the satisfaction of the desire that the criminal will face the moral truth of his crimes is shown to imply a wish that the criminal comes to share with the victim the impossible desire "to turn back time, to undo what had been done." This, again, explains what Améry meant when he demands that the torturers negate themselves and in the negation join their victim. If that would happen, two moral transformations would be made possible: the "rehabilitation" of the torturer into a "fellow man" and, through this, the release of the victim from his abandonment.

Améry neither rests content nor "wallows" in *ressentiment* (see Tudor [2001] on resentment). Instead he seeks redemption: a restoration of the trust and human community from which his experiences with torture and persecution have alienated him. But, even if the imagined transformation was to take place, would it imply a release from *ressentiment*? Considering the passage just quoted, the release from abandonment seems rather to imply that the perpetrator comes to share the wish otherwise carried solely by the victim. The "burden" so to say is shared. Still, when considered as the hostile attitude directed toward the torturer because of his loathsome and deeply offensive forgetfulness and neglect, *ressentiment* could and should be set aside. What remains is perhaps an anguished rather than resentful memory of the time that cannot be reversed and the past that cannot be undone.

According to Margaret Walker (2006b:142), Améry identifies the moral truth to be experienced by SS-man Wajs as the loneliness and abandonment experienced by Améry. Standing before the firing squad, Wajs too experiences the abandonment felt by Améry. It is understandable that the culprit facing execution might come to wish that he could turn back the clock and undo what had been done. It is also very possible that Wajs could feel abandoned. In fact, both of these cravings are entirely compatible with pure self-interest. If Améry's talk about moral truth and comprehension is to make sense, the moral truth to be experienced by the SS-man in order to transform him from anti-man to fellow man must involve a genuine moral acknowledgement of the moral nature of what he has done. If Améry "only" wanted to impart to Wajs the same feeling of loneliness and abandonment, the whole enterprise would not be far from the idea of revenge. As mentioned, one of the reasons why *ressentiment* is commonly considered as a degrading and mean emotional condition has to do with its involvement of a cluster of loathsome and mean desires: the desire for revenge or the imposition of suffering on others, the impulse to detract, *Schadenfreude,* and the like (cf. Scheler 1992). All such desires are apparently absent from the special kind of *ressentiment* defended by Améry. Nietzsche writes that the sullenly wrathful "will" wanted to impart to others the same wrath or antipathy against time and its irrevocable "it was." This, according to Nietzsche, was the very spirit of revenge. But Améry does not want a fellow sufferer but a fellow man. If his moral address to Wajs is to be seen as a kind of revenge, it is a justifiable variant of it.

We are, indeed, far away from Tutu's notion of reconciliation based on forgiveness and embrace. Instead of reconciliation and coexistence, the German word '*Verständigung*' (understanding, communication) covers an important part (but only a part) of what Améry hoped for, because his goal is not social harmony, consensus, and embrace, but rather dialogue and a shared moral understanding of the past and the responsibilities arising from it.[17] In Améry's moral vision, the victim will not answer the perpetrators' recognition of the moral truth and remorse and/or responsibility with a granting of forgiveness. But, and this is important, Améry seems as concerned as Tutu about the restoration or creation of a human community.

Améry could conceive of a moral conversion of SS-man Wajs, but Wajs was only one of a multitude: "if an entire inverted pyramid of SS men, SS helpers, officials, Kapos, and medal-bedecked generals had not weighed on me, I would," writes Améry, "have died calmly and appeased along with my fellow man with the Death's Head insignia. At least that is the way it seems to me now" (71). Even if Améry allows himself to believe in the moral conversion of Wajs, he still has to deal with the thousands of other torturers, those who helped them, and all those who stood by in silence. The problem is social and persistent: "the inverted pyramid is *still* driving me into the ground" (71, italics added). Clearly, how and why should the survivor "look but to the future," when he does not even know whether the mass of people, whose activity or passivity made the atrocity possible, would participate or stand by in silence yet again? Still living in Europe, Améry does not feel able to put his guard down; he lives in fear because he knows that the unthinkable is possible and in anger because he feels twice abandoned by the human community from which he expected better. On the basis of this understanding of the historical situation, Améry finds "scant inclination to be conciliatory" (71).

Rehabilitating the "Man of *Ressentiment*"

Desmond Tutu pictured anger and resentment as destructive forces, corrosive of the attitudes and acts that are praiseworthy and that sustain the intersubjective conditions of our common humanity. Like Tutu, many advocates of forgiveness tie the willingness or exercise of forgiveness to a realization of deep humanity and virtue. In forgiving, we "re-establish the deepest qualities of humanity" (Müller-Fahrenholz 1997:ix). "Exercising [forgiveness] people can liberate themselves, escape from the grasp of the past, and become more fully human" (Rigby 2001:191). Given such points of view, resentment often appears as an attitude that no sane or humane person would be willing to retain. Those who retain resentment or refuse to forgive are not likely to receive moral credit. Yet, as we have seen, philosophers like Adam Smith, Joseph Butler, and Peter F. Strawson maintain that resentment is part and parcel of our humanity (in the normative sense of "being human"), and in the works of Jeffrie Murphy, resentment can be "emotional testimony" of self-respect and a concern about the moral injury done to others or oneself.

Indeed, according to Murphy resentment also stands as testimony to "our allegiance to the moral order itself . . . an order represented by clear understandings of what constitutes unacceptable treatment of one human being by another" (Murphy 2003:20).

However, what about the victim trapped in the kind of *ressentiment* personified by Améry? In what category does this special kind of *ressentiment* belong? Is it like resentment proper; that is, something that can be retained by a morally decent person? In other words, is it possible to provide a moral rehabilitation of "the man of *ressentiment*"? In the part of the essay to which we turn in this section, Améry tries to undo the common assumption that humanity and moral virtue are automatically behind displays of a willingness to forgive, reconcile, and move on, whereas the prolonged display of *ressentiment* and irreconcilability are the reflex expressions of a morally flawed or deficient character; in other words, that the forgiving and conciliatory victim is realizing or manifesting something more honorable or humane in comparison with the person who retains resentment. Trying to counter this picture, Améry articulates his own view on the proper allegiances of what he calls "the moral person." The most central virtue he invokes is the "moral power to resist" (1999:72); in German *Sittliche Wiederstandskraft* (Améry 2002a:133). And *under the given historical circumstances,* what should be met with moral resistance is the social pressure on the victims to forgive and forget or to accept what happened because it is "already-being-long-past" (Améry 1999:71). Such pressure is, as Améry states, in itself immoral. To give in to it and its implied attitudes to individuality, morality, and time would constitute a moral lapse. He even states that the "loudly proclaimed readiness for reconciliation by Nazi victims can only be either insanity and indifference to life or the masochistic conversion of a suppressed *genuine* demand for revenge" (71).[18]

The unspoken question behind Améry's moral critique of the belief in the moral superiority of the forgiving and conciliatory Nazi victim is this: what kind of person would be able and willing to accept the call to forgive, forget, or reconcile in the given context; that is, under the circumstances of massive impunity and escapist forgetfulness? It is as if Améry asks, Is this what you want me to *be*? Here it is important to keep in mind the situated character of Améry's claims and arguments, lest one all too easily misconstrue his position. He is not the academic philosopher interested in a general, reasoned, and balanced concept of forgiveness or *ressentiment*. His primary aim is not to present a new concept of *ressentiment*, but to defend its moral necessity in the particular historical and social present in which he lives. Similarly, in relation to forgiveness, Améry does not do justice to the phenomenon and the concept. He criticizes the use of the term in the given context, but does not supply a more sound alternative. Yet, let us now examine

Améry's picture of the kind of person he would be if he gave in to the call to forgive and or forget:

> Whoever submerges his individuality in society and is able to comprehend himself only as a function of the social, that is, the insensitive and indifferent person, really does forgive. He calmly allows what happened to remain what it was. As the popular saying goes, he lets time heal his wounds. His time-sense is not dis-ordered, that is to say, it has not moved out of the biological and social sphere into the moral sphere. As a deindividualized, interchangeable part of the social mechanism he lives with it consentingly, and when he forgives, his behavior is analogous to the social reaction to crime, as the French trial lawyer Maurice Garçon described it in connection with the debate on the Statute of Limitations. "Already the child," so the *maître* instructs us, "who is reproached for a past lack of obedience answers: but that's already past. This already-being-long-past appears to the child in the most natural way as an excuse. And we, too, regard the remoteness through time as the principle of the Statue of Limitations. A crime causes disquiet in society; but as soon as public consciousness loses the memory of the crime, the disquiet also disappears. The punishment that is temporally far removed from the crime, becomes senseless" (Améry 1999:71).

Thus, Améry connects society's appreciation of the Nazi victim who forgives with a demeaning relinquishing of that individual's moral experiences and demands. The ease with which the deindividualized person forgives might be celebrated from the perspective of a societal interest in political stability and in nation building. Améry, however, insists on a moral position that upholds the legitimacy of the voice of the individual in spite of its uneasy attitude toward concerns about the social collective.[19] This plea on behalf of the moral standing and integrity of the individual must be understood against the historical background of a totalitarian regime under which the dignity and rights of the individual were completely demolished. This is another instance of the tension between the rights and needs of the individual and the good of society that was also pertinent to the discussion of the South African case.[20]

The "insensitive and indifferent person" (71) is furthermore characterized by his relationship to time and the healing it may bring about. As if he was a child, he allows what happened to remain what it was and lets time heal his wounds. According to Améry, this passivity is again an intolerable form of human subjugation (72); it is a moral capitulation to the social and biological or allegedly "natural" consciousness of time and the related normative implications of the passing of time. Améry stipulates as unworthy the attitude that the future per se should be considered more important than the past and that what is past should, simply because it is past, be considered unimportant. Equally incompatible with his notion of human dignity is the notion that one may allow the sheer passing of time to heal the wounds of the past. From within the "natural" perspective on time, forgetting and "the natural process of healing that time brings about" (77) may be suggested as a way to get over historical wrongs. As Francis Bacon put it, "That which is past is gone and irrevocable; and wise men have enough to do with things present and to come; therefore they do but trifle with themselves that labor in past matters" (Bacon 1625/1997:13). The "future-oriented person" (76) who allows "what happened to remain what it was [and] lets time heal his wounds" (71) might be considered healthy from a therapeutic perspective, but not, Améry retorts, on moral grounds:

> Man has the right and the privilege to declare himself in disagreement
> with every natural occurrence, including the biological healing that
> time brings about. What happened, happened. This sentence is as true
> as it is hostile to morals and intellects. The moral power to resist con-
> tains the protest, the revolt against reality, which is rational only as
> long as it is moral. The moral person demands the annulment of time
> (1999:72).

The demand of the moral person (who responds as befits a human being) coincides with the desire already presented as essential to the kind of *ressentiment* of which Améry speaks. This is, then, the point where Améry provides what might be called the ethical explanation for his *unwillingness* to "get rid" of his *ressentiment*. To let go (e.g., in order to be able to move on, feel relieved, be released of the pain, and so forth) would compromise human worth and virtue. In this way, the moral logic behind Améry's preservation of *ressentiment* overlaps with Jeffrie Murphy's (2003) argument for the connection between resentment and self-respect. The moral allegiance to a notion of human dignity and virtue is, however, only part of the explanation why Améry neither can nor wants to get rid of his *ressentiment*. There is also the desire to be released from the pain of abandonment.

The healing of the passing of time is amoral or even anti-moral; that is, contrary to the kind of settlement that "all those who wish to live together as fellow human beings"(xiv) ought to pursue. Améry thinks of his *ressentiment* as his "personal protest against the anti-moral natural process of healing that time brings about" (77).[21] Still, what Améry revolts against is not, as Margaret Walker (2006b) has also emphasized, the inexorability of time, but the "hol-low, thoughtless, utterly false conciliatoriness" (ix) that can be ascribed to human agents. What is under attack is, in other words, an unworthy attitude and the suggestion to leave it to time to heal the wounds of the past. And yet, to whom is the moral person's demand for an "annulment of time" (*Aufhebung der Zeit*) directed? Who is the proper addressee for this demand? If "ought implies can," we must wonder who can comply with this demand? How should we understand this demand —metaphorically or literally? At this point, the metaphorical interpretation gains validity again. Much depends, however, on another question. To the degree that the demand is directed toward society, and German society in particular, does Améry want society to satisfy his demand or does he want it to adopt it and share it with him?

Thus, to summarize: contrary to common beliefs in the moral superiority of the forgiving person, Améry posits that the preservation and voicing of *ressentiment* (against social pressure and in spite of the passing of time) can be a real moral and humane accomplishment. A bias toward the future and a concern about self-preservation might be natural, but as moral beings, human beings should be expected not to simply move on as if we were a piece of unaffected nature or nothing but a part of the social body. When Améry speaks of a wish for a "moralization of time,"[22] it is as much a wish for the moralization of his contemporaries' sense of time. A moralization of their sense of time would render impossible their appeal to let time do the healing. That seems to be his implicit hope.

Améry builds the case for his claim that there is more to the "twisted" sense of time than psychologists and moralists (influenced by Nietzsche) have been able to acknowledge by invoking a certain picture of the moral person and of the relationship among morality, society, and nature. He aims to show that we should praise, not chastise, the person who preserves *ressentiment* when moral repair fails to come about and when the voicing of resistance invites demonizing and pathologizing social responses. This kind of *ressentiment* should not be considered a moral taint, nor should it be reduced to a sickness to be treated. Insofar as one accepts the moral nature and legitimacy of *ressentiment*, it can also be the reflex expression of an honorable emotional response to inexpiable evil or wrongs and to legitimate moral expectations that have not been properly dealt with.

This brings us back to the question of the affinity between Améryean *ressentiment* and moral philosophical concepts of resentment, which I argue is based on their shared beliefs that legitimate expectations have been violated. One can both accept the notion of a *ressentiment* occasioned by a genuine moral wrong and still insist on the condemnation of the attitude, the reason being that the condemnable or regrettable aspect of *ressentiment* can be an effect, either of the excessive and gloomy nature of the way in which resentment is preserved in *ressentiment*, or of the vengeful desires to which *ressentiment* may give rise. In other words, persons plagued by *ressentiment* might reasonably believe that a serious moral wrong has been done, and at the same time, be appropriately criticized both for the way in which they hold on to their resentment and for the vengeful kind of retribution they wish to be inflicted on those responsible for the wrong in question.

The section of the essay considered in this chapter has shown that Améry in his *unwillingness* (rather than inability) to get rid of his *ressentiment* "cultivates" a special kind of *ressentiment*. (This idea presupposes that our emotions and the desires and beliefs involved can, to some extent, be molded). What first appears as a gloomy and unfocused uneasiness and hostility related to his dealings with the postwar Germans emerges—via the hermeneutical or phenomenological moral exercise of the essay—as a deliberate and focused moral-emotional attitude.

Wallace emphasizes the need to broaden the picture of the moral reactive emotions as more than expressions of blind hatred and vindictiveness. As he puts it,

> In expressing these emotions, then, we are not just venting feelings of anger and hatred, in the service of an antecedent desire to inflict harm for its own sake; we are demonstrating our commitment to certain moral standards, as regulative of social life. Once this point is grasped, blame and moral sanction can be seen to have a positive, perhaps irreplaceable contribution to make to the constitution and maintenance of moral communities; by giving voice to the reactive emotions, these responses help to articulate, and thereby affirm and deepen, our commitment to a set of common moral obligations (Wallace 1994:69).

Is Améry's deliberate preservation and public expression of his *ressentiments* in accord with this picture of the social function of the moral emotions? Améry, to paraphrase, is not just giving vent to envy, spite, and frustrated vindictiveness, and one does not need to accept Améry's moral convictions on the right and privilege of human beings or the value of resistance and individual integrity to accept that his preservation and expression of *ressentiment* demonstrate a commitment to certain moral standards and values that deserve to be answered—not treated.

Philosophical theories of resentment—as expounded by Butler, Strawson, Murphy, Wallace, and Walker—connect susceptibility to the reactive emotions with the stance of holding people responsible. This connection prompts recognition of an important point: in preserving and expressing his *ressentiments*, Améry is not simply experiencing and expressing an emotional reaction. He is doing something; he is performing a moral act. That is, he is holding those against whom his *ressentiments* are directed to the atrocities they have committed, failed to protest against, or forgiven or forgotten too hastily. As a character in one of Elie Wiesel's books says, it is perhaps not given to humans to efface evil, "but they may become the consciousness of evil" (cited in Ricoeur 1995:290). "In the midst of the world's silence," as Améry writes, "our *ressentiment* hold its finger raised" (78). The references to "consciousness" and the accusing finger of blame are very apt to his historical situation. Améry has no judicial or political power; he has no power to subpoena, and he does not speak to prompt trials or gain restitution. He "simply" maintains the stance of holding people responsible. This point draws our attention to a new problem: are all the people against whom his *ressentiments* are directed and on whom he imputes moral responsibility really blameworthy? More fundamentally, at whom is he pointing his finger?

11

Guilt and Responsibility

> *Morally speaking, it is hardly less wrong to feel guilty without having done something specific than it is to feel free of all guilt if one is actually guilty of something.*
>
> (*EICHMANN IN JERUSALEM*, ARENDT 1978:298)

Collective Guilt

At an earlier point in the essay, Améry accepts the obligation to clarify his *ressentiments* "for those against whom they are directed" (1999:67). But against whom *are* Améry's *ressentiments* directed, and are the implicit expectations and notions of guilt and responsibility themselves morally justifiable? Reading through the essay, one is presented with an international collection of resented individuals and groups: a SS-man Wajs from Belgium, a South German businessman, the philosopher Gabriel Marcel, the publicist André Neher, SS-men, Kapos, German bystanders, "former fellows in battle," and even "the world, which forgives and forgets." In addition, he mentions several individuals for their admirable or in other ways positive capacities: the few brave people he encountered ("the disabled soldier Herbert Karp," "Willy Schneider, Catholic worker from Essen" etc.) and the authors Thomas Mann and Hans Magnus Enzensberger.

Améry's *ressentiments* are not restricted to the Germans, but the Germans are the main addressee of his book. The essays were, as mentioned, originally written to be read for the listeners of a South German radio station. Améry holds "Germany against its twelve years under Hitler" (67), and throughout the essay we hear about the Germans (as the essay was originally entitled), the German people, German history, and Germany. At stake is not anything like the German national character (actually Améry thinks it is "sheer nonsense"(vii) to speak of one), but the conduct and attitudes of particular historical agents. It is the "inverted pyramid of SS men, SS helpers, officials, Kapos, and medal-bedecked generals" (70) that weighs on Améry. More than that, it is "the mass of the indifferent, the malicious and vile. . . . The far-too-many were not SS men, but rather laborers, file clerks, technicians, typists—and only a minority among them wore the party badge. All in all, for me they were the German people" (74). And Améry does not stop with the generation of "those who murdered or allowed the murder to occur" (75). Indeed, his concern is ultimately about German youth and their relationship to their national history.

However, such wide distributions of blameworthiness or responsibility are not promising with regard to the attempt to prove that the *ressentiment* under examination is of a special and more justifiable kind than its more well-known relatives. Has Améry, in spite of some promising surprises, given in to the familiar irrationality pertaining to people possessed by *ressentiment*? Perhaps we have reached a sore point in his attempt to delimit and defend *ressentiment*. Recall that when considered as a mood or a trait, *ressentiment* is commonly thought to involve an irrational and in some situations dangerous generalization of a more appropriately targeted resentment:

The person who feels anger toward someone in particular can be left in a mood of *ressentiment* through frustration of his desires, and this feeling—now less specifically towards things in general—can itself consolidate into a trait: he becomes a resentful person, habitually disposed to have resentful thoughts and feelings towards all sorts of specific persons and things" (Goldie 2002:150).

Likewise, Trudy Govier cautions that "bitter feelings may easily extend to others not responsible for the original wrong" (2002:54), and in an otherwise unusually approving analysis of bitterness, Lynn McFall argues that it can be difficult to contain, as it tends toward excess or overgeneralization. Bitterness, vindictiveness, and *ressentiment* are "liable to poison one's other perceptions, to corrupt one's judgments of people. . . . Instead of hating one's deserving wife or brutal husband, one hates all women, all men" (McFall 1991:152).[1]

Similar ideas of the connection between bitterness and corrupted judgment are found in many writings on the postgenocide context. Consider this 1977 statement in an Amnesty International report on postgenocide Rwanda: "In the climate of bitterness and suspicion which prevails after the genocide many defendants are considered guilty unless proven innocent" (cited in Bass 2000:307).

Améry acknowledges that whether his words will carry any weight will depend in some measure on whether he is able to "check"[2] his *ressentiments*—

"at least to the extent that they do not overrun their subject" (1999:72). Yet, this gesture to moderation and restraint is immediately contradicted, because Améry goes on with a declaration that if he is to delimit the "area" in which his *ressentiments* are active, he needs to endorse what he has "suggestively called collective guilt" (72). A term *less* indicative of rational judgment and moral sense is hard to come by (one could of course point to *ressentiment* . . .), and as Améry knew, "The word is forbidden, not just of today, but already since 1946. . . . Although I do not find it easy, I must stick to it. But first I must adequately define it, whatever the risk" (72).

Améry's endorsement of the idea of collective guilt does not, of course, come as a complete surprise. To the contrary; an adherence to a distribution of guilt run amok, collective guilt, seems precisely what is needed to explain a *ressentiment* directed against the German people. Much hinges on the possibility that the promised definition of collective guilt will reveal something surprising, because on the face of it, the term evokes, as the Israeli philosopher Abraham Zvi Bar-on puts it, the specter of "injustice, vindictiveness, blurring of distinctions" (Bar-on 1985:255).

When survivors and agents involved in transitional justice invoke the concept or problem of collective guilt, they do so typically to denounce it as a repugnant, irrational, and politically dangerous sentiment. Without a doubt, one of the most commonly voiced concerns arising in the wake of ethnic war and genocide is the presumption or fear that victim groups will hate and resent the entire national, religious, or political group, the members of which were responsible for the suffering and crimes inflicted on the victim group. The dangers of collective guilt explain why the ability to *individualize* guilt is one of the most common arguments for conducting trials of the perpetrators of mass atrocities:

> It is crucial to break the cycle of the collective attribution of guilt. Serbs, as a people, did not commit mass murder, torture, and rape in Croatia and Bosnia; rather, particular Serbs, and also particular Croats and Muslims, committed particular crimes. If those directly responsible are tried and punished, the burden of blame will not be carried indiscriminately by members of an entire ethnic group. Culpability will not be passed down from generation to generation. Trials will single out the guilty, differentiating them from the innocent (Neier 1998: 211).[3]

Assignments of collective guilt are built on a belief that all members of the resented group are properly seen as guilty or complicit simply by being members of that group. The guilt of the individual is determined by the acts of members of the group to which the individual, in the eyes of the accuser, belongs—without regard to the particular conduct, intentions, and circumstances of the person. Because assignment of guilt is not dependent on the conduct of the individual agent, assignments of collective guilt easily turn transgenerational. For example, the Bosnian Muslim born in the 1990s may be thought to inherit the alleged guilt of his imagined ancestry. The notion of transgenerational guilt has survived many centuries of criticism. Present-day statements of the need to individualize guilt in postconflict societies roughly echo appeals for restraint that have been voiced since the Old Testament. Just consider the words of the prophet Ezekiel: "The person who sins shall die. A child shall not suffer for the iniquity of a parent, nor a parent suffer for the iniquity of a child; the righteousness of the righteous shall be his own, and the wickedness of the wicked shall be his own" (Ezekiel 18:20; cited in Schimmel 2002:26).[4]

By assuming collective guilt, all the conditions that characteristically must be met if a person is to be found *guilty* in a legal and/or moral sense are set aside. According to Herbert Morris's reconstruction, legal guilt requires that the person has done a wrong or harm (or that one has culpably omitted to act); it requires fault or a culpability (a "guilty mind" and an opportunity to behave otherwise than one did). Guilt (unlike responsibility)[5] can never be vicarious, and if a person is deemed guilty because of the acts of another, a culpable relationship to the other person's conduct must be proved (cf. Morris 1992:118f). The ascription of guilt to individuals on the basis of their group identity diminishes the concept of guilt and debases the individual. The individual is blamed and perhaps "punished" not because of what he himself has done. People are seen and treated not as individuals, but simply as members of a group. Thus construed, the logic of collective guilt shares some of the aspects pertaining to the logic driving ethnic war and genocide.[6] "Genocide is," as Raphaël Lemkin wrote in *Axis Rule in Europe* (1944), "directed at the national group as an entity, and the actions involved are directed against individuals, not in their individual capacity, but as members of the national groups" (cited in Amann 2002:97, n. 12). It would, however, be misguided to say that the logic of collective guilt *is* genocidal in character. There is no necessary connection between a belief in collective guilt and advocacy for the total physical annihilation of the people who are seen as collectively guilty. Genocide requires the kind of group mentality connected with collective guilt, but collective guilt does not necessarily imply a genocidal intent or mentality.[7] Support of collective guilt does not necessarily imply more than the belief that every person within a given group deserves to be blamed, and that the group members should recognize their shared guilt and act so as to redeem themselves from it.

Still, contrary to ascriptions of shame or liabilities to provide reparations, ascriptions of *guilt* are tied to beliefs about culpability and desert, thus those who endorse notions of collective guilt prompt fear of future harsh treatment: mass sanctions, violent reprisals, and laws and practices of collective punishment. Setting out what is implied when ascribing guilt to someone, Herbert Morris (1992), among other things, points out that the person being held criminally guilty is seen to deserve not simply condemnation (the verdict) but also a response, essentially legal punishment, that cancels the improper arrogation of a position of superiority to others and the law. It might be bad enough when what is at stake is a claim of collective moral guilt, but the most pressing worries arise when the rhetoric of collective guilt appears as a preparation of collective punishment and a perversion of basic principles as to the "nexus" between *criminal* guilt and individual agency.

It is worth noting that assignments of collective guilt are not always meant to pave the way for harsh collective punishment. Appeals to collective guilt may just as well be used in campaigns intended to *undermine* efforts to secure accountability and punishment of the guilty. In the wake of genocide and other forms of mass crime, whether one looks at the history of Germany, Cambodia, the former Czechoslovakia, or South Africa, talk of collective guilt may reflect an attempt to allow the perpetrators and their accomplices to disappear in the midst of a collectively guilty people. Where all are guilty, no one in particular deserves to be punished, exempted from office, or the like.[8] With regard to the postwar German context, Norbert Frei has argued that the brandishing of the idea of a collective German guilt was first and foremost the result of German inventiveness: the expression of the bad faith of the Germans of the Adenauer period.[9] Why? Because, by insisting on the claim of being declared collectively guilty (by the victorious powers and in the very moment of utter defeat), one acquires an eminent pretext to push aside the question of personal guilt and instead wallow in resentment or a sense of being unjustly treated (cf. Frei 2000:170–71).

In short, the nightmare scenario of the belief in and the resentful promotion of collective guilt is a thoroughly irrational and immoral phenomenon. Whereas guilt feelings and the practice of blame and reproach that assigns guilt are normally valuable parts of our common moral life, both are perverted when collective guilt is claimed, whether to hide the guilt of individuals or to blame or incriminate the innocent.[10] This being said, the attempt to individualize guilt in courts of law is itself fraught with very difficult and complex problems. The jurisprudence from the Nuremberg and Frankfurt trials as well as the more recent ad hoc tribunals in The Hague and Arusha testify to the many problems faced as soon as individual accountability for state-sponsored mass crime is to be implemented. Where shall tribunals dealing with genocide draw the line between culpability and innocence? What are the fair conditions for assigning "command responsibility"? To what degree are principles governing the gradation of culpability and the mitigation of punishment in domestic criminal law applicable to these crimes? Can a person who participates in mass killings under threats against his own life be exempted from responsibility; that is, under the principle of duress? As Martha Minow cautions, the phenomena of mass atrocity might render problematic the assumptions normally sustaining the practice of imputing individual responsibility (cf. Minow 1998:46). Additionally, the sheer practical problems of proving participation in the atrocities, as well as the issues of time and resources, have sometimes prompted the inclusion of principles of prosecution and punishment that come hazardously close to the idea of collective guilt.

The prominence of the ideal of establishing individual accountability after mass atrocity and the murkiness of the "ideal type" picture of the assignment of collective guilt do not mean that all issues of guilt and accountability would be resolved, if and when matters of individual criminal accountability could be settled. As David Cohen puts it in a perceptive analysis of the problems of determining individual responsibility in modern warfare and mass atrocities, invocation of the principle of individualization of guilt can furnish a "perfect excuse to completely ignore the unique characteristics of mass murder carried out as a routine administrative function according to official governmental policies and organized bureaucratic procedures" (Cohen 1999:56). The issue is not simply that, given the thousands and thousands of possible defendants, such trials will always only prosecute a very small percentage of them. What matters is also that "the criminal law fails to reach many people who bear significant moral responsibility for what transpired" (Osiel 2000:125). And going beyond the scope of individual forms of guilt and responsibility, dealing with the legacy of genocide and other forms of mass crime perhaps necessitates a focus on the responsibility of states and organizations, and even on such "vague" concepts as the ways in which societies or nations relate to their history and ethical-political identity.[11] One may recognize the reality and value of individual responsibility and accountability and still see the need to address and deal with different kinds of collective, political, and institutional responsibility.

With this background in mind, let us return to Améry's essay. In the earlier retrospective account of the years during which his *ressentiment* increased, Améry admits that the talk about the collective guilt of the Germans in the immediate postwar period and the general contempt directed against Germany were fine with him. It matched his experience of the crime as a collective enterprise, committed, supported, or indifferently looked at by the overwhelming majority of the German society. In the eyes of Améry, the German people were "laden with collective guilt" (65), and he concurs, it seems, with the so-called Morgenthau plan that Germany should be pastoralized as the "potato field of Europe" (65). That Améry agrees with the most controversial aspect of Henry Morgenthau Jr.'s[12] plan for defeated Germany shows his desire for a response that goes way beyond legalistic and pragmatic considerations.[13] Yet, the problem facing Améry when he wrote this essay (that is, 1965) is the German nonacknowledgment of guilt and the pinning of the blame on Hitler as the arch-criminal who (allegedly) seduced and victimized the Germans, who had never really been committed to the National Socialist regime, who had only obeyed orders, and the like. Améry states that it is *he*, not the Germans, who is burdened with collective guilt or, more precisely, with the knowledge of its reality (this must, to return to an earlier issue, be part of the "moral truth" to which Améry is captive). The present has "proclaimed the collective innocence of the Germans" (75), and "the world which forgives and forgets" (75) has sentenced Améry; he is, he writes, condemnable as Shylock, "but already cheated of the pound of flesh too" (75).

Now, how does Améry define the kind of collective guilt that he advocates? Considering the genuine dangers inherent in the concept of collective guilt, it is not promising that Améry begins his presentation speaking as if the reasons why the term has been tabooed all have to do with Cold War politics. Still, let us now find out what he is up to:

> Collective guilt. That is naturally sheer nonsense if it implies that the community of Germans possessed a common unconsciousness, a common will, a common initiative to act, and therein became culpable. But it is a useful hypothesis if nothing else is meant by it than the objectively manifested *sum* of individual guilty conduct. Then there grows out of the guilt of individual Germans—guilt of deed, guilt of omission, guilt of utterance, guilt of silence—the total guilt of a people [die Gesamtschuld eines Volkes]. Before the concept of collective guilt can be applied, it must be freed of myth and mystification. Then it will lose its dark, ominous tone and be useful in the only way that it can: as a vague statistical statement (72–73/135).

The question is whether the concept of collective guilt *can* be rehabilitated, including whether it is conceptually compatible with the idea of a "vague statistical statement." The passage offers a peculiar mix of clarity and cognitive dissonance. Améry's idea of collective guilt seems to be reducible to different kinds of individual guilt pertaining to "the generation of destroyers—the gas chamber constructors, those ready at any time to sign their name to anything, the generals duty-bound to their Führer" (75). Thus, when Améry speaks of collective guilt, the claim involved is that an overwhelming majority of Germans of age between 1933 and 1945 conducted themselves in a manner that makes it appropriate to declare them individually guilty (vs. innocent) of the Nazi crimes. A *massive assemblage* of individual guilt is a more precise expression of Améry's allegation of a collective German guilt. Améry's vague statistical judgment may be empirically untenable, and one may dispute the implicit standards of what people can be expected to risk for each other (when it is fair to ascribe guilt for knowledge resisted and acts omitted, etc.). But so far the reconstructed position is not conceptually confusing. Améry does not ascribe guilt to anyone on the basis of acts or omissions not attributable to the individual; guilt stays strictly personal—there is just a huge sum of individually guilty conduct. Améry does not consider different degrees of guilt and kinds of guilt, but neither does he call for a Draconian punishment of all the individuals comprised in the sum total.

Considering the examples—perpetrators as well as bystanders—running through the essay, the summation of individually guilty conduct comprises both instances of strictly moral guilt only and instances where moral guilt overlaps with criminal guilt. The guilt of the greater part of the majority of the "generation" in question may be strictly moral. Nonetheless, it remains individual guilt, because it is tied to individual conduct. The individuals in question should acknowledge their guilt, and the *ressentiment* occasioned by their second moral failure to do so is in principle justified. Even though thousands and thousands of people had participated in the "joint criminal enterprise," Améry's previous focus on the desire that the guilty face the "moral truth" of their conduct suggests that it is their moral acknowledgement of guilt—contrition, repentance, restoration of damaged relationships, and the like—that matters to him rather than the need to punish the guilty as such.[14] In sum, it is possible that Améry succeeds both in avoiding the hazards commonly connected with the assertion of collective guilt and in controlling in his *ressentiment*, thereby avoiding the pitfall of overgeneralization, as pointed to by Peter Goldie, Trudy Govier, Lynne McFall, and others.

But it makes sense to say that the majority of Germans of age under the rule of Hitler all had some share of guilt to deal with, and here it is important that Améry's notion of guilt includes the moral guilt incurred by the bystander to atrocity. Granted this, his point of view is shared by Primo Levi, Hannah Arendt, Karl Jaspers, Günther Grass, and others who have attributed widespread moral guilt for passivity and omission.[15] Keeping in mind the way in which declarations of collective guilt are connected to the exculpation of individuals and the blurring of the difference between those who should be punished and those who are simply blameworthy, one can object that Améry should have distinguished more clearly among different kinds and degrees of individual guilt. His concern in the essay is, however, not about justice, and his business is only to *actualize* the problem. He wants to *initiate* a public, national confrontation with the guilt incurred by the conduct of the past. The nuances would—one hopes—arrive later. One may still insist that Améry exemplifies the same kind of careless and offensive judgmentalism as referred to in the statement from the Amnesty International report (guilty until proven innocent). His claim concerning the mass of individually guilty conduct is based on, as he writes, a vague statistical assessment, rather than either the adversarial process of legal prosecution that properly separates the legally guilty from the innocent or a personal knowledge of the acts and attitudes of each single responsible individual.

Yet, the point just mentioned—that Améry's quest is to provoke or stir up a confrontation with the question of guilt—does not necessarily justify the lack of distinctions among degrees and kind of individual guilt. Karl Jaspers too wanted to prompt a German debate on the guilt question, but interestingly he used a reference to an American postwar poster reminiscent of Améry's posture in its accusatory coarseness:

> In the summer of 1945, when in all towns and villages the posters hung with the pictures and stories from Belsen and the crucial statement, "You are the Guilty!", consciences grew uneasy, horror gripped many who had indeed not known this, and something rebelled: who indicts me there? No signature, no authority—the poster came as though from empty space (Jaspers 1946/2000:41).[16]

Against this background, Jaspers introduces his landscape of different kinds and forms of guilt. (This being said, one should add that Jaspers was also aware that the very drawing of distinctions could facilitate evasion). Améry knew and appreciated Jaspers' book, and I am inclined to stick to the pragmatic justification of Améry's lack of subtlety: he wants to *initiate* a confrontation with the past.

Yet, the real confusion, or at least my confusion, emerges because Améry does not stay with the claim of a massive assemblage of individually guilty conduct after all. In the excerpt cited above, he claims that *out of the individual guilt of a mass of Germans emerges the total guilt of a people*. Now, Améry's approach comes close to what Margaret Gilbert has called "the reductionist critique" (2000:142f) of collective guilt. The confusion enters as it seems that Améry wants to stick to a claim ("the total guilt of a people") that his reductionism should have made untenable. In Gilbert's exposition, the reductionist critique is not just a critique of a particular definition of collective guilt, but rather a *reductio ad absurdum* of the very idea of collective guilt. As Gilbert points out clearly, when the claim of collective guilt is construed on reductionist grounds, it might become perfectly intelligible, but the reductionist explanation immediately reveals that assertions of the collective guilt of entire nations or ethnic groups are simply unbelievable or at least unlikely to be true. Technically speaking, they imply that *every* single member of the group has some share in the total sum of guilt. But as Gilbert writes, "many citizens are likely to be morally blameless in relation to the wars their nations undertake. Some citizens may not know the war is taking place, others may attempt to stop it, and so on" (2000:142).

The strange thing is that Améry is perfectly aware of such exceptions. He has not forgotten the few brave people he met. For example, he mentions "the disabled soldier Herbert Karp from Danzig who in Auschwitz-Monowitz shared his last cigarette with me; Willy Schneider, a Catholic worker from Essen, who addressed me by my already forgotten first name and gave me bread" (73). One may even say that Améry has a charitable eye for the smallest acts of resistance or expressions of concern. His requirements are minimal: "an angry glance at the SS Roll Call Officer . . . a compassionate smile for us . . . a lowering of their eyes in shame" (73). In other words, on the basis of the very reductionist definition offered by Améry, the sum of individually guilty conduct is not total, as Améry has made perfectly clear. The leap from the many to all is bad moral mathematics. It is understandable if Améry wants to attribute some kind of liability to the German society and citizens, but there needs to be a new category to indicate that the responsibility ascribed to the collective as a whole is something other than the guilt ascribed to a certain part of its members. The reality of a kind of responsibility beyond guilt and innocence is the subject of the next chapter.

In *Die Schuldfrage* (*The Question of Guilt*) from 1946, Karl Jaspers writes that "the categorical judgment of a people is always unjust. It presupposes a false substantialization of 'a people' and results in the debasement of the human being as individual" (cited in Fletcher and Weinstein 2002:604). Yet, the weird leap made by Améry from the vague statistical statement to the categorical judgment of the total guilt of the people is not a false substantialization. Améry is as "antiholistic" as Max Weber when the latter states that "there is no such thing as a collective personality which 'acts'" (cited in Gilbert 2000:143). What is at stake must be extracted from the following passage:

> My good comrades are not to be blamed, nor am I, that their weight is too slight as soon as they stand before me no longer in their singularity but in the midst of their people. . . . Whether the victim wanted to or not, he had to believe that Hitler really was the German people. My Willy Schneider and Herbert Karp and Foreman Matthäus did not stand a chance of prevailing against the mass of the people. . . . I, too, had to determine the quantity of good comrades on the one hand and of the scoundrels and indifferent ones on the other when, in the midst of the German people, I had to reckon every moment with falling victim to ritual mass murder. Whether I wanted it or not, I had to accept the notion of statistical collective guilt (1999:74–75).

Améry appeals to the reader's ability to comprehend that the Jew struggling to survive in Hitler's Europe *had* to fear and to mistrust any and all German citizens of the Third Reich. Even knowing that very few Germans tried to resist and help, the persecuted Jew *had* to act as if there was total complicity. This is why Améry feels justified speaking of the collective guilt of the German people (still identified not as all Germans at any time, but as the generation of those who did it and those who let it be done) and why he is concerned with the people as a whole.

Thus, one readily understands why the individual struggling to survive during the war had to calculate that there was total complicity. But why uphold this attitude twenty years later? I first thought that Améry needed to justify the leap to the declaration of a justifiable presumption of collective guilt in order to legitimate *Beyond Guilt and Atonement* as an open letter— *J'accuse*—to German listeners and readers. The problem is that this actually does not explain why Améry, fully conscious of what he is doing, still *has* to calculate as he did during the time of persecution. Pondering this issue, I have come to the conclusion that Améry still "calculates" because he still lives in fear and mistrust; he is still not confident that things and people have changed. He has not been assured that the German ex-Nazis and ex-bystanders have acknowledged their fault and that they would not participate in mass murder or allow mass murder to take place again. As Améry said in an interview in 1978, he feels the need to probe every single German over a certain age: what did you do and what did you not do back then? (cf. Hermann 1992:82). His position is an assumption of guilt until otherwise has been proven. Yet, what does he want from the Germans—except for the contrite acknowledgment of personal guilt or complicity? This is the question of responsibility to which we now turn.

Heirs to Responsibility

You don't want to listen? Listen anyhow. You don't want to know where your indifference can again lead you and me at any time. I'll tell you. What happened is no concern of yours because you didn't know, or were too young, or not even born? You should have known, and your youth gives you no special privilege, and break with your father (Améry 1999:96).

Observing that the generation laden with guilt is "growing old with honor" (75),[17] Améry turns his attention to the young Germans, but does he hold them responsible for the guilt of the older generations? Before we proceed with this issue, let me dispel the possible misgiving that this chapter's elaborations on guilt and responsibility are not that important to the question of the moral nature and value of *ressentiment*. I have already argued that the question whether Améry attributes guilt irrationally is interesting in relation to the common expectation of overgeneralization. The reflections on guilt and responsibility are, however, also relevant because they offer an extraordinarily accurate picture of what resentful victims may actually want; that is, over and beyond the commonly expected desire for compensation and revenge.

The attitudes of German youth to the Nazi past are clearly of concern to Améry. For example, he cites a letter from a young man from Kassel who was "sick and tired of hearing again and again that our fathers killed six million Jews" (75). More important, in the preface to the German reprinting from 1970, Améry stresses explicitly his hope that *Beyond Guilt and Atonement* would reach those young Germans who thought it was time to put an end to the talk of the Nazi past. Yet, what can he expect or demand from those born after the war and under a new political constitution?

> To accuse the young would be just too inhuman. . . . Only stagnant, Old Testament, barbaric hate could come dragging its burden and want to load it onto the shoulders of innocent German youth. Accordingly, segments of the young people, fortunately not all, do protest with the sound consciousness of justice possessed by those who stand on the solid ground of their natural time-sense (75).

Améry has to rebut the assumption that an imposition of responsibility on the young generations reflects an ascription of transgenerational guilt. If so, then any such imposition would be unjust and barbaric, and the youth should be seen and treated as free of any responsibility in relation to the past at all. Why not let them move on and leave the ghosts of the past to the parties involved in the horror? If Améry has a bone to pick, it must be between people like him and those who committed, supported, or made possible the crimes of the past. And yet,

> It is understandable that the young people are free of individual guilt and of the collective guilt that results from its summation. I must and want to, grant them the advance in confidence that is due to the future-oriented person. But possibly one can expect of these young people that they do not lay claim to their innocence as vigorously and impudently as the letter writer quoted above. For as long as the German nation, including its young and youngest age groups, does not decide to live entirely without history—and there is no sign that the world's most history-conscious national community suddenly would assume such a position—it must continue to bear the responsibility [Verantwortung tragen] for those twelve years that it certainly

did not terminate itself. German youth cannot cite Goethe . . . and ignore . . . Himmler. It will not do to claim national tradition for oneself where it was honorable and to deny it where, as dishonor incarnate, it cast a probably imaginary and certainly defenseless opponent from the community of man (76/140).

The excerpt involves three steps in the sequence of reasoning: first, a reassuring declaration that Améry does not consider the young Germans guilty; second, an assertion of a collective and transgenerational German responsibility (a responsibility not simply incumbent on the young Germans, but on any German citizen; that is, it is also relevant in relation to those with a share of guilt); and third, a suggestion that the responsibility in focus involves an obligation to integrate the Nazi past into a collective historical self-understanding. I now comment on all three points in the opposite order, because it makes most sense to begin the explanation with the practical conclusion.

Let me begin, then, at the end and elaborate on the third point: Améry's injunction that German youth cannot cite Goethe while ignoring Himmler. Nations traditionally collect memories of great heroes and victories or—sometimes equally "great"—defeats and martyrs and victims (that is, the victims of the nation, not the victims of the crimes committed by the nation).[18] However, in the last part of the second half of the twentieth century, "negative" remembrances of crimes and victims have been collected in the public commemorations and memory culture of several countries. The recognition of guilt and the willingness to engage in reparations to the victims or the descendants of the victims have, for example, been described in Elazar Barkan's *The Guilt of Nations* (2002). As Barkan points out, this new phenomenon (tied to what he calls "liberal humanist guilt") began with the German postwar reparations to the state of Israel. Germany is also the "forerunner" in terms of the ability and willingness of a nation to scrutinize its own past. As James E. Young argues in *The Texture of Memory: Holocaust, Memorials and Meaning*, Germany has shown "that a negative memorial legacy can be sustained, . . . even cultivated as a basis for national identity" (1993:53).

Returning now to Améry, we are, however, only at the turning point where the decades of silence slowly began to be replaced with the kind of apologetic (contrite) remembrance characterizing Germany today. Even if one may doubt whether any development would ultimately satisfy Améry, his demands have been met to a degree that he could not have foreseen. What did he demand? That the German nation had to reclaim (instead of repress and hush up) "the twelve years that for us others really were a thousand" and claim them "as its own realized negation of the world and its self, as its own negative possession" (78); that the German people should "remain sensitive to the fact that they cannot allow a piece of their national history to be neutralized by time"

(78); and that Auschwitz should not be placed in "the cold storage of history" (xi). For Améry, these demands sum up what German responsibility involves: not monetary compensation or the establishment of monuments or annual commemorations, but an obligation to include the Nazi past as an inalienable and indelible part of the collective political-ethical identity and memory. Améry's call for a moralization of history is a plea for the awakening of a political community willing to assume responsibility for its Nazi past.

The idea of a collective and transgenerational German responsibility for Auschwitz has been claimed repeatedly by Jürgen Habermas, who appears something like the ideal respondent of Améry's essay. For example, in an essay on the German Holocaust monument in Berlin, Habermas wrote that the monument represented a collective political self-understanding according to which the crimes of National Socialism are continuously remembered and acknowledged among present German generations – as Habermas puts it: "burnt" into this self-understanding as a persistent worry and as a reminder of the horrible crime that was done to the victims (Habermas 2001a:49–50).

This normative statement expresses what, according to Habermas, the Germans *ought to* feel and think as to the meaning of the *Denkmal*. Yet, this is not necessarily what characterizes the majority opinion, which mattered most to Améry; the danger came from the mass. However, James E. Young's empirical study of Holocaust memorial work in Germany after 1989 comes close to Améry's and Habermas's pleas for an emotionally inflected memory. According to Young, the memory of the Holocaust in Germany remains a tortured and self-reflective exercise, and, as he underscores with a point coming close to the demand raised by Améry, "it may also be true that the surest engagement with memory lies in its perpetual irresolution" (Young 1993:21).[19] More than ten years have passed since Young wrote his classic, *The Texture of Memory*, but it seems that new controversies continually erupt in German society over how to deal with the Nazi past (cf. for example Niven 2002). During the last couple of years, German victimization and the humanity of the perpetrators have become prominent issues on the public scene. I guess that Améry would have found sufficient reasons to retain his mistrust.

The second assertion of a collective and transgenerational German responsibility first appears as a hypothetical imperative. It seems to offer the premise for the assignment of responsibility to the German nation. So long as being German includes a consciousness of national history, the Germans must continue to bear the responsibility for the part of their past that runs from 1933 to 1945. If a complete amnesia and a genuinely new start post-1945 had been imaginable, then forgetting Auschwitz *too* would, perhaps, have been acceptable. The Germans could have lived, à la Morgenthau, an unhistorical minimalist life as the farmers of the potato fields of Europe. The implicit thought seems to be that if any part of the historical culture in which

Auschwitz became possible is going to be continued (and the "if" is of course purely contrafactual), then Auschwitz, and what led to it, must be incorporated in that culture. In consideration of the breakdown of civilization caused by the Nazi genocide, the German people cannot continue its collective historical tradition and self-understanding without the inclusion of Auschwitz. If this is correct, Améry mirrors what Arendt wrote in the preface to the first edition (1950) of *The Origins of Totalitarianism*:

> We can no longer afford to take that which was good in the past and simply call it our heritage, to discard the bad and simply think of it as a dead load which by itself time will bury in oblivion. The subterranean stream of Western history has finally come to the surface and usurped the dignity of our tradition. This is the reality in which we live. And this is why all efforts to escape from the grimness of the present into nostalgia for a still intact past, or into the anticipated oblivion of a better future, are in vain (Arendt 1976:ix).

In contrast to Améry, Arendt expresses a much broader concern with Western history and tradition, of which Germany is only a part. Whether discussing totalitarianism, responsibility, or the nature of the Nazi crimes, Arendt attempts to untie the thinking about these subjects from their national "containers." The Nazi crime, she argues, was a crime against humanity and insofar as German anti-Semitism had an explanatory role to play, it was only with regard to the choice of victim. My question here is whether Améry should be placed on the opposite end of the spectrum from Arendt. Was he blind to international participation in the Holocaust? Did he think that only the Germans would be able to engage in another genocidal project? Why did he not speak of a European or universal responsibility to avoid its repetition? When considering these questions, one should, first, be aware that the consciousness of the Holocaust as a global or at least European issue is a recent phenomenon and the result of a predominantly American universalization of the "lessons" of what happened. Second, the Holocaust *was* after all, as Habermas has put it, "planned, executed, and passively supported or tolerated by others within a national framework" (2001b:173). Third, *Beyond Guilt and Atonement* was written for and read to a German audience. Quite naturally, it deals with the problem of German forgetfulness and responsibility.

The plea that, so long as the German nation does not decide to live *entirely* without history, it must continue to bear responsibility, also expresses a moral demand in relation to the German politics of the past. That is, if Germans "want" to live historically at all, if there is to be anything like a continued German collective memory, then one thing to be included for sure must be the twelve years from 1933 to 1945. Thus construed, it reflects a call for an acknowledgment of the significance of what happened then in comparison with all other parts of German history: Auschwitz was not a "parenthesis" or a mishap or nothing out of the ordinary. If *anything* is to be remembered and paid heed to, then Auschwitz and the Nazi past more generally must be it. The reasoning here is not very sophisticated or elaborate. It simply asks for a response that recognizes and assumes responsibility for the overwhelming negative importance of what happened. It reminds me of Primo Levi's "prayer" prefacing *If This is a Man*: "You who live safe. . . . Consider if this is a man / Meditate that this came about: I commend these words to you. . . . Repeat them to your children, / Or may your house fall apart, / May illness impede you, / May your children turn their faces from you" (Levi 1947). Améry does not add the threats articulated by Levi, but in both instances, we are faced with vehement responses to an experience of abandonment, disregard, and forgetfulness.

Claims of a duty to remember are often put forth with reference to prospective consequentialist justifications (i.e., there is a need to remember in order to avoid its repetition). The idea of a duty to remember might also be explained as a debt or a duty owed to the dead (cf. Jankélévitch 1996). Améry, too, invokes the justification of the prevention of further evil (see his 1970 preface to *Beyond Guilt and Atonement*, Améry 2002a:628). However, Améry's call for recognition or solidarity and responsibility reflects, I think, a more basic and more personally urgent need among survivors of mass atrocity. In short, the reasons to remember are plural. They can include ideas of a debt owed to the dead and considerations of how to avoid new atrocities, but, as Habermas once stressed, a most fundamental reason is a concern for the survivors and descendants. Addressing his fellow citizens, Habermas stressed,

> There is an obligation incumbent on us in Germany . . . to keep alive, without distortion and not only in an intellectual form, the memory of the sufferings of those who were murdered by German hands. It is especially these dead who have a claim to the weak anamnestic powers of solidarity that later generations can continue to practice only in the medium of a remembrance that is repeatedly renewed, often desperate, and continually on one's mind. If we were to brush aside this Benjaminian legacy, our fellow Jewish citizens and the sons, and daughters, and grandchildren of all those who were murdered would feel themselves unable to breathe in our country (Habermas 1989:233).

Améry does not ask the Germans as a group to keep alive the sense of being guilty. The guilt remains with a specific number of individuals. Instead, he maintains that Germany and the Germans, including those born well after the genocide, continue to bear responsibility for the Nazi past. The distinction between guilt and responsibility is evidently important. There is, as Arendt has argued, "such a thing as responsibility for things one has not done" (1968b:147). Unlike guilt, responsibility can be vicarious and thus collective. "Citizens of a political community must," as Habermas writes, "'answer for' its violations of human dignity" (1998:20).[20]

In short, what Améry presumes—in his address to the Germans in general—is not a particularly radical notion of responsibility. Indeed, Améry's insistence on an awareness and historical-cultural practice of liability for the Nazi past has for many years been the official "default" position in public German memory culture.[21] Substantially, it implies a responsibility to integrate the Nazi past into the historical consciousness and identity of the national community. Insofar as the later-born Germans are responsible *for* something, it is more strictly speaking not the Nazi past but the way in which they deal with it as part of the legacy of the historical and political community in which they live. Améry thinks of this acceptance of historical and political responsibility as involving a certain mistrustful and critical attitude to national mores, history, and traditions. Shame might be there too, but I tend to think that *mistrust* is the more apt term.

Whether one ultimately can endorse Améry's attempt to "check" the scope of his *ressentiments* or not, he does provide a contra-example to the ordinary picture of the bitter or resentful person as someone disposed to corrupt judgments of other people. More important, Améry's reflections in this part of the essay should also give pause to the rhetorical construal of resentment or *ressentiment* as closely related to dehumanization and revenge. In his account of the relationship between responsibility and the moral sentiments, Richard J. Wallace (1994) theorizes that victims' susceptibility to resentment and indignation is the emotional correlate of a belief that certain moral expectations or demands have been breached. As Wallace emphasizes, the value of his framework lies in its focus on resentment as an aspect of the stance of holding people responsible and that it is not simply an expression of a retributive impulse. Holding the Germans to account in relation to certain normative expectations, Améry demonstrates a commitment to basic social-ethical standards not yet in "place" (see Wallace 1994:69 and Honneth 1995:163).

12
Wishful Thinking?

*If, in the midst of the world's silence, our ressentiment holds its finger
raised, then . . .*

A Moral Daydream

Améry defends both the refusal to let time heal all wounds and the
refusal to forgive or forget as being the right and privilege of the
moral person. He characterizes his unwillingness to move on or
to let go of his *ressentiments* as a display of personal moral virtue, rather
than as a failure to be condemned or treated. In fact, he ties the special
kind of *ressentiment* harbored by the survivor of the Holocaust to different kinds of virtues and values: a protest against forgetfulness and shallow
conciliatoriness, a struggle to regain dignity; an acute sense of the inexpiable nature of what happened, the instrument with which to make the
criminal understand the reprehensible moral nature of his actions, and
the key to a vision of a rehumanization of relationships.[1] Still, whether or
not one grants this conception, can *ressentiment* really play a constructive
role in relation to the larger social realm? More specifically, can *ressentiment* play a positive role in dealing with the unresolved moral-social conflict between the survivors of the Nazi genocide and the German people?
In the field of transitional justice studies, the social or political significance of interethnic resentment for social reconstruction is often considered, but almost always in a purely negative way: resentment is considered
as a health problem, a sign of impending cycles of violence, something
that trials might placate, and the like (see Chapter 1). The idea that
ressentiment could play a constructive role as an indirect instrument of

reconciliation between groups is hard to come by. Yet, *ressentiment*, Améry hopes, might be about more than a private protest and struggle for personal dignity. As clearly shown in the last chapter on guilt and responsibility, what weighs on Améry is not primarily this or that wrongdoer, but the multitude of wrongdoers. It was the participation and passivity of an entire society and a state that made possible the Holocaust. Therefore, Améry craves a society-wide reformation catalyzed—fantastically—through *ressentiment*.

In his comparison of Tutu and Améry, David Heyd writes that "only Tutu strives to use [the personal response of the individual] as a lever for a new social order" (Heyd 2004:196). I offer here a different assessment: Améry too *strives* to use a personal attitude as a lever for a new social order. In contrast to Tutu, Améry was not in a position to believe that his project could prove successful, but he did invest his *ressentiments* with a sociohistorical task:

> Were it to fulfill the task that I set it, it could historically represent, as a stage of the world's moral dynamics of progress, the German revolution that did not take place. This demand is no less absurd and no less moral than the individual demand that irreversible processes be reversible (Améry 1999:77).

That demand *is* absurd, and it took a couple of readings for me not to turn it into a statement of a hope that *ressentiment* would "only" *cause* or *arouse* a German revolution. Yet, Améry does say "represent," and the thought seems to be that *if* the Germans really came to share the *ressentiment*-full victims' desire that what happened had not happened, then it would be *as if* a German revolution had happened. It should be clearly stated that Améry is not just talking about a sentimental ("inner") revolution. The revolution in question includes the acceptance of the kind of historical collective responsibility addressed in the previous chapter. In this way, the change in attitude is tied to a change in historical practice: an overcoming of repression and hushing up of the Nazi past and an acceptance of "Auschwitz" as an indelible part of Germany's past, present, and future (a formula Améry assigns to Hans Magnus Enzensberger). What would occur if this happened?

> On the field of history there would occur what I hypothetically described earlier for the more limited, individual circle: two groups of people, the overpowered and those who overpowered them, would be joined in the desire that time be turned back and, with it, that history become moral. If this demand were [sic] raised by the German people, who as a matter of fact has already been rehabilitated by time, it would have tremendous weight, enough so that by this alone it would already be fulfilled. The German revolution would be made good,

Hitler disowned. And in the end Germans would really achieve what the people once did not have the might or the will to do, and what later, in the political power game, no longer appeared to be a vital necessity: the eradication of the ignominy (Améry 1999:78).[2]

This is a vision, then, of the conditions for a moral rehabilitation of the German people, but, as Améry indicates, also an idea of the restoration of a shared relationship to the past; "a settlement in the field of historical practice" (77). If the German people in this way rejected "everything that was carried out in those twelve years, [it] would be the negation of the negation: a highly positive, a redeeming act" (79). And then follows a statement that could hardly have been anticipated just a few pages before: "Only through it would our *ressentiment* be subjectively pacified and have become objectively unnecessary" (79).

This, then, is Améry's proposal for an externalization and actualization, as he puts it, of the conflict or rupture between survivors and the people of the perpetrators. This is the specification of the earlier stated programmatic demand that the "pile of corpses that lie between them and me" (69) can only be removed if those responsible (in one sense or another) for the Nazi crimes "negate themselves and in the negation coordinate with [their victims]" (69). It is a surprising and interesting "model" of the restoration of coexistence in several respects. Albeit transposed to a social level, Améry's vision of the transformation of Germany's relationship to the past mimics the earlier picture of the transformation of the SS-man, Wajs. Again, *ressentiment* appears as the key instrument with which to catalyze the process. Once more, the persons who bear the guilt or the responsibility—this time the Germans as a group— are thought to join the victims as their fellow human beings and to share with the victims the demand for a moral turning back of the clock. And yet again— but this time more clearly—the change of affairs makes appropriate an abandonment of *ressentiment*. At least as an attitude directed toward the Germans, Améry's *ressentiments* are not brandished as something that in principle *never ought* to be set aside. Yet, in the most stark contrast to current notions about the role of resentment in relation to all the noble goals of rehumanization and reconciliation, *ressentiment* is *not* held forth as a "plague to be avoided" or a prime obstacle to the promotion of coexistence, but to the contrary as a necessary part of a positive transformation. Insofar as *ressentiment*, as an attitude directed toward the Germans, can be satisfied at all, it seems to imply that "its" demand cannot be impossible to meet and also that there is some aspect of the given predicament that can be overcome. This is where the figurative interpretation of the absurd demand comes into prominence. Yet, one has to keep in mind that the vision of reconciliation between peoples is pictured as a result of their being "joined in the desire that time be turned back" (78). In other words, the absurd demand is still part of the game.

Resentment and Self-Preoccupation

Some accounts of resentment (including *ressentiment*) picture an emotion that is essentially tied to its holders' concerns about their own selves.[3] In Trudy Govier's account of resentment, the self-preoccupation of the resentful person is even represented as deeply inflected with a certain envy of those other people who have not, like oneself, been victimized, because "most fundamentally, we resent the fact that these bad things happened *to us*" (Govier 2002:51).

> Characteristic or resentment is the tendency to dwell on ourselves and our sense that *we* have been "hard done by" and have not received our fair share. . . . We easily become preoccupied with aspects of our own suffering while gaining little perspective as to how the wrongs done to us fit into the larger scheme of things (Govier 2002:52).

The picture fits of course part of the reality, but it seems to me misleading insofar as it is offered as a general description of victims' resentment. In relation to our case at hand, Améry is evidently personally concerned about the issue, and he has clearly articulated what is at stake for him: the release from abandonment, self-respect, a struggle to regain dignity, and the like. But his concern is not why *he* had to endure all the horrors visited on millions. His *ressentiments* are about what happened—more precisely, what was willed and allowed to happen—and they are about the attitudes of the German society. They are not simply about *his* fate in comparison with others. Second, any careful reader of the essay must be struck by the repeated references to what Améry posits as a common concern. The lingering conflict between Jews and Germans is introduced as "our problem" (69), the upholding of *ressentiment* is declared also to be "for the good of the German people" (80), and the call for an "externalization and actualization" of the unresolved conflict is put forth as necessary "if both the overpowered and those who overpowered them are to succeed in mastering the past, a past that, despite its extreme oppositeness, they still have in common" (77). The problematic (collective) self-preoccupation pertains to those who have the nerve to tell the survivors to "look but forward, to a better, common future!" (69). There can be no *common* future as long as the relationship between the overpowered and those who overpowered them has not been restored.

As long as surviving victims of mass atrocity have not been reassured what happened could not as easily happen again with the participation, consent, or indifference of their contemporaries, so long will the talk of a common future be hollow and offensive, not the least in its blatantly self-preoccupied disregard of the real condition of the victims (cf. Chaumont

1990). The responsible parties and third parties might be able to "let bygones be bygones," but the survivor lives in the fear pertaining to the experience of abandonment. Here it seems appropriate to consider the title of the essay collection. What is at stake is not simply the question of guilt and atonement of the responsible agents. *Beyond Guilt and Atonement* is an attempt to overcome the chasm or conflict damaging not only the lives of the survivors (living with a sense of abandonment) but also—surprisingly—the perpetrators, accomplices, bystanders, and their descendants.[4]

Awakening

"But what an extravagant moral daydream I have abandoned myself to!" (Améry 1999:79). Thus Améry opens the final part of the essay. In spite of continued vigilance, in the end his *ressentiment* plays a trick on him and makes him see time turned backward: "Did not a German tear from SS-man Wajs the shovel he used as a tool for beating?... What didn't I see in the unbridled past, which in the future was transformed and from then on was overcome truly and forever" (79). Awakening from his moral daydream, Améry dismisses the vision of a German revolution as completely unrealistic: "natural time will reject the demands of our *ressentiments* and finally extinguish them.... Germany will not make it good, and our rancor will have been for nothing" (79).[5] The victims will be seen as the "truly incorrigible, irreconcilable ones" (80).

We have returned to the original point of departure. In the opening sequence, Améry writes: "I travel through a thriving land. . . . I feel uncomfortable in this peaceful land" (62–63). Now, at the end, he "travels through the thriving land, and . . . feel less and less comfortable as I do" (80). The whole tone has become darker: "some stand eternally in the light and others eternally in the darkness" (80). Truth, if that was what was recovered through the examination, has not been redemptive. Throughout the essay, Améry tries to express the degree to which the Nazi past is (with William Faulkner's famous words) "not dead. It is not even past." Améry slips repeatedly from present to past and vice versa; for example, when the psychological concept of the "warped" survivor causes him to recall how his arms were twisted behind his back when he was tortured. Likewise, in the end, his travels in the present, from Frankfurt to Stuttgart to Cologne, where Améry gives his talks to the Germans, slip into the memories of the way in which Améry traveled "in the evacuation trains that, under the pressure of the final Soviet offensive, carried us from Auschwitz westward and later from Buchenwald north to Bergen-Belsen" (80). So, Améry still travels, but apparently the traveling leads nowhere except deeper into bitterness—and into a state where the "fusion" of past and present apparently intensifies.[6] The *conditio inhumana* of the survivor of Auschwitz includes, it seems, a present invaded by the past. This is also clear in a nightmare forcefully recounted by Primo Levi as the last words of *The Reawakening:*

> A dream full of horror has still not ceased to visit me. . . . It is a dream, within a dream, varied in detail, one in substance. I am sitting at a table with my family, or with friends, or at work, or in the green countryside; in short, in a peaceful relaxed environment, apparently without tension or affliction; yet I feel a deep and subtle anguish, the definite sensation of an impending threat. And in fact, as the dream proceeds, slowly or brutally, each time in a different way, everything collapses and disintegrates around me, the scenery, the wall, the people, while the anguish becomes more intense and more precise. Now everything has changed to chaos; I am alone in the centre of a grey and turbid nothing, and now, I know what this thing means, and I also know that I have always known it; I am in the Lager once more, and nothing is true outside the Lager. All the rest was a brief pause, a deception of the senses, a dream; my family, nature in flower, my home. Now this inner dream, this dream of peace, is over, and in the outer dream, which continues, gelid, a well-known voice resounds: a single word, not imperious, but brief and subdued. It is the dawn command of Auschwitz, a foreign word, feared and expected: get up, "Wstawàch" (*The Reawakening*, Levi 1993:207f).

The final part of the essay conveys Améry's searing bitterness caused by the prospect that his moral address will not be answered and by his powerlessness to change the situation. In an essay from the year of his death, 1978, he writes of the way in which anger when combined with a sense of powerlessness leads to resignation. More specifically, it is the sense of powerlessness connected to the experience of speaking without being heard.[7] In the essay written in 1966, Améry has not entirely given up hope. The organs of public opinion-making buy his voice, but no one wants to relieve him of his *ressentiment.* That is, he seems to feel that his experiences are consumed, not answered: "I must encapsulate my resentments. I can still believe in their moral value and their historical validity. Still, but how much longer?" (80). The essay ends as follows:

> Our slave morality will not triumph. Our *ressentiments*—emotional source of every genuine morality, which was always a morality for the losers —have little or no chance at all to make the evil work of the overwhelmers bitter for them. We victims must finish with our retroactive rancor. In the sense that the KZ argot once gave to the

word "finish"; it meant as much as to "kill." Soon we must and will be finished. Until that time has come, we request of those whose peace is disturbed by our grudge that they be patient (80–81).

Is there anything blameworthy about Améry's persistent *ressentiments* or bitterness? Would a more self-beneficial or forgiving stance have been more humane? Indeed, are the moral considerations underlying the belief that the preservation of this bitter protest is a moral necessity confused or unjustifiable? As is clear from the preceding chapters, I do not think so. The moral stance of Améry might be psychologically burdensome, even so onerous that the position cannot be claimed as a moral duty of anyone else but oneself. But his *ressentiments* are justified as a protest against the "impossible" attitudes of his German contemporaries. As succinctly formulated by Pamela Hieronymi, a past wrong that has not been appropriately recognized as a wrong makes a claim:

It says, in effect, you can be treated this way, and that such treatment is acceptable. That—that claim—is what you resent. It poses a threat. In resenting it, you challenge it. If there is nothing else that would mark out that event as wrong, there is at least your resentment. And so resentment can be understood as a protest (Hieronymi 2001:546, cited in Walker 2006b:128).

The ordeal of Améry, left in mistrust and abandonment and intensified by unanswered calls for repair and reassurance, is first fully expressed in the essay that follows "*Ressentiments*." The last essay of *Beyond Guilt and Atonement*, is entitled "On the Necessity and Impossibility of Being a Jew." Only in the end are we faced with the victim's being-in-*ressentiment* in its most complete sense as an "existential determinant" (64) and as part of the *conditio inhumana* of the victim of the Third Reich. In stark contrast to the passages presenting the vision of a restoration of human solidarity and responsibility, the final essay brings forth the point of view of a person who has almost become resigned to the bitter sense of inescapable abandonment:

Every day anew I lose my trust in the world. . . . My neighbor greets me in a friendly fashion, *Bonjour, Monsieur*; I doff my hat, *Bonjour, Madame*. But Madame and Monsieur are separated by interstellar distances; for yesterday a Madame looked away when they led off a Monsieur, and through the barred windows of the departing car a Monsieur viewed a Madame as if she were a stone angel from a bright and stern heaven, which is forever closed to the Jew. . . . Without trust in the world I face my surroundings as a Jew who is alien and alone, and all that I can manage is to get along within my foreignness. . . . I was unable to force yesterday's murderers and tomorrow's potential aggressors to recognize the moral truth of their crimes, because the world in its totality did not help me to do it. Thus I am alone, as I was when they tortured me. Those around me do not appear to me as anti-humans, as did my former torturers; they are my co-humans, not affected by me and the danger prowling at my side (Améry 1999: 94–96).

We sometimes apply the notion of hopelessness without paying attention to the radical implication of the literal sense of the word. The last lines of Améry's essay are arguably not evidence of a person in despair or without hope entirely. Améry has not given up insisting on what is right. The very publication of *Beyond Guilt and Atonement* as a whole is evidence of this point. As Margaret Walker has put it, "In bitterness, one insists on what is right but with a sense of futility and alienation; in despair, one gives up on insisting on what is right" (2006b:108). Despair is not far away, but the onus should not be on the victim to move on or forgive, but on the others—to whom resentment's protest is directed—to provide the long-awaited response.

Yet, given the way in which the essay has developed one must ask whether it would not be fair to say that actually Améry "wallows" in his *ressentiments*. If one does not believe that reassurance will be forthcoming, is it not irrational and a kind of "wallowing" not to let go and move on? Améry touches on this question in the last essay of his book:

Often I have asked myself whether one can live humanly in the tension between fear and anger. Those who have followed these deliberations may well see their author as a monster, if not of vengeance, then at least of bitterness. There may be a trace of truth in such a judgment, but only a trace. . . . But this does not mean that fear and anger condemn him to be less righteous than his ethically inspired contemporaries are. . . . Because it became hard for me to be a human being does not mean that I have become a monster (100).

There is a difference between wallowing in resentment and enduring with resentment. To illustrate this difference, let me quote a passage from Steven Tudor's study, *Remorse and Compassion*:

The lucidly remorseful person must not necessarily believe that perfect redemption is always *possible*. Someone might *wish* for it while justly believing his crimes to be so heinous that he could never truly or completely re-enter the world to be with his fellow human beings.

However, such a person is different from the chronically remorseful person in that he is not "content" in his remorseful suffering, and still undertakes atoning acts in order to go at least some way toward redemption (Tudor 2001:191).

Even if Tudor is speaking of the person who has done wrong rather than the person who has suffered wrong, the passage is helpful in our understanding the victim who seems to indulge or to be "content" in his grievances or *ressentiments*. That is, even if the release from abandonment is not thought to be possible, the preservation of the protest is not necessarily a symptom of a kind of wallowing in *ressentiment*. Améry does not take pleasure in his *ressentiment*; he does not want there "to be nothing that would give him a reason to be less resentful" (Thomas 2003:205). He harbors *ressentiment*, but in the wish that it would become unnecessary—at least insofar as *ressentiment* is directed toward the Germans (with regard to *ressentiment* as a certain kind of relation to what happened, the question is more murky, yet "wallowing" seems anyway inappropriate). Yet, the preservation of *ressentiment* is not only *compatible* with a wish that the resented persons would make the *resentment* inappropriate. More than that, one might even say that his ressentiment is *expressive* of a stubborn holding on to a demand that the communities of judgment from which he expected better will change: joining the victims' desire or attitude with regard to the ruined past, the Germans would release the survivors from the sense of loneliness and abandonment. What the victims, according to Améry, can do to promote this outcome is solely to keep alive and express their *ressentiment*. This is the *objective* task of the victims' publicly manifested *ressentiments*: to make the crime a reality to the perpetrator and to catalyze *self-mistrust* among the broader masses of German citizens. The German revolution must, according to Améry, be goaded not by a hollow conciliatoriness, but by the "spurs" of the victims' *ressentiment*: "If, the midst of the world's silence, our *ressentiment* holds its finger raised, then Germany . . ." (78). In this way Améry actively uses his *ressentiments* to promote a process aimed at their overcoming. A "politics of *ressentiment*" *can* be combined with a vision of reconstructing the relationship between antagonistic groups; more precisely, between "all those who wish to live together as fellow human beings" (xiv).

13

A Multifarious Reception

Resistance quand meme . . . is the essence of Améry's philosophy.

(SEBALD 2003:155F)

A morality . . . of despair and resignation
(HEYD 2004:196).

It is easy to agree that Améry's "*Ressentiments*" is a controversial upside-down perspective on *ressentiment*, resentment, forgiveness, reconciliation, and the ways in which they relate to one another. In a letter written on November 24, 1965, Améry informs the South German radio station that was broadcasting the essays that a fourth essay entitled "*Ressentiments*" was on its way. It is, writes Améry, "starker Tobak (tough stuff)—hopefully not too tough for your listeners. It's just that such an essay could either be written in all honesty, or it could not be written at all" (cited in Heidelberger-Leonard 2004:123, trans. Claudia Welz).[1] Améry was of course thinking of the public articulation of his animosity against his contemporaries. However, seen as a rejoinder to common understandings of what is appropriate, laudable, and healthy with regard to victims' responses to past violations, the essay is as timely and stimulating today as it was fifty years ago. Améry presents a moral perspective on victims' needs and reconciliation that is often not even considered possible by many scholars and students in the field of transitional justice today. In relation to the emergence of the rhetoric of healing and closure and the new prominence accorded to forgiveness in psychological counseling, as well as in contemporary thinking about reconciliation after mass atrocity, Améry proposes a valuable cautionary view to be taken into consideration.

However, over and above the basic consensus that Améry's essay is refreshingly different and a source of interesting debates on social reconstruction after mass atrocity, more elaborate attempts to pin down his position veer in several directions. The complex structure of "*Ressentiments*" and its wealth of only rudimentarily articulated ideas have ensured a multifaceted reception.

In this chapter I discuss several philosophical analyses of "*Ressentiments*"; first and foremost: "*Ressentiment* and Reconciliation: Alternative Responses to Historical Evil" by David Heyd (2004) and "Geschichtliche Verantwortung und menschliche Würde bei Jean Améry" ("Historical Responsibility and Human Dignity in Jean Améry") by Jean-Michel Chaumont (1990). In addition to these two essays, several works include Améry's defense of *Ressentiments* as an illustrative case or use his stance as support of an argument, and so forth. In this chapter we shall look at four of these works: Giorgio Agamben's 1999 critique of Améry's defense of *ressentiment* as a misguided response to Auschwitz (*Remnants of Auschwitz: The Witness and the Archive*); Susan Neiman's use of Améry in a reflection on the (im)possibility of reconciliation with the evils of history (*Evil in Modern Thought*, Neiman 2002); Margaret Urban Walker's inclusion of Améry in an investigation of the moral work performed by resentment in social life (*Moral Repair: Reconstructing Moral Relations After Wrongdoing;* Walker 2006b); and Jan Phillip Reemtsma's remarks on "*Ressentiments*" in an analysis of Améry's use of the first person "I" ("172364: Gedanken über den Gebrauch der ersten Person Singular bei Jean Améry" ["Reflections on the Use of First Person Singularis by Jean Améry"] Reemtsma 1996). Of course, this is not an all-inclusive list, but it encompasses the works that analyze the reasoning of "*Ressentiments*" in ways that call for discussion in this study.[2]

The critical reception of Améry's essay encompasses quite divergent pictures of his thinking. In this chapter I show that it is possible to group the essays mentioned above in two broad clusters, with each cluster being concerned about exactly those parts of the essay that the other cluster leaves in the margins, and with both clusters being insufficiently attentive to the tensions in the text. I surmise that a more complex and interesting picture emerges when one adopts a more comprehensive perspective and keeps in sight the loose ends and ambiguities of Améry's reflections. This is not only important as a matter of doing justice to the text but also in terms of contributing to the task of understanding victims' responses to mass atrocities. In relation to this last point, I want to raise the question whether the split in this critical reception reflects a certain shortcoming in our approaches to or notions of victims' possibilities of response.

Heyd and Chaumont

David Heyd (2004) contrasts Améry and Tutu as "two radically different moral approaches to the question of the right response to historical evil" (187). Heyd is interested in the forward- and backward-looking perspectives of morality, and his paper begins with an intriguing reflection on the story of Lot and his wife as they flee the destruction of Sodom and Gomorrah. Whereas Lot looks only ahead, his wife disregards God's command not to look back and turns into a pillar of salt (Genesis 19:26). The point, playfully extracted by Heyd, is that "looking backward is in itself a petrifying act, particularly when the object of gaze is past trauma from which one is trying to escape" (185). In Heyd's use of the story, Lot is the survivalist and the negotiator, preoccupied with the future and moving with time. Lot's wife, to the contrary, exemplifies the vindictive impulse and the inability to forget the evils of the past. Her backward-looking gaze is numbing; she "becomes a timeless witness" (186) to evil. Heyd's comparison of Tutu and Améry is not intended to show that one is morally justifiable and the other is not. We are presented with *two* deep and partly irreconcilable moral responses to historical evil. Yet, whereas Tutu is more sophisticated than Lot (that is, he is more than a forward-looking survivalist), Améry comes out very much like the wife, fixed and fossilized as she is in the backward-looking perspective.

Jean-Michel Chaumont begins his 1990 paper by asking why *Beyond Guilt and Atonement* ends with an essay on the necessity and impossibility of being a Jew. Considering Améry's desire to reach young Germans, Chaumont wonders why the essay collection did not end with *"Ressentiments"* in which Améry addresses the reasons why German youth should assume responsibility for the past. The purpose of Chaumont's paper is to demonstrate that, far from being an arbitrary appendix to the book, the last essay is instead a masterpiece in which Améry successfully brings together his thoughts on the existential condition of the victim and his injunction to the (young) Germans to take historical responsibility for the Nazi past. I will leave it to the reader to consult Chaumont's paper to learn why he believes that Améry's last essay deepens and sustains the call for responsibility issued in the essay on *ressentiment*. What is important in this context is rather Chaumont's understanding of Améry's reflections on *ressentiment*: its *raison d´être* and its relationship to reconciliation.

Heyd's and Chaumont's interpretations seem nearly like mirror images of each other. The picture Heyd paints of Tutu—depicted in his essay as the inverse reflection of Améry—resembles in several ways the picture Chaumont provides of Améry. In Heyd, Améry comes out as the staunch defender of unending *ressentiment* and as the uncompromising adversary of reconciliation. In Chaumont, Améry is driven by a desire to be released from his social and emotional ordeal, and reconciliation is the ultimate goal of his endeavors. Now, to start with, let us consider the difference between Chaumont's and Heyd's considerations of the meaning hidden in the title of the essay collection; that is, other than the obvious connotation to Nietzsche. Heyd suggests that the title, *Beyond Guilt and Atonement*, alludes to Améry's wish to go beyond a legal and theological vocabulary geared to deal with guilt that can be balanced with punishment and sin that can be atoned for. The limits of the morality of guilt and atonement have to do with their connection to a logic of closure and expiation. Beyond guilt and atonement, Heyd places a past that cannot be undone and a *ressentiment* that "should persist as long as possible, down into the long future of German society" (2004:193). Chaumont, on the other hand, argues that Améry's choice of title expresses a conviction that—far beyond the need to deal with the guilt and atonement of particular and individual perpetrators—"it is in the interest of every single person that the bonds between the severed parts of the society are re-established, since their breach damages the common foundation of their existence and, as a result, is harmful to all of them" (Chaumont 1990:36, trans. Claudia Welz).[3]

In Chaumont's paper, *ressentiment* serves as the instrument of Améry's upright desire for reconciliation or the restoration of the relationship between Jews and Germans (1990:32). Chaumont's Améry opposes the call simply to look to the future because of a conviction that a shared future will only be possible if the relationship between the surviving victims and the people of the perpetrators is re-established. He strives, as Chaumont emphasizes, for the restoration of the "we" without which there can be no individual "I" (cf. Chaumont 1990:36). Chaumont brings into focus the Améry who is ready to abandon his *ressentiments* if and when the Germans come to assume the responsibility to which he holds them. In this perspective, Améry is against premature, thoughtless, and hollow conciliatoriness as well as the pathos of forgiveness and reconciliation, but he is not against reconciliation that is properly understood and premised. Thus Améry's essay appears as a poignant attempt to sketch out the moral terms of a shared overcoming of the legacy of the past: "a reconciliation of the living, which does not take place at the expense of the dead" (40, trans. Claudia Welz). Chaumont's presentation of Améry is deeply influenced by his observation of the Hegelian vocabulary used by Améry to articulate his demands and visions. The whole language of negation, overcoming, and reconciliation permeates Améry's essay.[4] What Chaumont sees as the most important Hegelian strand in Améry's reasoning is his acknowledgment of the social—intersubjective—conditions of individual identity and self-respect: infringing the conditions of mutual recognition can severely damage our lives (Chaumont 1990:36).[5]

In short, Chaumont accentuates Améry as a Hegelian thinker of reconciliation; first and foremost concerned with the question of how to overcome—in a morally justifiable way—the conflict between Jews and Germans. Heyd, on the other hand, puts emphasis on an Améry who is primarily occupied with the question of how to respond—in a moral way—to an evil past. The most salient aspect of Heyd's presentation of Amery is the image of the individual defending the *indelible* preservation of *ressentiment* as a matter of the human right and privilege of the moral person: "For Améry it is human to feel *re*-sentiment as an ongoing and self-perpetuating response to evil which cannot be undone" (Heyd 2004: 197). "The wound should," as Heyd puts it, "remain open, indefinitely" (196). Since the teleological or forward-looking aspects of Améry's preservation of his *ressentiments* (i.e. his desire that they will tug the unrepentant into the truth of their atrocity and his dream that they will be instrumental to a release from his loneliness) are not considered in Heyd's essay, Améry comes out as what one might call a moral *retrospectivist*; that is, one for whom "the response to the past, primarily of crimes and atrocities, has priority over the attempt to shape the future" (191). "He knows," writes Heyd, "that resentment means staying behind. But he will not give in, since this is in his mind the only way to respond in a *moral* way to historical evil" (191). Indeed, Améry is on a "*self-imposed* mission [to] stop the natural process of healing, forgetting and forgiveness" (191, italics added).

Thus, Heyd depicts Améry's entrapment in *ressentiment* as a function of the decisiveness of Améry's moral convictions: the indelible preservation of resentment simply is the appropriate moral response to historical evil. This fits perfectly well with the *Zustand* passage, with the passage that asserts *ressentiment* as the right and privilege of the moral person, and with the essay's final picture of a *ressentiment* that will be preserved in spite of its inefficiency. It also captures those parts of Améry's essay that deal with the relationship to the Nazi atrocities of the past. The problem is simply that it leaves out, more or less, the parts of Améry's essay in which he presents his *ressentiments* as the result of the postwar "management of the past," in which he envisions the possibility of an abandonment of *ressentiment* and where his unwillingness to get rid of his *ressentiments* has more to do with the indifference of his contemporaries than with the "self-chosen" perseverance in resistance to reconciliation with the past. Even if Améry's *prospective* vision of a situation where he would no longer need to hold his *ressentiments* against the Germans is revealed as a daydream, it remains an important part of his reasoning.

The risk tied to Heyd's representation of Améry becomes evident in the introduction to the anthology in which Heyd's paper is published. As emphasized by the editor, Améry (that is, as presented by Heyd) insists on unchanging and constantly renewed *ressentiment* as the only morally appropriate attitude of victims aimed purely at keeping the memory of the horrible past alive and preventing victims from partaking in any transitional agenda (cf. Meyer 2004:46). Arguably, this description could fit the stance adopted by Vladimir Jankélévitch in his intervention in the debate on the statute of limitations (cf. Chapter 9). Again, it captures an aspect of Améry's position, but at the cost of being blind to the original way in which Améry combined the unreconcilable attitude to the past with an agenda of transition in relation to his German contemporaries.

The full implications of Heyd's construction of Améry in the image of the deontological retrospectivist appear through the comparison with the alternative moral approach of Tutu. According to Heyd, Tutu is the mirror image of Améry in several ways. In contrast to Améry, Tutu sees truth as "the instrument of moral reform and mutual reconciliation of the victim with the perpetrator. . . . Unlike Améry, Tutu wants closure, a 'settlement,' since it is the only way to open a new page for a society with such a troubled moral history" (Heyd 2004:193–94). Tutu's is a morality of hope, whereas Améry's is one of "despair and resignation. . . . Only Tutu strives to use [the personal response of the individual] as a lever for a new social order" (196). Unlike Améry, Tutu "aspires to be freed from the risk of being enslaved to the past by feelings of bitterness and resentment" (195–96). Only Tutu is able to let forward- and backward-looking perspectives reinforce each other.[6] Finally, Améry's moral approach is said to preclude him from having a moral vision of reconciliation. He is therefore caught in the choice between "the necessity of resentment or the pragmatic acceptance of sheer compromise" (195). The problem is that Améry *does* see moral truth as transformative, does strive to use his *ressentiment* as a lever to bring about new social relationships. He *does* desire to be released from abandonment, does speak of a settlement in moral terms, and does hope that the Germans would pay heed to his *ressentiment* in such ways that he could get rid of it (not in relation to the past, but indeed in relation to the indifferent and forgetful among his contemporaries). Améry's morality is not one of hope, but neither is it one of resignation. He was brought to despair, but his morality is one of revolt and resistance. Why does Améry resist a settlement? Because, as he writes, "nothing is resolved, no conflict is settled" (Améry 1999:xi). But this is not equal to a principled moral exclusion of the very notion of a settlement. Améry rejects *conciliatoriness* as the path to a settlement, not, as Heyd, paraphrases his point, reconciliation. One can desire reconciliation and reject a plea that one should adopt a conciliatory stance toward an unrepentant perpetrator-group. As W.G. Sebald puts it,

> One of the most impressive aspects of Améry's stance as a writer is that although he knew the real limits of the power to resist as few others did, he maintains the validity of resistance even to the point of

absurdity. Resistance without any confidence that it will be effective, resistance *quand même*, out of a principle of solidarity with victims and as a deliberate affront to those who simply let the stream of history sweep them along, is the essence of Améry's philosophy

(SEBALD 2003:155F).

When Améry's position is presented as a radicalization of the retrospective aspect of morality, what is left out then is not only a cluster of actually present forward-looking considerations but also Améry's critical attention to the acts and omissions of the communities and agents toward whom the resentment of the victim is directed and because of whom it was first stirred up.[7]

Chaumont, on his side, quotes the *Zustand* passage, but he does not dwell on its absurd demand or elaborate on the degree to which Améry's *ressentiments* take on the character of an indelible outrage over the unacceptable Nazi past. Also, he does not deal much with the last part of the essay: the awakening from the moral daydream and the disheartening prospect of never-ending *ressentiment*. In Améry, the whole restorative enterprise is bitterly denounced as a moral daydream; de facto only *ressentiment* remains. In Améry the entire Hegelian apparatus is set in motion in a gigantic moral vision, but it falls to the ground. One might say that Chaumont's reading of Améry moves too quickly past the radically negative disruption to which Améry in the end gives voice. It is not that Chaumont does not refer to the abandonment and estrangement of the victim; rather, he simply—and in a way this is completely in the spirit of the essay—responds to the call to the reader to assume responsibility insofar as he assumes the position of the "we" addressed by Améry. He turns the discussion into a discussion focused on "us"—the ones to whom the victim's call for reassurance is directed.

In sum, both parties neglect the tensions of the essay. Between the deontological and teleological, the retro- and prospective, the ontologically absurd and the politically absurd, Chaumont's interpretation loses sight of the despair and the absurdity, and Heyd's reading fails to see that part of the ordeal is a consequence of the social failure.

Neiman and Agamben

Does the split between Heyd and Chaumont represent a fundamental division in the interpretation of Améry's thinking more generally, with each side bringing out an important aspect of the essay and consequently marginalizing what the other brings to the fore? To answer this question, let us consider two works that seems to be in accord with Heyd's perspective. Susan Neiman and Giorgio Agamben both present Améry's *ressentiment* as the emotional aspect of the survivor's categorical refusal to accept, or reconcile with, the irreversible evils of the Nazi past; both ignore the degree to which Améry's reflections on *ressentiment* are also tied to concerns about social abandonment and the moral repair of social relationships. This brings Neiman and Agamben close to the picture offered by Heyd—Améry as the anti-Nietzschean—but much more than Heyd, they identify Améry with an abstract moral position or condition.[8] Agamben refers, very briefly, to the refusal to accept that what happened did happen. Neiman introduces Améry as captured by the impossible—yet perfectly moral and humane—wish to undo the past reverse time:

> [S]ome evils produce states that cannot be overcome. Améry saw himself as a prisoner of events he could not undo and would not accept. Any diagnosis that tried to liberate him merely points out that his wish to undo the past conflicts with reality. But for Améry . . . the whole worth of morality lies in that conflict (Neiman 2002:265).[9]

Agamben brings Améry into focus to set the stage for what he considers to be Primo Levi's more apt understanding of "the ethical problem" raised by the reality of Auschwitz. Proceeding on a demonstration that Nietzsche's proposal to overcome *ressentiment* through *amor fati* lost whatever power it might have had before Auschwitz, Agamben declares that Améry's response to Nietzsche—and Auschwitz—is misguided[10]:

> The failure of Zarathrustra's lesson [does not imply] the pure and simple restoration of the morality of resentment—even if, for the victims, the tempation is great. Jean Améry was thus led to formulate a genuine anti-Nietzschean ethics of resentment that simply refuses to accept that "what happened, happened" (Agamben 1999:100).

Agamben leaves out the postwar/social reasons why Améry is led to defend *ressentiment*. Moreover, he also takes away the wish to undo the past; what remains is only the refusal to accept what happened. Améry thinks, according to Agamben, that "the ethical problem" after Auschwitz is "a matter of holding fast to the unacceptable through resentment" (1999:102). Améry is, however, holding fast to something that "*has never ceased to take place; it [Auschwitz] is always already repeating itself*" (101). Agamben seems to suggest that "Auschwitz" is emblematic of our condition in a Hobbesian sense—not implying the absurdity that Auschwitz is still functioning, but rather that "Auschwitz" after Auschwitz is a permanent possibility with which we need to reckon. But, then it becomes difficult to explain what possibility Améry has not grasped. Améry was all too intimately aware that the social order *can* fall apart and disintegrate in the insanity of mass murder. Indeed, *Beyond Guilt and Atonement* can be seen as an agonized first-person account of Agamben's point that Auschwitz "is always already repeating itself" (cf. Chapter 12 in this book). But to have this perspective, one needs to appreciate the degree to which Améry's *ressentiments* are tied to a revolt not only against an irreversible past but also an intolerable present.

Walker and Reemtsma

When I first learned about Margaret Walker's philosophical account of resentment, I was surprised by the extent to which the points she made about resentment provide a generalized theoretical account of central features of Améry's defense of his *ressentiments*.[11] In *Moral Repair* (Walker 2006b), Walker has incorporated an interesting analysis of Améry. The analysis is brief as its purpose is mainly to use Améry to reveal the conditions under which *intractable* resentment might be morally justified. Walker's account of resentment (to which I referred in Chapter 1) fits very well with the reasoning and the cravings presented in Améry's essay and is much better indeed than accounts of resentment or *ressentiment* as only about the self-esteem of the offended person or as something purely personal if not asocial. Walker uses Améry's case to show that, where there is a failure to achieve validation or assurance from the relevant communities of judgment, where victims feel abandoned, as Améry certainly does, resentment may fester: "Where victims feel forgotten and deserted . . . resentment persists as an unfulfilled demand" (Walker 2006b:142–43). Walker suggests that Améry's account can be read "as a lesson in how resentment over horrific injustice might nonetheless be *answered* even if it seems impossible or unconscionable to extinguish the resentment and the underlying outrage itself" (2006b:141). Indeed, as we know from the previous chapter on collective historical responsibility, the "answer" (suggested by Améry) involves the cultivation of a certain kind of "negative" collective memory of the outrageous past (that is, an unreconciled memory inflected by *ressentiment*).

Like Chaumont and Walker, the German writer Jan Philipp Reemtsma connects Améry's *ressentiments* to the ruin and repair of the "social contract" (a term used by Améry in the essay on torture); what matters is the response of society, and like Walker, Reemtsma focuses on the need to assume certain obligations at the same time as it has to be recognized that no response will ever be adequate. What happened cannot be made good again, but *this* fact can be acknowledged, *and* it can be acknowledged that *that* fact is no excuse for just moving on as if nothing had happened. Thus, like Chaumont and Walker, Reemtsma focuses on the "nexus" between Améry's *ressentiments* and the repair of socio-ethical relationships. The social response cannot undo what has happened, but—and this is a most important point—if nothing is done, the "work of destruction" will be *continued* (Reemtsma 1996:81).[12] This insight is extremely precise, not only in relation to Améry's essay but also with respect to responses to mass atrocity more generally.

Like Chaumont, both Walker and Reemtsma share a focus on "*Ressentiments*" as a moral address and an expression of a desire for some kind of reassurance or restoration of relations of trust and hope. What is left— more or less—in the margins in this part of the critical reception is the question of the moral nature and significance of *ressentiment* as "embodying" the wish to undo the past and as a revolt against certain attitudes to the passing of time (that is, what was most central to Heyd, Neiman, and Agamben).

Perhaps the divide in the critical reception of Améry's essays simply reflects the differing concerns of his readers. Some have been interested in issues of time and ethics in relation to responses to past evil. Others have approached Améry from a more social-ethical perspective and focused on the significance of *ressentiment* (as conceptualized by Améry) in relation to the moral repair of social relationships after mass atrocities. Perhaps, the tensions between the different parts of the reception reveal that any attempt to use Améry, or to think *straight* about the issues at hand, must choose one of the two possibilities. In this book I have proceeded on the assumption that something significant could be brought out by trying to hold together and keep in sight the—dialectical—tensions or ambiguities in the essay: for example, between the temporal and social aspects of *ressentiment* or reconciliation or between the *ressentiment* that feeds on a particular past wrong and the *ressentiment* that is tied to the failure of relevant others to provide a corrective response to that wrong (this is where the idea of compounded or nested resentments enters). What is at stake here is not only the question of doing justice to the complexity of the essay. In the end what is probably more important is the need to keep in mind such tensions if we want to try to understand victims' responses to violations that seem to transcend the boundaries of what can be forgiven, punished, and repaired. In this perspective, it is worth asking whether the divide in the critical reception reveals inherent limits of given schemes through which we understand victims' responses to mass atrocity. At least, insofar as we struggle to understand victims' emotional responses to mass atrocities, there is a need to develop perspectives that can reach across the realms of the philosophy of time, memory, and history, on the one hand, and the ethics of emotions and social relations on the other hand.

14
Epilogue

As for this word "reconciliation"—I almost feel it should be banned from the English language. These family members will never lose that pain of having lost a loved one. So who are they supposed to reconcile with? And why should they? They don't really have to reconcile [with] anybody. They were wronged. What they are asking for is justice.

(ERIC STOVER, IN A 1999 INTERVIEW)[1]

After working extensively with the problems facing postwar countries and with victims in particular, Eric Stover, in a 1999 interview, expressed fatigue with reconciliation talk.[2] His comments came after the interviewer characterized Stover's work with forensic investigations and postwar reconstruction as part of a process of reconciliation. I wrote this book because I felt a similar fatigue with the rhetoric of forgiveness, closure, and reconciliation, and I wanted to challenge a certain cluster of unquestioned assumptions and implied inferences. This book offers examples from various contexts, but the rhetoric and logic against which it objects are part of a global discourse of forgiveness and reconciliation. Consider this passage from *Justice and Reconciliation: After the Violence* by Andrew Rigby (2001):

> Individuals, like collectives, for the sake of peace must somehow become capable of accepting loss and moving on. This ability to let go of the pain of the past is at the heart of what many understand to be forgiveness. Hatred and the quest for revenge can consume people, turning them into mirror images of those whom they hate . . . At the core of any reconciliation process is the preparedness of people to anticipate a shared future. For this to occur they are required not to forget but to forgive the past, and thus be in a position to move forward together (Rigby 2001:12).

The intentions are of course all to the good. But what is tiring is the repetition of the same cluster of pieties: the rhetoric of moving on, the all too easy denouncements of negative emotional responses, the appeal to surviving victims not to turn into "mirror images" of those who persecuted or tried to exterminate them or their entire group, and indeed the repeated assumption that reconciliation or a shared future requires forgiveness. Of course, anger and resentment can be mobilized and used in the instigation of mass violence. As Elisabeth Neuffer writes about the genocide in Rwanda, "the incessant propaganda, mixing truth with rumor, myth, or outright falsehood, cleverly stirred up all the age-old resentments and fear of the RPA, the Tutsi-led army" (Neuffer 2001:119). Yet, the belief that emotion as such—construed as the antithesis to reason or rationality—is the problem with which our attempts to prevent genocide or rebuild societies has to deal, is in error.

I hope that with this book I have provided a constructive complement to writings that dismiss various kinds of resentment and refusals to forgive only as the negative to be overcome. Its most important aim would be met if it prompts a more probing and open-ended discussion of the moral nature and value of the negative emotions in postconflict societies. It is, however, not only about a sufficiently nuanced approach to various emotions and attitudes as such. What matters to me most fundamentally is the way in which victims who hold these emotions or attitudes are understood and treated. Looking back on the reading of Améry's essay, I think it is fair to say that—sometimes—the preservation of outrage or resentment and the refusal to forgive can be the reflex expression of a moral protest and ambition that are as permissible and admirable as the willingness to forgive or forgiveness proper. When this possibility is neglected—and I surmise that it is neglected often—it can do real harm to the survivors. Margaret Walker's and Jan Phillip Reemtsma's shared argument is important here. The societal response to mass destruction cannot undo the past or restore what has been ruined, but when a response that captures the outrage of what happened is not forthcoming, the work of destruction is *continued*. The "claim" inherent to the original atrocities stands uncorrected, the survivor's sense of continued abandonment is legitimate, and the threat of "license with impunity" (Walker 2006b) is fulfilled. The special kind of resentment or *ressentiment* harbored by the survivor in this social situation should not be pathologized or denounced without scrutiny; the moral right of the individual to protest against the politics of national stability and reconciliation should not be relinquished.

On the other hand, a too narrow focus on the individual as individual only is also dangerous. After mass atrocities occur, the voice and problems of the individual are closely interwoven with the entire social and political context.

Having been targeted because of one's membership in a given group, rather than as an individual, survivors' considerations about how to respond may involve notions about what they owe to the group or those who were murdered; this is one reason why pleas made to individual victims to forgive in this context should be hedged very carefully —that is, if they should be made at all. What makes it so difficult or even impossible for survivors of mass atrocity to extend forgiveness is not necessarily anything connected with their individual trauma. In such contexts, an overly individualized perspective on the victims' resentment and resistance to forgiveness and reconciliation becomes blind to some of their central concerns.

The spirit of forgiveness, healing, and reconciliation is perhaps challenged more deeply by the heinous nature and long-term effects of genocide and crimes against humanity. After crimes that shock the conscience of humanity, "healing" appears like a fantasy and complete forgiveness might neither be possible nor desirable. "Reconciliation" should perhaps be replaced by less "thick" concepts like "coexistence," but that depends on how one further qualifies the terms. Whether one thinks of the Holocaust or the genocides in Rwanda and Bosnia, such systematically organized mass atrocities leave behind a measure of devastation that is hard to fathom. In countries like Poland, Germany, Cambodia, Rwanda, and Bosnia-Herzegovina, the material remainders of an atrocious past—the vast and barren landscape of Birkenau, the marks of shelling in Sarajevo, the corpses and bones still visible in Rwanda—are there for all to see. The emotional remainders left in surviving victims are less visible than concentration camps and mass graves. Yet, as we have seen in this study, whereas the passing of time brings decay even to chambers made of concrete, it does not necessarily diminish the anguish and resentment of the surviving victims. Even where impunity and silence are replaced with various kinds of acknowledgment and accountability, the outrage, grief, and fear of the surviving victims of mass atrocity can seem inextinguishable. Sometimes the demands voiced by survivors are absurd or impossible to satisfy. Yet, even if the relevant authorities or communities simply cannot satisfy the wishes in question, their very recognition that what happened cannot be repaired, forgiven, or reconciled and that responsibilities will be taken seriously can be of significant value.

Recognizing that unforgiving and irreconcilable victims may be morally justified and worthy of serious consideration does not imply a commitment to give absolute moral or political priority to a policy of "resentment satisfaction." In the transitional justice context, there are other values than those tied to resentment and indignation, and there are other factors to consider than securing a response to the past that will provide repair and reassurance to the victims.

Between Resentment and *Ressentiment*

As mentioned in Chapter 1, Améry's "special kind" of *ressentiments* seems to lie somewhere between more well-known or conventional concepts of resentment and *ressentiment*. Let me briefly tie some of the threads of the previous chapters together and summarize in what ways "Améryean" *ressentiments* relate to resentment and *ressentiment*, as they are typically understood.

Améry's *ressentiments* share several similarities with resentment as conceptualized in the philosophical tradition. Both stem from a belief that a moral wrong has been committed or a normative expectation has been violated. At stake are a cluster of deeply ethical concerns about dignity and humanity, moral acknowledgment and repair. These concerns are reflected in Améry's attempts to explain why he does not want to get rid of his *ressentiments* and in his desires to restore a common life with the group against which his *ressentiments* are directed. This leads directly to a second, often noted point about moral resentment: it is misguided to picture it as intrinsically related to a desire for revenge. Indeed, Margaret Walker's point that resentment seeks assurance from offenders or from others that they can be trusted again echoes the basic impetus of Améry's undertaking. There is also a congruence between Améry's concerns about guilt and responsibility and Strawson's and Wallace's concept of resentment as part of the stance of holding others responsible. A range of philosophers agree that resentment is about more than what concerns the victim's self. Adam Smith, Joseph Butler, and others all emphasize the ways in which the expression of resentment may also stem from perceived violations of normative expectations or the moral order; thus, resentment is an emotion that performs a valuable socio-ethical function. Like resentment thus conceived, Améry's *ressentiments* are not only about his struggle to regain his personal dignity but also about what he returns to repeatedly as "our" problem: the conflict related to the Nazi past. Moreover, Améry wishes his *ressentiments* to contribute to moral repair on the socio-historical level. Finally, a central endeavor of the ethical-philosophical approach to resentment is to show that resentment can be felt, expressed, and retained by a morally decent person. As we have seen, this was also a strong concern of Améry's. Like the holder of resentment, the person who retains the special kind of *ressentiment* depicted by Améry is not someone who has "failed" to feel and do something more appropriate or humane. Améryean *ressentiments*—like resentment proper—can be testimony of a moral character worthy of respect.

So far, Améryean *ressentiments* seem to be morally and functionally equivalent to resentment proper. Therefore one might be tempted to say that had

Améry known the works of Adam Smith and Joseph Butler, he would have found conceptual support and a reason to dismiss the concept of *ressentiment* as inapplicable to his case. Améryean *ressentiment*—if it is to be categorized as a kind of *ressentiment* at all—is certainly of a special kind. It is not fueled by spiteful and malicious envy—which is often used to distinguish *ressentiment* from resentment—and it is not characterized by an excessive self-concern. It does not crave revenge, its attributions of guilt and responsibility are not expressive of a blind and unjustifiable generalization of blame, and Améry does not seem to take secret delight in the continuation of his *ressentiments*. Also unlike the conventional image of the "man of *ressentiment*," Améry's anger and fear are not expressive of an irrational or disturbed understanding of the social reality.

Should we simply say that Améry presents a case where what appears like *ressentiment* actually is resentment proper? First, let us consider some important "family resemblances" between conventional notions of *ressentiment* and Améryean *ressentiments*. Unlike resentment proper, but very much like *ressentiment*, Améryean *ressentiments* also refer to an "existential determinant" (1999:64) that has taken hold of the person. In addition, like Nietzsche and Scheler, Améry ties the being-in-*ressentiment* to an irrational craving and an inability to let go of the past. Finally, unlike resentment proper, but like conventional understandings of *ressentiment*, Améry's *ressentiments* harbor a vivid sense of what has been violated; *ressentiment* relates to discussions about memory and history in ways that are far from the ethical and social concerns of philosophers of resentment.

So, is it a special kind of *ressentiment* or a special kind of resentment or a new kind in its own right? Ultimately, the taxonomical issue is not the main concern here. What is more important than choosing the most appropriate term is the acknowledgment of the limits of our vocabularies or of the need to think about their limits. Yet, let me return to the suggestion made earlier to uncouple the concept of *ressentiment* from a specific set of particularly disagreeable emotions including spite, malice, and envy. Doing so would provide conceptual space to understand Améry's predicament as an example of *ressentiment* inflected by fear and resentment or indignation but not spite, not malice, and not vengefulness. Rethinking *ressentiment* in this way would also challenge the monopoly that Nietzsche's construction has apparently gained on the meaning of *ressentiment*. The suggestion not only builds on the reflections of Améry and Jankélévitch. It is actually a plea to *revive* a real and more capacious pre-Nietzschean use of the term. According to the article on "*Ressentiment*" in the *Historisches Wörterbuch der Philosophie*, the noun "*ressentiment*" can be found in French literature since the sixteenth century, and like the historical as well as current use of the verb from which it is derived (i.e., *resentir*, "to re-sent," to feel again), its older use did not have the strongly negative connotation it acquired later. In accordance with the verb, "*ressentiment*" was not defined by a certain cluster of nasty emotions, but rather as a peculiar form of "keeping" or "enduring" a given emotion; a particularly strong and enduring feeling.[3]

In Chapter 1, I mentioned a cluster of objections to the very attempt to use a reflection on *ressentiment* after the Holocaust in relation to present discussions of responses to mass atrocity more generally. Indeed, Améry himself questions repeatedly the application of abstract and generalizing approaches to the ordeal he personally suffered. His aim was to illuminate concrete events and experiences and to face up to particular socio-political realities. Thus, his concern about the moral significance of the passing of time did not arise from readings of Heidegger. It was, at least in part a moral response—from the perspective of the victim—to one of the most important public debates in West Germany of the 1960s, namely the controversy over whether to extend the statute of limitations on the crime of murder (cf. Herf 1997:335). One should take care trying to "apply" Améry's thinking more generally or to stipulate an identity between Améry and the morality of resentful victims more broadly considered. At the same time, it would be wrong to insulate his reflections. Salient features of his social predicament and of the attitudes against which he voiced his protest and moral vision are comparable to the situation facing other survivors in the aftermath of state-sponsored mass atrocities.

More generally, societies tire of the angry and accusing voices of survivors who cannot or will not forget and reconcile with the past. When reconciliation has become the order of the day, victims who persist in their demands are seen as "imprisoned in the past, as hostages to their own memory, and therefore obstructions to the process of selective forgetting advocated by reconciling national political leaders" (Hamber and Wilson 2002:45). What Améry adds to various anecdotal representations of victims' refusal to forgive is an articulation of the possible moral sources for the preservation of resentment or the resistance to forgiveness. Moreover, the pressures and perspectives addressed by Améry—the therapeutic reduction of anger and resentment and the pressure on victims to forgive, move on, or look but to the future—are even more alive today than they were in the 1960s.[4] Still, and of course, Améry's reflections are not a blueprint to be applied across times and borders. If nothing else, then the untidiness and ambiguities of his reflections make that clear.

One might object that at least the boosters of forgiveness and reconciliation offer a measure of hope and moral optimism, whereas all I offer is mere negativity and pessimism. Yet, with regard to the question of what constitutes optimism, let me end this book with a passage from the *Ethics* of John Dewey:

In fact a certain intellectual pessimism, in the sense of a steadfast willingness to uncover sore points, to acknowledge and search for abuses, to note how presumed good often serves as a cloak for actual bad, is a necessary part of the moral optimism which actively devotes itself to making the right prevail. Any other view reduces the aspiration and hope, which are the essence of moral courage, to a cheerful animal buoyancy; and, in its failure to see the evil done to others in its thoughtless pursuit of what it calls good, is next door to brutality, to a brutality bathed in the atmosphere of sentimentality and flourishing the catchwords of idealism (cited in Putnam 2004:11).

Appendix I
Overview of Jean Améry's "Ressentiments"

Setting the Stage (Améry 1999: pp. 62–64): Améry introduces who speaks to whom about what and why. He first declares the essay to be aimed at clarification and second to be a justification of *ressentiment* addressed to moralists, who see it as a taint, and psychologists, who see it only as a sickness.

Looking Backward (pp. 64–67): Améry offers a narrative account of the historical development that led to the formation of his *ressentiment*. The narrative begins in 1945 and leads up to the time of the essay. At this point, Améry's *ressentiments* are presented as caused by contemporary German attitudes to the Nazi past.

Restating the Task (pp. 67–68): The task of the essay is given an additional twist. He identifies Friedrich Nietzsche and modern psychology as alternative explanations against which Améry must delimit and defend the kind of *ressentiments* harbored by the Nazi victim under the given historical circumstances.

Being-in-*Ressentiment* (p. 68): In a short, but very significant, passage, Améry explains why the man of *ressentiment* cannot look to the future. The very brief explanation gives prominence to the idea of a certain absurd demand (for a reversal of time and an undoing of the past) and to a notion of a twisted sense of time. The focus seems changed from the relationship to the Germans to the relationship between the victim and his ruined past.

A Controversy to be Settled? (pp. 69–71): The essay slips into a consideration of how to imagine an overcoming of a lingering conflict between Holocaust survivors and

Germans. This is one of the most thought-provoking parts of the essay. Améry refuses not only to let bygones be bygones or to "internalize" his *ressentiment* in silences. More than that, his model of "reconciliation" involves a dismissal of calls for objectivity and compromise. Améry wants the responsible parties to face the "moral truth" of what happened and to assume the responsibility that follows .

The Right and the Privilege of Human Beings (pp. 71–72): Améry tries to undo the common assumption that humanity and moral virtue automatically underlie displays of a willingness to forgive, reconcile, and "move on," whereas the prolonged display of *ressentiment* and irreconcilability are the reflex expression of a morally flawed or deficient character. Trying to counter this picture, Améry articulates his own normative view on the proper allegiances of what he calls "the moral person." The most central virtue invoked is the "moral power to resist" (72): to resist the natural sense of time (healing time, the passage of time as a reason to leave an issue behind) and to resist the social pressure to forgive and forget.

Collective Guilt and Historical Responsibility (pp. 72–76): Améry explains and defends his widespread distributions of blameworthiness. First he deals with his idea of the collective guilt of the wartime generations; second he articulates his thoughts about the historical responsibility of all Germans, the younger generation included.

A Moral Daydream (pp. 77–79): Near the end of the essay, Améry considers whether the victims' *ressentiment*s can play a constructive role in relation to the social conflict between Holocaust survivors and the Germans. Améry imagines what it would take for his *ressentiment* to be pacified. If the German people came to join the victims' desire that time be turned back, then *ressentiment* would become unnecessary.

Awakening (pp. 79–81): But Améry is convinced that his moral daydream will never come true. The last part of the essay (and some parts of the following, last, essay of *Beyond Guilt and Atonement*) presents the full meaning of the *conditio inhumana* that obtains when victims are abandoned by the societies from which they expect a reassuring response to an atrocious past.

Appendix II
Genocide and Crimes Against Humanity

As mentioned in Chapter 1, this book is focused squarely on the aftermath of mass atrocities. It is about the ethics of moral repair and responses to mass atrocities. Readers are assumed to have a general knowledge of the mass crimes that form the background of the discussion. However, one of the problems plaguing some discussions of resentment and forgiveness stems from a lack of appreciation of the radical nature of what is supposed to be forgiven, particularly when belief in the relevance of forgiveness and other conflict-resolution techniques is built primarily on an acquaintance with small-scale conflicts and isolated criminal offenses. Thus, in an attempt to keep in mind that we are talking about crimes rather than conflicts, I offer here a very brief overview of the meaning of "crimes against humanity" and "genocide" in international criminal law.

CRIMES AGAINST HUMANITY

The term "crimes against humanity" is older and broader than "genocide." As mentioned by legal scholar William A. Schabas, the French revolutionary Maximilien Robspierre (1758–94) described King Louis XVI as a "[c]riminal against humanity" (Schabas 2006), and in 1890, an American observer traveling in the Congo—George W. Williams—wrote a letter to the U.S. Secretary of State, declaring that "crimes against humanity" were committed by the Belgian King Leopold's regime (cf. Hochschild 1998:111–12). Yet, most significantly, in May 1915, the governments of Great Britain, France, and Russia issued a declaration in response to the genocide of the Armenian population, denouncing the "new crimes of Turkey against humanity and civilisation" (cited from Schabas 2006, cf. Orentlicher 1998).[1] The notions of crimes against humanity have their historical wellspring in the much older natural law tradition, the legacy of which is clearly visible in modern statements about the "laws of humanity" or "conscience of mankind."[2]

As a part of positive law, however, crimes against humanity first came into existence with the 1945 Charter of the International Military Tribunal in Nuremberg. Article 6c of the Charter defines the three crimes over which the tribunal was given jurisdiction: crimes against peace, war crimes, and crimes against humanity. The last category included murder, extermination, enslavement, deportation, persecution, and "other inhumane acts." According to some jurists, the category of crimes against humanity was thought to encompass the phenomenon of genocide.[3] However, the Nuremberg Charter did not acknowledge Nazi genocide as an independent crime. According to Hannah Arendt, the Charter even left the nature of the Nazi crimes in "a tantalizing state of ambiguity" (Arendt 1978:257f) insofar as it made the Nazis' plan to annihilate the Jews appear as a matter of criminal excess in the pursuit of war and victory" (257).[4] That was because the article included a "nexus requirement" that restricted the Tribunal's power to prosecute crimes against humanity to cases where they were committed "in execution of or in connection with" either war crimes or crimes against peace. Yet, the main reason behind the nexus requirement was arguably not the lack of understanding of the nature of the Nazi crimes against their own population, but rather a concern—shared among the victorious powers—about becoming vulnerable to prosecution themselves. Without that requirement, the new crime would have infringed too openly on the principle of national sovereignty (cf. Orentlicher 1998). Thus, the nexus requirement allowed the victorious powers to interfere with the crimes of a government against its own people—without having to worry whether they would be brought to, court for lynchings, colonialism and deportations (cf. Schabas 2006).

The requirement of a nexus between crimes against humanity and international armed conflict has been eliminated in the most recent definition of crimes against humanity in international law—Article 7 of the Rome Statute of the International Criminal Court (1998): Individuals can be prosecuted for crimes against humanity whether or not they were committed in times of peace or during war or international conflict. Article 7 lists a long number of acts that may count as crimes against humanity. It includes murder, extermination, enslavement, deportation or forcible transfer of population, imprisonment or other severe deprivation of physical liberty in violation of international law, torture, persecution (against any identifiable group on political, racial, national, ethnic, cultural, religious, gender or other grounds), enforced disappearance of persons, the crime of apartheid, and "other inhumane acts of similar character intentionally causing great suffering, or serious injury to body or to mental or physical health."[5]

Even a quick glance over this list of criminal acts (actus reus) reveals that crimes against humanity are extremely reprehensible, malevolent, and harmful or—as the statute puts it—"inhumane" acts. It is not only the extreme cruelty or malevolence of a crime that makes it prosecutable as a crime against humanity. To count as a crime against humanity, it must have been "committed as part of a widespread or systematic attack directed against any civilian population" (Article 7). Thus, the crime committed by the man who captures, rapes, and murders a number of children is a "common" crime, not a crime against humanity. The crimes in focus here "are not isolated, random acts of individuals but rather result from a deliberate attempt to target a civilian population" (Cassese 2002a:367, referring to ICTY Tadic case, Judgments, para. 653) and are typically sponsored and/or perpetrated by states or groups acting under their provision (paramilitary units etc.).

This "objective" requirement—that the crimes committed must be part of a widespread attack—is related closely to the nature of the criminal intent (mens rea) required for crimes against humanity. According to Antonio Cassese, the mens rea of crimes against humanity "involves both the intent to bring about a certain result and the awareness of the factual circumstances which make up or are required for the actus reus" (2002a:362). This means, that the defendant must not only have intended to rape or murder his victims, he must furthermore have been aware that he was participating in a widespread or systematic attack on a civilian population; in Cassese's words, "the agent must be cognizant of the link between his misconduct and the policy or the systematic practice" (362).[6]

Today, crimes against humanity are commonly understood as offenses against humankind, thus indicating the ideal of the notion of universal jurisdiction. As set out in the sentencing judgment in the Tadic case, the crime against humanity is seen as "a crime against more than just the victims themselves but against humanity as a whole" (ICTY, Tadic, Sentencing Judgment 15 July 1997, para. 73). Yet, the preservation of the term "inhumane acts" from Article 6c in the Rome Statute testifies to the viability of the precedent understanding according to which crimes "against humanity" means offenses against "humaneness" or "inhumane acts."[7] Arendt scorned the language of "inhumane" acts "as though the Nazis had simply been lacking in human kindness, certainly the understatement of the century" (1978:275). Whether the use of the concept in this sense is tenable or not, to characterize an act as "inhumane" suggests more than a lack of kindness; that is, it connotes cruelty, absence of empathy, disregard of the humanity of the victim, and the like.

GENOCIDE

It was when the Nazi regime declared that the German people not only were unwilling to have any Jews in Germany but wished to make the entire Jewish people disappear from the face of the earth that the new crime, the crime against humanity . . . appeared. Expulsion and genocide . . . must remain distinct (Arendt 1978:268).

The word "genocide"[8] was coined in 1944 by the Jewish jurist and refugee Rafael Lemkin in *Axis Rule in Occupied Europe*. In a now-classic passage, Lemkin writes, "New conceptions require new terms. By 'genocide' we mean the destruction of a nation or an ethnic group"(1944:79). The word was mentioned and sometimes discussed in Nuremberg, but it did not become a distinct crime until the UN General Assembly adopted the Genocide Convention in 1948.[9] The legal concept of genocide has much in common with the concept of crimes against humanity, and many feel that genocide is not different in kind from crimes against humanity, but rather the worst among them: "the crime of crimes."[10] As Cassese has it, we are—however —in both cases confronted with "offenses that shock our sense of humanity in that they constitute attacks on the most fundamental aspects of human dignity" (Cassese 2002b:339). In both cases there is a scenario or history of large-scale atrocities, and both crimes are "usually carried out with the complicity, connivance, or at least the toleration of the authorities"(339).

Other common features are manifest in the status of these crimes in international law and in the principles for the prosecution and punishment of these crimes Genocide and crimes against humanity are both part of international customary law and regarded as jus cogens,[11] they both give rise to efforts to promote universal jurisdiction, defenses like "acts of state" and "due obedience" are nonapplicable, and statutory limitations do not apply.

Now, what is the reason for two categories of crimes? Why cannot the crimes against humanity category suffice? And what accounts for the idea that genocide is somehow morally worse than crimes against humanity? The most influential answer points to the nature of the intent with which genocide is committed; for example, the Nazis' intent to annihilate the Jews as expressed in Himmler's address to SS officers in Poznan 10 June 1943: "The hard decision had to be made that this people should be caused to disappear from the earth" (cited in Lang 1999:21).[12] Thus, the Nazis were not only persecuting parts of the civilian population, and they were not only massively persecuting these civilians; they were massively persecuting civilians with the intention of destroying—in this extreme case, annihilating—the existence of the group to which the individuals were seen to belong. Thus genocide differs both from war crimes and crimes against humanity because its perpetrators act with the intention to destroy the targeted group as such. What makes the writing of Rafael Lemkin so outstanding is exactly that he, in the words of Michael Ignatieff, "imagined an abominable new intention when others saw only immemorial cruelty" (Ignatieff 2001).[13] It took nonetheless fifty years from the adoption of the Convention until the first conviction of genocide was presented in a courtroom. The following passage from this first judgment of genocide at the International Criminal Tribunal for Rwanda (ICTR) illustrates the central role of intent in the legal definition of genocide. The judgment was pronounced on September 4, 1998: a Rwandan bourgmestre—Jean-Paul Akayesu—was convicted of genocide for his role in the 1994 mass slaughter of Tutsi civilians:

> In the opinion of the Chamber, there is no doubt that considering their undeniable scale, their systematic nature and their atrociousness, the massacres were aimed at exterminating the group that was targeted. Many facts show that the intention of the perpetrators of these killings was to cause the complete disappearance of the Tutsi. In this connection, Alison Desforges, an expert witness, in her testimony before this Chamber on 25 February 1997, stated as follows: "on the basis of the statements made by certain political leaders, on the basis of songs and slogans popular among the Interahamwe, I believe that these people had the intention of completely wiping out the Tutsi from Rwanda so that-as they said on certain occasions—their children , later on , would not know what a Tutsi looked like, unless they referred to history books" (Judgment of Akayesu, ICTR 1998).

Now, let us turn to the 1998 Rome Statute for the International Criminal Court to see how intent figures in its definition of genocide. The Rome Statute reproduces the central parts of the UN Genocide Convention from 1948: according to Article II, five kinds of prohibited acts (actus reus) have to have been committed with a special intent (mens rea) to count as acts of genocide:

> any of the following acts committed with the intent to destroy, in whole or in part, a national, ethnical, racial, or religious group, as such:

(a) Killing members of the group
(b) Causing serous bodily or mental harm to members of the group
(c) Deliberately inflicting on the group conditions of life calculated to bring about its physical destruction in whole or in part
(d) Imposing measures to prevent births within the group
(e) Forcibly transferring children of the group to another group.[14]

Legally, the mental element required for genocide—the intent to destroy—amounts to a so-called dolus specialis. Explained by Cassese, this means that "an aggravated criminal intent must exist in addition to the criminal intent accompanying the underlying offense" (Cassese 2002b:338, italics added). Thus, it is not sufficient to prove that the defendant intended to kill, to cause serious harm, or the like. In addition, it must be proved that such acts were intended and committed with the intent to destroy a particular group as such.

Whereas the dehumanization of entire groups and the degrading treatment of the individual as nothing but an exemplar of the hated group are certainly central elements of genocide, such dehumanization and degradation can also pertain to persecution (as a crime against humanity) and even to so-called hate crimes within domestic criminal law. The difference between the persecutor (not perpetrator) and the génocidaire is that the latter acts with the intent to destroy (in whole or in part) the group as such: to eliminate it from the surface of the earth and annihilate any sign that "they" ever existed. In other words; the difference between a defendant accused of genocide and one accused of crimes against humanity can, in principle, boil down to the question whether the defendant tortured, murdered, raped etc. (a) with the awareness that he participated in a widespread and systematic attack or (b) with the intent to destroy the group attacked as such. Given the actual scale of genocidal violence, the person accused of genocide will most probably also be aware that he has participated in a widespread and systematic attack, but what matters is the nature of the intent.

This is not the place to discuss the merits and flaws of the Genocide Convention; let me just mention its most discussed controversial issues, some of which have some bearing on the scope of this study. The Convention's exclusion of political groups from the number of groups protected has for a long time been a target of criticism, as have the limits set on the acts that may constitute genocide. Another "classic" concern is the question whether so-called cultural genocide—that is, the destruction of a group as such by, in Lemkin's words, the "elimination of its cultural attributes, as opposed to the physical destruction of the group"(Lemkin 1944:79) —can count as genocide.

More recently, the work of two international tribunals[15] has brought to the fore a number of difficult conceptual, legal, and moral issues arising from their application of the law. It is, for example, clear that these cases are never about intent in and of itself; rather, intent is contextualized in or inferred from the circumstantial evidence (e.g., to the quantitative scale and geographical scope of the destruction). Other unresolved questions include the following: What percentage of a targeted group must be killed to count as genocide? Is it genocide when the perpetrators "only" intend to destroy the part of an ethnic group that lives in one region of a country? Can a person be convicted of genocide if he is the sole perpetrator who kills with the intent to destroy the group as such?

These "technical" legal issues have repercussions beyond the legal realm. Even though the absence of a conviction for genocide does not mean that genocide did not happen, but rather that it could not be proved that the defendant was guilty of it, the trial has gained more and more prominence as the place where an authorized truth and final verdict on what happened are issued. In the context of this study's focus on the negative emotions in the aftermath of genocide and crimes against humanity, such legal issues should be recognized as one important source of anger in victim groups struggling against officially supported denial.

In a sociological perspective, the crime of genocide enjoys, finally, the dubious status of "the crime of crimes." One consequence of the idea that there is a hierarchy of crimes is that genocide convictions are seen to offer victims groups not just the important public recognition that they were, indeed, victims of a crime, but also that they have suffered the "ultimate" crime. The question in what sense—if at all—it makes moral sense to say that genocide is worse than crimes against humanity is complex, and any abstract comparison of the two crimes "as such" will probably not facilitate greater understanding. Yet, the great significance attached to this question is a reality. For example, the debate whether the indictment of Milosovic for genocide was perhaps going to be withdrawn (due to extra-legal considerations) created a global response. In a 2004 article in the Los Angeles Times, Samantha Power wrote,

> Victims all over the world who have been targets of genocide pine to be anointed with the international recognition [that] they have suffered the ultimate crime, so the Bosnian Muslims are going to say: 'What? Are you saying we suffered less?' And an acquittal will be a victory for Serb nationalists loyal to Milosovic, who will take it as proof they didn't commit genocide, that it was just a war."

I fully recognize the political repercussions of acquittals, and I agree that to acquit defendants for crimes they have in fact committed because of the benefits of plea bargaining or considerations of time and resources is deeply problematic, particularly in historic trials. But the idea that the legal difference between genocide and crimes against humanity determines degrees of victims' suffering, or that it signals what requires intervention and what does not, is equally disturbing. Mass atrocities should not have to be genocidal to be taken seriously, and any comparison of the aggregated suffering of various kinds of victim groups soon runs into conceptual and moral problems. There are many reasons to take a closer look at the moral assumptions behind the idea of the "crime of crimes.[16]

Notes

PREFACE AND ACKNOWLEDGMENTS

1. The three quotations all appear on the blurb of the paperback edition of *At the Mind's Limits* (Améry 1999).

CHAPTER 1 TRANSITIONAL JUSTICE AND THE ETHICS OF ANGER

1. For the purposes of this book, a "victim" is simply a person to whom a crime has been committed. A "survivor" is a victim who escaped being murdered. Thus, I use both terms without the import of normative connotations of a special dignity, insight, heroism, or weakness.

2. "Transitional justice" is the kind of justice or, more broadly speaking, the range of societal responses that can be found in phases of political transition from violence and instability to democracy, the rule of law, and reconciliation. Roughly speaking, one may define transitional justice literature as works that address how societies can or should deal with their atrocious past.

3. The claim that acts and agents of revenge are not necessarily as bad as we are often told is of course compatible with a recognition that much of what we are often told is true, but it is just not the whole truth. Indeed, any attempt to explore the possible moral dimensions of vengeance should keep in mind suggestions like the following. In 1997, an elderly Cambodian woman told a journalist that "each of the ten million Cambodians alive today should be given a razor blade, and Pol Pot should be brought before the people, with each Cambodian allowed to make one cut" (Etcheson 2003).

4. I use the term "postconflict" occasionally because it is ordinary usage. However, it has to be said that there is something ironic about the term "postconflict" because the

actual situation in many "postconflict" societies is riddled with conflicts. Moreover, talking about "conflict resolution" or "postconflict" societies is—strictly speaking—problematic when what happened was a not a conflict (with two parties who are both somewhat responsible and both have claims in need of compromise etc.), but rather crimes with perpetrators and victims.

5. As an international development worker in Rwanda said, "Can't someone ask these survivors to stop wailing and move on" (cited in Smith (2004:36).

6. David Cesarani has examined the public debates preceding the ratification of the War Crimes Bill in Britain in 1991. According to Cesarani, several prominent Christian theologians opposed the bill on the following grounds: "First of all, it was possible that the guilty men suffered inner torment. And if they were guilty, would it not be better to let God punish them in the next world? After such a long period of time, it was better to forgive, if not forget. . . . Advocacy of forgiveness was frequently coupled with the claim that the campaign for war crimes trials was driven by motives of revenge. This in turn was indissolubly lined to the characterization of the campaign as Jewish, the product of a 'Jewish lobby' and the exemplification of an Old Testament approach to justice" (Cesarani 2001:254).

7. A systematic discussion of the emotional aspects of reconciliation and postwar reconstruction can be found in Halpern and Weinstein (2004).

8. The most prominent examples are the South African Truth and Reconciliation Commission and the international criminal ad hoc tribunals set up in The Hague and in Arusha to deal with war crimes, crimes against humanity, and genocide in the former Yugoslavia and Rwanda.

9. As an example: "We see the cycle of hatred at work at every level of violence. . . . Crimes of hate have a past; sadly, they have a future, too, as each contributes to the climate of demonization and the desire for revenge. Perpetrators become victims, victims avengers. The cycle extends across generations" (Rosenblum 2002:1). For an excellent critique of thinking in terms of "cycles of violence," see Walker (2006a).

10. There is, according to Martha Minow, a "striking prevalence of therapeutic language in contemporary discussions of mass atrocities . . . in contrast to comparable debates fifty years ago" (1998:22). Or as Fletcher and Weinstein (2004:597f) put it, "The transitional justice literature is replete with discussion of the need for societies to 'heal' after mass violence. Writers frequently employ a biomedical model of trauma treatment to conceptualize the tasks of social recovery for a country that experienced mass violence. Trials are promoted as a way for societies . . . to achieve 'closure,' and to rebuild a 'healthy society.'"

11. An assumed ability to assert what *will* happen can result in depictions of a nearly mechanical positive development from which the unpredictability and possibility of dissent disappear. During one of the hearings of the TRC, Desmond Tutu preached that "[f]orgiveness *will* follow confession and healing *will* happen, and so contribute to national unity and reconciliation" (Tutu 1999:120, italics added). In a comparable mode, summarizing the contributions of legal justice to peace and reconciliation, Antonio Cassese claims, "Justice dissipates the call for revenge when the victims' call for retribution are met; by dint of dispensation of justice, victims are prepared to be reconciled with their erstwhile tormentors, because they know that the latter have now paid for their crimes" (cited in Stover 2003:10).

12. See http://www.victimstrustfund.org (accessed November 25, 2004).

13. Another example is "Progress and Humility: The Ongoing Search for Postconflict Justice" by Neil Kritz (2002).

14. In the field of the philosophy of emotion, especially with respect to the role of emotions in ethics and law, Martha Nussbaum has probably been the most prolific and influential voice behind an apparently global rehabilitation of interest in the emotions as an enrichment of moral understanding and reasoning (cf. Nussbaum 1992, 1994, 2001, and 2004). Yet, Nussbaum is of course not the only—or the first—philosopher who has argued the need to pay heed to the emotions. Among many others, consider, for example, Williams (1973), Strawson (1974), and Lamb and Murphy (2002).

15. For example, Joseph Butler, Reinhold Niebuhr and—with a leap to a current theologian—Nigel Biggar. A favorite textual ground for all of these is a line in a letter from Paul to the Christians of Ephesus: "Be angry, but do not sin." For an excellent and richly detailed account of ancient ideologies of absolutist anger "control," see Harris (2001).

16. The Aristotelean "tradition" —defined simply by its refusal to define anger absolutely as bad or mad—includes philosophers like Adam Smith, Peter F. Strawson, Jeffrie Murphy, Margaret Walker, and Richard J. Wallace.

17. Cf. "When resentment is guarded and qualified in this manner, it may be admitted to be even generous and noble" (Smith 1854/2000:50f).

18. "To encounter the Holocaust philosophically, one must study what happened, to whom, where, when, and how" (Roth 1999:43).

19. The approach, and what it makes possible, is close to what Michael Walzer defended in his considerations on how to write about toleration: "I shall not attempt a systematic philosophical argument, though in the essay as a whole all the necessary features of such an argument will at least make an appearance: readers will find some general methodological indications and reasons here, and then an extended illustration with historical examples, an analysis of practical problems, and a tentative and incomplete conclusion, which is all that the approach allows" (Walzer 1997:1–2).

CHAPTER 2 COMMISSIONING ANGER

1. Roland Palm spoke these words during an amnesty hearing in Cape Town on October 28, 1997. His daughter was one of the victims of a massacre on the Heidelberg Tavern, and the passage is part of his address to the amnesty applicants.

2. Another example of high rhetoric can be found in an essay by theologian Alan J. Torrance: "One ingredient in the remarkably peaceful transition from tyranny to democracy was the capacity of Desmond Tutu to tap resources deep within the faith of people and subliminal in their attitudes to their oppressor. Through his spiritual leadership of a people, most notably through the unique dynamics of the Truth and Reconciliation Commission, Desmond Tutu capitalized on those theological resources. The man who embodied his insistence that 'without forgiveness, there is no hope' may well be argued to have exemplified the capacity of forgiveness to realize hopes that transcend the expectations of the most optimistic political realist" (Torrance 2006:45).

3. On the use of the rhetoric of "closure" and "healing" or "catharsis" in relation to international criminal tribunals, cf. Stover (2003). Concerning critical surveys of victims

attitudes to the TRC and the TRC in general, cf. Chapman (2001), Graybill (2002), Hayner (2002), and Verdoolaege (2006).

4. The amount of literature on the TRC is enormous, but philosophical studies or reflections are comparatively limited in number. Jacques Derrida's essay, *On Cosmopolitanism and Forgiveness* (2001), offers a brief critique of Desmond Tutu's well-intentioned but "confused" introduction of the discourse of forgiveness to a public and political institution. David Crocker (2000) has critically assessed Desmond Tutu's statements about justice, retribution, and revenge, and Susan Dwyer (1999) has written an interesting article on the concept of reconciliation (both appear in Prager and Govier 2003). Contextually grounded philosophical analyses of the TRC can be found in the edited volume, *Truth v. Justice: The Morality of Truth Commissions* (Rotberg and Thompson 2000). The same volume includes an article by Elizabeth Kiss that was most inspirational for this study. The article is about restorative justice and the TRC more generally, but in a comment to the TRC report, Kiss remarked it should have included a clear statement "acknowledging that anger was not only understandable but morally justified" (Kiss 2003:85). There are extensive sources that cite the work of the TRC, and the list above is not comprehensive.

5. The Interim Constitution, the Promotion of National Unity and Reconciliation Act, and other aspects of the legal background of the TRC can be retrieved from the home page of the commission: http://www.doj.gov.za/trc/trc_frameset.htm

CHAPTER 3 THE HEARINGS

1. Tutu's talk of the "many" forgiving victims is not empirically accurate. Cf. studies of victim responses to the TRC among the online publications of the Centre for the Study of Violence and Reconciliation in Johannesburg and Cape Town, http://www. csvr.org.za/pubslist/pubstrc.htm (accessed December 5, 2004).

2. The question whether the criminal trial can/should pursue therapeutic aims or how to make the criminal trial as victim-friendly as possible without compromising other important concerns has been interestingly discussed by Dembour and Haslam (2004) and Stover (2005). Aldana (2006) offers a critical and focused discussion of the claim that commissions are more victim-friendly than prosecutions. Brudholm (2007) reviews some of the issues arising from the extraordinary character of genocide trials.

3. In the context of the amnesty hearings, victims were asked how they felt about the granting of amnesty (cf. R. Wilson 2001:120).

4. Here I am at odds with Alex Boraine (former deputy commissioner at the TRC) who has argued that the TRC only provided a platform that made forgiveness possible for those who wanted to forgive (Boraine 2000). Yet, other commissioners have protested that it should have been considered the victims' "right to hate the perpetrators. From the Reparations Committee the view is "Have you hugged a perpetrator yet today?" (Russel Ally, quoted in R. Wilson 2001:108).

5. The research for the chapter began with extensive browsing in the transcripts of the TRC hearings. Yet, to avoid the danger of relying on purely anecdotal and possibly unrepresentative examples, I have drawn on the findings of scholars who have approached the question of the place of anger and resentment in the TRC on empirical grounds; for example, Chapman (2001), Graybill (2002), Hayner (2002), Verdoolaege (2006), and R. Wilson (2001).

6. Throughout I bring the quotes from the transcripts as they appear on the TRC home page httop://www.doz.gov.za/trc/trc_frameset.htm. Using the references to place, date, and identify the given kind of hearing (human rights violation [HRV] or amnesty), it is easy to find the original transcripts on the home page. I have left grammatical errors uncorrected. Also, for the purposes of this book, I have chosen to use the term "commissioner" throughout, although a given quote might have been said by a committee member, not by one of the commissioners. What matters here is first and foremost what the representatives of the TRC said and did.

7. This has been argued convincingly, for example, by Jeffrie G. Murphy (2003) and David A. Crocker (2000).

8. The victims or relatives who were to appear at the public hearings had been interviewed and had given statements before they came to the hearings. Annelies Verdoolage (2006) points to examples where commissioners used such statements to remind the hesitant victims about their earlier clear statements in support of forgiveness and reconciliation.

9. The question posed to them was like the following: "I have no questions in re-examination, but I do have a question which is not evidence inasmuch as I think it is important to hear what the witness's view is regarding this application. What her feeling is about amnesty, and I would like to just give her an opportunity to express a view of the application, if I may. Could you please advise the members of the Committee how you feel about the amnesty application which has been brought regarding the assassination of your son."

10. Amnesty hearing in Johannesburg, October 21, 1996; can be retrieved from http://www.doj.gov.za/trc/trc_frameset.htm

11. HRV hearing, in Durban, Vryheid, April 16, 1997. The case is considered in Verdooelaege (2006).

12. A similar observation can be found in Annalise Acorn's comparison of the ways in which retributive and restorative justice relates to victims' vindictive passions. Restorative justice, according to Acorn, "humours" victims' anger and it might provide victims with an opportunity to "blow of steam." Yet, at the same time anger is invalidated and seen as something to be purged as part of the restoration of the dignity of the victim and of the right relationship between victim and offender (cf. Acorn 2004: 53f).

CHAPTER 4 THE THERAPY OF ANGER

1. Desmond Tutu's propensity sometimes to give way to wishful thinking can also be considered with the following "rosy" depiction of what happened in the TRC. A blood bath had been expected, but "instead there was this remarkable Truth and Reconciliation Commission to which people told their heartrending stories, victims expressing their willingness to forgive and perpetrators telling their stories of sordid atrocities while also asking for forgiveness from those they had wronged so grievously" (Tutu 1999:261).

2. The state leader's plea for a privileging of the collective good is of course not exceptional. During heated French debates of the question whether an amnesty should be provided for the French-Alsatians who had participated in the horrible massacre on the inhabitants of Oradour, General de Gaulle appealed for understanding of the French-Alsatians in the interest of national unity: "In this serious affair what we have to avoid,

above all, is that . . . France lets a bitter wound be inflicted on the national unity." (Farmer 2000:210).

3. Staub et al. (2005), Berliner (2006), Kaplan (2002), Herman (1992) all present and discuss the possibilities and limits of various psychological approaches to rehabilitation and trauma treatment after mass atrocities.

4. Thanks to Inge Genefke from the International Rehabilitation Centre for Torture Victims in Copenhagen for discussion about this point.

5. Interesting discussions about the use of forgiveness in psychotherapy and counseling of victims can be found in Lamb and Murphy (2002).

CHAPTER 5 DESMOND TUTU ON ANGER

1. For example, several times Tutu has told about a hearing about the so-called Bisho massacre, in which South African security forces killed thirty unarmed participants in a protest march. Tutu tells of the tensions building up during the hearing. Yet, because one of the former perpetrators made an unexpected apology, a startling change of mood allegedly took place and the audience broke out in "thunderous applause. . . . It was as if someone had waved a magic wand which transformed anger and tension into display of communal forgiveness and acceptance of erstwhile perpetrators. We could only be humbled by it all" (Tutu 1999:151).

2. On political forgiveness, cf. Digeser (2001) and Schaap (2005). For a discussion of the illiberal nature of the public promotion of forgiveness (from a pro-promotion perspective), see Philpott (2006).

3. The statement (from Tutu's foreword to the TRC's report) is repeated in several variations. Here is another example: "You encounter people who, having suffered grievously, should by rights have been riddled with bitterness and a lust for revenge and retribution" (Helmick and Petersen 2001:xi).

4. Cf. the delimitation of four aspects of religion in Bruce Lincoln (2003).

5. For an anthropological critique of Tutu's use of *ubuntu* as an ideological construct, cf. R. Wilson (2001). It is interesting to note that a Bosnian-Muslim counterpart to *ubuntu*—*merhamet* —has likewise been used in the Bosnian context to find a local—customary—explanation of the reason why some Bosniaks are able and willing to forgive and move on. Cf. Weine (1999).

6. To be sure that the line of reasoning was not just a "whimsical" stream of words in a specific interview, one might check its reiteration in several other contexts: "[*Ubuntu*] speaks of the very essence of being human. . . . It is to say, 'My humanity is caught up, is inextricably bound up, in yours'" . . . Social harmony is for us the *summum bonum*—the greatest good. Anything that subverts, that undermines this sought-after good, is to be avoided like the plague. Anger, resentment, lust for revenge . . . are corrosive of this good. To forgive is not just to be altruistic. It is the best form of self-interest. What dehumanizes you inexorably dehumanizes me" (Tutu 1999:31). And: "God has given us a great gift *ubuntu*. . . . *Ubuntu* says I am human only because you are human. If I undermine your humanity, I dehumanize myself. You must do what you can to maintain this great harmony, which is perpetually undermined by resentment, anger, desire for vengeance" (reported in *Mail and Guardian* on March 17, 1996 and cited in R. Wilson 2001).

7. Even though, sometimes, social cohesion seems to be a function of shared hatred and resentment. Thanks to Jeffrie Murphy for suggesting this point to me.

8. For a modern philosophical examination of anger as a deadly vice, cf. Taylor 2006. Nussbaum (1994) includes several articles on the topic of anger in the Stoic tradition.

9. In the TRC Report, forgiveness is defined as the overcoming of resentment (TRC Final Report 1998, ch. 5, para. 48).

10. The literature is constantly growing and too large to refer to in too. Key examples from recent years and with attention to moral horrors or mass atrocities include Card (2002) Derrida (2001), Digeser (2003), Garrard (2003), Murphy (2003), Roth, Thomas (2003), and Walker (2006b).

11. Yet, sometimes it seems that what motivates the talk of "forgiving the unforgivable" would be captured more accurately as an insistence that forgiveness deals with wrongs that are inexcusable and unjustifiable (and thus genuine occasions of anger and resentment).

12. I am here inspired by Michael Walzer's talk of moral minimalism and maximalism in Thick and Thin: Moral Argument at Home and Abroad (1994).

13. In one of the many languages used in the context (i.e., Xhosa), the word chosen for "reconciliation" was according to Nomfundo Walaza "much closer in meaning to 'forgiveness'" (Krog 2000:243).

14. For reflections on the relationship between forgiveness and reconciliation, cf. Morton 2004:14ff, Ignatieff 2003, Schimmel 2002, Helmick and Petersen 2001, and Dwyer 1999.

15. Tutu is probably thinking of the words: "Father forgive them for they know not what they do."

16. See http://www.virginia.edu/nobel/transcript/tutu.html. The example is also given in a section on Tutu in Wiesenthal (1998) and several other places (e.g., Tutu 1999:146).

17. A similar example of the blotting out of the negative can be found by comparing Tutu's accounts of a series of encounters between former perpetrators and victims that was seen on the BBC with the response of Jonathan Freedland. A forceful critique of the use of narrative of magic moments can be found in Annalise Acorn's (2004) *Compulsory Compassion*.

CHAPTER 6 LAYERS AND REMAINDERS

1. The reasoning of the court can be compared with the way in which spokesmen from the ANC and the TRC saw the families bringing the lawsuit as "anti-reconciliation" because of their legal challenge. As Richard Wilson writes, "Their actions outraged Desmond Tutu who bitterly denounced them in a press hearing, saying, "I hope they get their come-uppance. I am annoyed and very hurt for the many people I know who want to tell their stories" (R. Wilson 2001:172).

CHAPTER 7 CONTEXTUALIZING "*RESSENTIMENTS*"

1. If the Holocaust was unique (not in the trivial sense in which any event is unique, but in the sense of incomparable or incommensurable with anything else in any sense),

192 / Notes to chapter 7

then any comparative study and any talk of the Holocaust as "a genocide" would reveal a lack of understanding. For an excellent discussion of the idea of uniqueness, see Geras' "In a Class of Its Own?" in Garrard and Scarre (2003).

2. The essays were presented for the listeners in 1964 to 1965. Cf. Heidelberger-Leonard 2004.

3. In the literature on Améry, one finds references both to "Maier" and to "Mayer." The confusion is well founded! On his birth certificate Améry was named "Hans Maier," on a class list from primary school he was registered as "Hans Mayer," and in high school it was "Johann Mayer"; as editor of the journal *Brücke* in the early 1930s, Améry used "Hanns Mayer" (cf. Heidelberger-Leonard 2004:359, note 1).

4. The first book-length biography is Irene Heidelberger-Leonard's *Jean Améry* (Heidelberger-Leonard 2004). A much shorter alternative is Susan Neiman's "October 1978: Jean Améry takes his life" (Neiman 1997). Friedrich Pfäfflin's "Jean Améry— Daten zu einer Biographie" combines factual biographical information with quotes from Améry's writings in a chronologically structured exposition (in Steiner 1996, 265–80).

5. Brudholm (2006a) examines Améry's reflections on the homesickness and exile of the Nazi victim.

6. The passage can be compared to Primo Levi's recounting of an episode in which he and another inmate "transcend" camp reality by recalling a stanza from Dante's *The Divine Comedy*. Cf. Levi: "'Think of your breed; for brutish ignorance / Your mettle was not made; you were made men, / To follow after knowledge and excellence.' As if I also was hearing it for the first time: like the blast of a trumpet, like the voice of God. For a moment I forgot who I am and where I am" (Levi 1987:103). One should, however, add that Levi ends the chapter with another quote: "And over our heads the hollow seas closed up" (105).

7. Cf. bibliography in Steiner (1996). Améry's collected works are now being published in Germany in nine volumes by Klett-Cotta.

8. Pendas (2006) provides an excellent and comprehensive historical analysis and contextualization of this most important and complex postwar German trial of Nazi criminals.

9. The opposite strategy would be to try to establish an understanding of the event consonant with a given worldview. Lawrence Langer has spoken of attempts to "pre-empt the Holocaust"; by this he means "using—and perhaps abusing—its grim details to fortify a prior commitment to an ideal of moral reality, community responsibility, or religious belief that leaves us with space to retain faith in their pristine value in a post-Holocaust world" (Langer 1998:1). The rescue of the Danish Jews in October 1943 has also been held forth as "the light in the darkness" that allowed Christians to sustain the faith challenged by the catastrophe in general (cf. Brudholm 2007a).

10. Jan Philip Reemtsma's "172364: Gedanken über den Gebrauch der ersten Person Singular bei Jean Améry" (1996) explores the substantial underpinnings of Améry's use of different grammatical cases. Reemtsma argues that Améry's work can be seen as an attempt to recapture the capability to say "I" —to be an individual—on the background of a wholesale devastation of the social preconditions of individuality. Cf. Susan Neiman (1997): "questions about the nature and meaning of the subject, the relation of subjective

experience to a reality which is impervious to it, are probably the most central in Améry s work" (775).

11. The problems of the term "Bewältigung" in relation to the Nazi past have been the inspiration for several titles and comments. There is for example the historian Charles Maier's classic entitled *The Unmasterable Past: History, Holocaust, and German National Identity* (1997) and Arendt's comment that "this past could not be 'mastered' by anybody" (Arendt 2003:55).

12. *Vergangenheitsbewältigung*, according to the Swedish historian Kristian Gerner, "means roughly 'to come to terms with the past, confess a collective guilt for the Holocaust and be reconciled with the duty always to remember it'" (Gerner 2003:119). Although this is a sensible stipulation of the current meaning of the concept, the use of the term "collective guilt" is problematic. Speeches at commemorations assert repeatedly that what the present generation has inherited is a collective responsibility, not a collective guilt. The use of the term "reconciled" is also somewhat insensitive to what might be called the "agonistic" nature of the duty to remember.

13. Compare Adenauer's first *Regierungserklärung* (policy statement): "The government of the Federal Republic, in the belief that many have atoned for a guilt that was not heavy, is determined where it appears acceptable to do so to put the past behind us [In German: Vergangenes vergangen zu lassen]" (Herf 1997:271).

14. "Regierungserklärung" does not have a precise English equivalent and "policy statement" should, strictly speaking, be rendered, as "statement of the policy directions of the incumbent government." Thanks to Dietrich Jung for urging this point on me.

15. Adenauer's speech was promptly gainsaid by the leader of the Social Democratic fraction of the Bundestag, Kurt Schumacher. Schumacher noted that Adenauer had not uttered a word either about the victims of fascism or about the resistance to Nazism within Germany (Herf 1997:273). More on Adenauer in Herf (1997:299, 378).

16. Kellenbach (2001b) gives a more detailed examination of the reaction of the Evangelical German Church.

17. A brief comparison of postwar Germany and postapartheid South Africa can be found in Theissen and Hamber (1998).

18. The escape from reality (cf. *Eichmann*, Arendt 1978:50ff) was, according to Arendt, more fundamentally an escape from responsibility (cf. 1994:250). Arendt's following words about the "irritation that comes when indifference is challenged" (when stating the obvious; that is, that one is a Jew): "This is usually followed by a little embarrassed pause; and then comes—not a personal question, such as 'Where did you go after you left Germany?'; no sign of sympathy, such as 'What happened to your family?'—but a deluge of stories about how Germans have suffered (true enough, of course, but beside the point); and if the object of this little experiment happens to be educated and intelligent, he will proceed to draw up a balance between German suffering and the suffering of others, the implication being that one side cancels the other and that we may as well proceed to a more promising topic of conversation" (Arendt 1994:249).

19. In German: "das lange Schweigen, Vertuschen und Schönfarben der Vergangenheit durch die Führungseliten und ihr fehlender Wille für mitverschuldetes Unrecht einzustehen" (Fischer 2003:11).

CHAPTER 8 OPENING MOVES

1. David Heyd (2004) uses the comparison with the wife of Lot in a paper on Améry.
2. One finds similar considerations in Theodor W. Adorno's classic essay with the title, "What Does Coming to Terms With the Past Mean," from 1959. Adorno writes, "National Socialism lives on, and to this day we don't know whether it is only the ghost of what was so monstrous that it didn't even die off with its own death, or whether it never died in the first place—whether the readiness for unspeakable actions survives in people, as in the social conditions that hem them in" (Adorno 1986:115).
3. In the original German: "Kein vages Versöhnungspathos klingt durch seine Über-legungen, sondern jene radikale Aufrichtigkeit, die allein das Feld bereiten kann für einen künftigen Dialog" (Améry 2002b:623).
4. Cf. similar reservations with regard to vengeance: "'vengeance' is not the name of an emotion as such, nor is there any single emotion name that corresponds to vengeance" (Solomon 1999:124).
5. Other times to issue a warning or express fear. The existence of deep and some-times highly cultivated *ressentiment* between ethnic groups is also used to call masses to participate in (alleged retributive) ethnic cleansing and genocidal violence. In the former Yugoslavia, inflammatory nationalist anti-Muslim and anti-Croat propaganda stirred up "old grievances that Serbs had carefully collected since World War II, like misers hoard-ing their coins" (Neuffer 2001:34), and in Rwanda, "the incessant propaganda, mixing truth with rumor, myth, or outright falsehood, cleverly stirred up all the age-old resent-ments and fear of the RPA, the Tutsi-led army" (Neuffer 2001:119).
6. Lynne McFall's rehearses these and other regular arguments against bitterness in "What's Wrong With Bitterness" (1991).
7. In the original preface, Améry even characterizes *Beyond Guilt and Atonement* as a whole as a "personal confession refracted through meditation" (xiii).
8. In "On Humanity in Dark Times: Thoughts About Lessing," Hannah Arendt expresses a similar thought and principle of opposition. She writes that "for many years I considered the only adequate answer to the question, Who are you? To be: A Jew. That answer alone took into account the reality of persecution. As for the statement which Nathan the Wise (in effect, though not in actual wording) countered the command: "Step closer Jew"—the statement: I am a man—I would have considered as nothing but a grotesque and dangerous evasion of reality. . . . The basically simple principle in question here is one that is particularly hard to understand in times of defamation and persecu-tion: the principle that one can resist only in terms of the identity that is under attack. Those who reject such identifications on the part of a hostile world may feel wonderfully superior to the world, but their superiority is then truly no longer of this world; it is the superiority of a more or less well-equipped cloud-cuckoo-land" (Arendt 1968:17–18).
9. In a study of trauma victims and politics, Jenny Edkins underlines that "the only words they [i.e. survivors of mass atrocity] have are the words of the very political com-munity that is the source of their suffering. This is the language of the powerful, the words of the status quo, the words that delimit and define acceptable ways of being human within that community" (2003:8).
10. German postwar historian Norbert Frei finds it improbable that the very term *"ressentiment"* would have been in common use in the postwar discourse. "The term

"*Ressentimentträger*" belongs more to the world of academic analysis than to the post-war public discourse" (e-mail correspondence, quoted with permission).
11. The essay was first published as "Pardonner?" (Éditions Le Pavillon) in 1971, but it discusses interventions in French public debates in 1965 (same year as the publication of *Beyond Guilt and Atonement*) regarding statutory limitations. I have not been able to find any evidence of a relationship between Améry and Jankélévitch.
12. I have made a little but important correction in the translation. It has to do with the translator's (Ann Hobart) inconsequential translation of the French *ressentiment* and of Jankélévitch's use of scare quotes to indicate the difference between the ideology of the advocates of statutory limitations and the reality of the emotional/anamnestic stance of the "ressentir" of the "homme de cœur" (39). Jankélévitch writes: « on peut du moins ressentir, inépuisablement. C'est sans doute ce que les brillant avocats de la prescription appelleront notre *ressentiment* [...] Le voilà notre « *ressentiment* ». Car le « *ressentiment* » peut être aussi . . . » (Jankélévitch 1986:62). Ann Hobart translates: "We can at least feel, inexhaustibly," "this is what the . . . advocates . . . will call our resentment." And finally: "This is our "resentment" [*ressentiment*]. For *ressentiment* can also . . ." (the bracketed insertion is Hobart's).
13. The nature of Améry's critique of Nietzsche in *Beyond Guilt and Atonement* can be put in perspective by comparing it with the recently published drafts written by Améry in 1945 as Hans Mayer. Mayer does not accept the thought that the National Socialist use of Nietzsche was all due to a vulgar interpretation of his works. Cf. "Zur Psychologie des Deutschen Volkes," *Werke* (Améry 2002b: 500–34). The statement of a need to "answer Nietzsche" has, by the way, been resumed by Jonathan Glover in his recent *Humanity* (cf. Glover 2001:40f).
14. Cf. "Whereas all noble morality grows out of a triumphant yes-saying to oneself, from the outset slave morality say 'no' to an 'outside,' to a 'different,' to a 'not-self': *this* no is its creative deed"(*Genealogy*, Nietzsche 1887:19).
15. Nietzsche describes the human beings of *ressentiment* as the "physiologically failed and worm-eaten ones, a whole trembling earth of subterranean revenge, inexhaustible, insatiable in outbursts against the happy . . . when would they actually arrive at their last, finest, most sublime triumph of revenge? Undoubtedly, if they should succeed in *shoving* their own misery, all misery generally *into the conscience* of the happy: so that the happy would one day being to be ashamed of their happiness" (Nietzschc 1887/1998:89).
16. Cf. the fantastic section 14 in the first book of the *Genealogy* where it is revealed how the humans of *ressentiment* "fabricate ideals on earth." Cowardice is turned into patience; misery becomes blessedness and revenge is disguised as justice: "Bad air! This workplace where they *fabricate ideals* – it seems to me to stink of sheer lies." (Nietzsche 1887/1998:27).
17. As aptly demonstrated by Niederland's analyses of a host of "patients," the psychological perspective is internally capable of distinguishing between the question whether the patient's suffering is owed to delirium and psychosis or whether it is the effect of real proceedings (cf. Niederland:188). In "Trauma and Reintegration," Bruno Bettelheim remarks that the state of mind of the concentration camp survivor may be likened with "that of an individual suffering from a depressive or paranoid psychiatric

disturbance" (1980:29). But Bettelheim adds that there is a crucial difference between the psychotic person and the survivor: "while the psychotic person only delusionally believes that there are all-powerful figures who control his life and who plan to destroy him, the concentration camp survivor observed correctly that those in whose absolute power he was actually had destroyed others like him, and were bent on destroying him too. Thus the crucial difference between the prisoner and the psychotic is that the first assessed his situation realistically, the second delusionally" (29).

18. Cf.: "Those were no hysteric hallucinations when I heard the Germans call for the Jews to "die like a dog!" and, in passing, heard how people said that there really must be something suspicious about the Jews, because otherwise they would hardly be treated so severely.... I am thus forced to conclude that I am not deranged and was not deranged, but rather that the neurosis is on the part of the historical occurrence" (96).

19. Cf. Kali Tal: "Bearing witness is an aggressive act. It is born out of refusal to bow to outside pressure to revise or repress experience, a decision to embrace conflict rather than conformity, to endure a lifetime of anger and pain rather than to submit to the seductive pull of revision and repression. Its goal is change. If survivors retain control over the interpretation of their trauma, they can sometimes force a shift in the social and political structure" (cited in Edkins 2003:191).

20. A public health perspective on conflict and reconciliation can be found in Halpern and Weinstein (2004). The authors see hatred and fear as part of the "health effects of intra-ethnic conflict": "The profound effects of war and conflict on the health of survivors are a significant public health concern.... This paper argues that healthy psychological and physical functioning requires overcoming the hatred that pervades the relationships between ethnic groups, and that, in turn, this depends upon seeing their recent enemies in human terms" (2004:562). As indicated by the last part of the sentence, the article represents an interesting mix of a moral psychological and public health perspective.

21. Primo Levi might, again, provide an exemplary illustration of the phenomenon. In the chapter "Chemical Examination," Levi describes the look of Doktor Pannwitz as he examined whether Levi was a chemist: "[T]hat look was not one between two men; and if I had known how completely to explain the nature of that look, which came as if across the glass window of an aquarium between two beings who live in different worlds, I would also have explained the essence of the great insanity of the third Germany" (Levi 1987:96).

22. The inclusion of the retrospective narrative can be seen to illustrate Peter Goldie's claim about what it takes to make sense of one's emotional life: "It is the notion of narrative structure which ties together and makes sense of the individual elements of emotional experience.... To make sense of one's emotional life, including its surprises, it is thus necessary to see it as part of a larger unfolding narrative" (Goldie 2002:5).

23. The "world" did not unanimously join in such attitudes at any point of time. Jonathan Bass's account of the internal fights between the Allies and between the advisors of Roosevelt is enlightening. Still, Améry probably grasps the general mood of the period (cf. Bass 2000 and Deák et al. 2000).

24. "It seemed to me as if I had experienced their atrocities as collective ones. I had been just as afraid of the Germans on the small passenger platform where, from the cattle cars of our deportation train, the corpses had been unloaded and piled up; not on a

single one of their stony faces was I able to detect an expression of abhorrence [Abscheu]"
(65f/122f).

25. At http://www.victimstrustfund.org/info/abouticc.html.

26. Cf. Nussbaum (2004) on disgust. The moral philosophical importance of the
sense of horror is examined in Robert M. Adam's *Finite and Infinite Goods* (2002). A classic source on the horrible is Spinoza, who defines the concept in his *Ethics* (cf. Spinoza
1677).

27. Améry is alluding to the proposal of the Secretary of Treasury, Henry
Morgenthau Jr. to turn Germany into an agricultural society (cf. Bass 2000:150,152).

28. German: "die Vergangenheit zu [...] bewältigen"(125). Améry illustrates the
wrongs and failures of the German *Vergangenheitsbewältigung* of the 1950s and 1960s by
pointing to the fact that only a few of Germany's postwar politicians had distinguished
themselves in the resistance movement. He draws attention to the lack of prosecutorial
zeal and to a number of particular episodes.

29. Cf. Philip Fisher's (2002) thoughts on the "Paths among the Passions."

CHAPTER 9 FACING THE IRREVERSIBLE

1. The notion of the "captivating" force of the passions or emotions is in itself a con-
testable idea. According to Robert Solomon, emotions are something we choose, and
metaphors like "driven by anger," "paralyzed by fear," and—we can add—"trapped in
ressentiment" betray "a faulty philosophical analysis" (2003:224).

2. The one serious consideration I have in mind is a short passage in a manuscript
by Arne Grøn (2006).

3. Cf. Derek Parfit in *Reasons and Persons* where he emphasizes that a "bias toward
the future" is commonly (and, according to Parfit, wrongly) assumed to be a straightfor-
wardly rational attitude to time (Parfit 1984:177). Améry does not mention Martin
Heidegger, but there is an affinity between Heidegger's concept of *Dasein's* future-
directedness and the bias toward the future. Heidegger's "bias" toward the future is critically considered in Ricoeur (2004).

4. In her monograph on *Transitional Justice*, Ruti Teitel explains the paradoxical
operation of time in the context of reparatory transitional justice by referring to the special problems that pertain to the possibility of achieving justice after the commission of
state crimes. Our intuitions about time are ill suited to account for what should be considered the state's compensatory obligations and the victims' rights in such cases, because
time does not diminish, but rather facilitates the conditions of justice (cf. Teitel 2000).

5. In the original German: "Sie ist sich klar darüber, dass alle diese Ereignisse viele
Jahre zurückliegen und kann doch von den Erinnerungen und quälenden Fantasien nicht
loskommen. Sie lebt in anderen Worten immer noch im Konzentrationslager..."
(Niederland 1980:101).

6. Cf. Anthony Kenny on the role of desire in the understanding of emotion: "one
emotion differs from another because of the different sort of things it makes one want to
do" (2003:70).

7. "Aufhebung" is "Hegel's term for the dialectical transition in which a lower stage
is both annulled and preserved in a higher one" (Taylor 1979:49). One may notice that
"Ableben" means "deceased." What is "abgelebt" if not simply what is "past" (as the trans-

lation has it), but what is decrepit or obsolete. The phrase "Rückgang ins Abgelebte" thus alludes to the very point of contestation (i.e., the question whether the Nazi past is really past).

8. The connection between Améry's rejoinder to Nietzsche and this part of Nietzsche's writings was first noticed in Agamben (1999) and Neiman (2002).

9. The moral revolt embraced by Améry might be compared to the "moral embitterment" or "revolt of the good spirit" in Hegel's *Philosophy of History* (cf. 2001:35).

10. The metaphorical understanding of "undoing" does not necessarily mean to concede that reconciliation with the past events would be possible. Arendt understood figuratively the power of forgiveness to "undo" the deeds of the past, but she also insisted on the limits of this power in the face of radical evil. In sum, one should take seriously exactly what Améry writes.

CHAPTER 10 RESTORING COEXISTENCE

1. "To the very same that for me a fresh, calm look toward the future is too difficult, my persecutors of yesterday manage to find it too easy" (Améry 1999:69).

2. Tim Judah (2004:25) reports an instance of resistance to reconciliation from Bosnia premised on the assumption that the parties have to meet halfway: "I," says the Bosnian interviewee, "am against reconciliation as seen from The Hague perspective. I never wronged anyone. I did nothing wrong. Reconciliation means we have to meet halfway, but that's offensive. I was wronged and almost my entire family was killed. I care about justice and truth."

3. Another forum could, of course, have been the courtroom, but the issue of *ressentiment* is more about moral recognition and remembrance than criminal punishment and justice.

4. Améry richly illustrates Axel Honneth's claim that some social conflicts are genuinely moral in nature. Cf. Honneth (1995), *The Struggle for Recognition: The Moral Grammar of Social Conflicts.*

5. The translation of "Untäter" into "monster" was, on the other hand, a problematic radicalization.

6. For a more general comparative perspective, during and after state-sponsored mass atrocity, perpetrator groups "tend to be resistant to acknowledging their wrongdoing" (Govier 2002:25). The absence of (public) moral acknowledgment of wrongdoing and responsibility is generally a matter of great importance to survivors of genocidal violence. Without such acknowledgment the surviving victim understandably and legitimately remains "unable to trust, unable to forgive, and unable to reconcile. . . . What victims see [when acknowledgment remains absent] is persons or groups who have committed serious wrongs—but seem not even to be aware of what they have done" (Govier 2002:146).

7. Cf. Ralph Giordano, another victim of Nazi persecution and a critic of the politics of memory in postwar West Germany. In a commentary to the Auschwitz trial in Frankfurt (from 1965), Giordano recognizes the danger that such trials can reduce national responsibility for mass crimes to the miniscule group of perpetrators who actually come to stand trial. In the face of the failure of the Auschwitz trial to arouse a sense of responsibility among the Germans more generally, Giordano concludes that the only option—for the surviving victims—is to "live with Auschwitz" (cited in Pendas 2006:268).

8. As shown by Niederland, through his analysis of postwar psychiatric assessments of applicants for economic compensation, it took years before the field of psychiatry recognized the possibility that the injuries done to the victims during the years of persecution could be indelible (Niederland 1980).

9. Cf. the so-called Brahimi Report on UN peacekeeping operations (the particular case in question was the fall of Srebrenica): "In some cases, local parties consist not of moral equals but of obvious aggressors and victims, and peacekeepers may not only be operationally justified in using force but morally compelled to do so. Genocide in Rwanda went as far as it did in part because the international community failed to use or to reinforce the operation then on the ground in that country to oppose obvious evil. Impartiality for United Nations operations must therefore mean adherence to the principles of the Charter: where one party to a peace agreement clearly and incontrovertibly is violating its terms, continued equal treatment of all parties by the United Nations can in the best case result in ineffectiveness and in the worst may amount to complicity with evil. No failure did more to damage the standing and credibility of United Nations peacekeeping in the 1990s than its reluctance to distinguish victim from aggressor" (Executive Summary, para. 50). The report can be accessed at http://www.un.org/peace/reports/peace_operations/.

10. A possible philosophical spelling out of Améry's statements could come close to the position adopted by Charles Taylor in *Sources of the Self* (Taylor 1989:6ff).

11. The German text can be found in full in Lanzmann's *Shoah* (1985:141–44). On the cultivation of emotional "coldness," see Schwan (2001).

12. Resentment "is to be considered as a weapon, put into our hands by nature, against injury, injustice, and cruelty" (Butler 1897:121).

13. Cf. psychologist Sharon Lamb contesting the advocacy of forgiveness as a universal good by some American counselors: "For some people, there is a legitimate need for continued resentment, and in some situations, the withholding of forgiveness can encourage a wrongdoer to repent" (Lamb and Murphy 2002:11).

14. This explains, I guess, why Améry first suggested that the book be entitled *Ressentiments*—it even provides a possible explanation why he keeps using the possible but unusual plural form of the noun (when referring to the series of essays in the book).

15. The question of Jewish revenge after the Holocaust is much more complicated than Améry seems willing to admit; cf. Lang (1999) and Tobias and Zinke (2000).

16. In the essay "In the Waiting Room of Death" (from 1969, reprinted in *Radical Humanism*, Améry 1984), Améry argues that the desire and act of revenge under extreme circumstances can become admirable and genuinely moral. The essay focuses on the conditions of the Jews in the ghettos established by the Nazis and on ways in which the Jews responded to the dehumanization process. Revenge enters in this context as a response that belongs on the top of an eventual moral hierarchy of more and less worthy or valuable responses. In this essay, Améry conceptualizes revenge as "avenging violence that is intended as the nullification of the oppressor's violence. . . . For one moment he [i.e. the Ghetto Jew] became the hunter, not for the joy of hunting but from the will to remain who he was and at the same time become another" (Améry 1984:26).

17. In an interview with Ingo Hermann in the summer of 1978, Améry talks of an earlier longing for a new German generation with which it could be possible to come to an understanding (cf. Hermann 1992:82).

18. The italicization of "genuine" alludes to the hypothetical allegation that Améry's *ressentiment* is nourished by a lust for revenge.

19. In regard to his upholding of the experience and demand of the individual moral subject, Améry can be compared with the Hungarian writer and Holocaust survivor Imre Kertész. The press release announcing that Kertész won the Nobel Prize in Literature in 2002 stated that he received it "for writing that upholds the fragile experience of the individual against the barbaric arbitrariness of history." In his writing Imre Kertész explores the possibility of continuing to live and think as an individual in an era in which the subjection of human beings to social forces has become increasingly complete" (Nobel Committee 2002).

20. Sebastian Haffner's posthumously published memoir of the prewar years, especially of his stay in the SA (the storm trooper) training camps, is just one testimony of the background against which Améry's plea for the moral standing of the individual is best understood. Haffner vividly documents the progressive destruction of individuality and independent moral thinking and the formation of comradeship (see Haffner 2003).

21. As Jankélévitch has it: "It is in general incomprehensible that time, a natural process without normative value, could have a diminishing effect on the unbearable horror of Auschwitz" (1996:556–57).

22. In a letter to the publisher of *Beyond Guilt and Atonement* Améry writes that the problem of the experience of time is the very concern of the essay and that the victim's *ressentiment* will be understood as a wish for a moralization of time or time reversal (cf. Améry 2002b:626).

CHAPTER 11 GUILT AND RESPONSIBILITY

1. Another example: "The vengeful impulses that *ressentiment* generates are not directed exclusively toward those who have violated demands in their treatment of the person in its grip (Wallace 1994:247).

2. In German: "zu zügeln" (i.e., bridle or rein; Améry 2002a:134).

3. In fact, the idea of a trial's ability to individualize guilt is far from self-evident or nonproblematic. The conventional criminal trial—through its focus and procedures—does individualize guilt. It is about the guilt or innocence of a particular individual; the defendant in the dock. Yet, even a quick glimpse at the history of genocide trials reveals that they have always been about more than the particular individuals at trial. Indeed, the trials in Nuremberg, Frankfurt, Jerusalem, and The Hague have typically pursued a "two track" approach, trying at once to establish individual guilt and to teach a history lesson. Indeed, the idea that trials individualize guilt is often first and foremost expressive of a hope as to their effects on relevant groups, rather than a reference to the focus and procedures of the criminal trial as such. In any instance, the struggle to individualize guilt has to be complemented with a struggle to facilitate collective responsibility. That is, there is a danger that trials too effectively individualize guilt and facilitate a sense that only the "monsters" who came to trial were responsible; see Cohen (1999), May (2004), Minow (1998), and Brudholm (2007).

4. Actually, the Hebrew Bible includes both ideas of transgenerational guilt and injunctions not to harm children for the sins or crimes of their parents. Schimmel (2002:26) points to Deuteronomy 24:16 ("Parents shall not be put to death for their children, nor shall children be put to death for their parents; only for their own crimes may

person be put to death.") and Ezekiel 18:13–14, 20 ("The person who sins shall die. A child shall not suffer for the iniquity of a parent"). As an example of the opposite, the most notorious passage is probably, the will of the Lord to "have war with Amalek from generation to generation" (Exodus 17:8–16) and the responsibility of the Israelites not to forget what the tribe of Amalek did to them, but instead to await the moment when they shall "blot out the remembrance of Amalek" (Deuteronomy 25:17–19, cited in Schimmel 2002:25).

5. "Responsibility" covers two completely different things. On the one hand, it signifies a condition for the attribution of guilt to an individual. The assignment of guilt requires that the agent can be treated as a responsible person or that he acted responsibly in the sense that he knew what he did, could have acted otherwise, etc. On the other hand, "responsibility" may signify the having of an obligation, and "being responsible" may signify a special kind of character virtue. Cf. Jonas 1984:90–98 and Scanlon 2000, ch. II, 6.

6. In a speech to the Society for Christian-Jewish Cooperation in December 1949, former *Bundespräsident* Theodor Heuss stressed that the term "collective guilt" relies on simplifications and perversions comparable to the way in which the Nazis approached the Jews; as if the very fact of being a Jew in itself implied being personally guilty (see Frei 2000:176, n. 29).

7. This is why a proponent of collective moral guilt like Ralph Giordano can arouse strong indignation by his very comparison of his claim of the collective guilt of the German wartime generation and the Nazi logic and practice of collective guilt and punishment (Giordano 2000: 245–66).

8. Hannah Arendt was among the first to put emphasis on this "paradox of collective guilt" (see, for example, her 1945 article, "Organized Guilt and Responsibility," reprinted in 1994: 273–83).

9. The title of Frei's article is "Von deutscher Erfindungskraft oder: Die Kollektivschuldthese in der Nachkriegszeit" (Frei 2000).

10. See Adorno's poignant remarks, from 1959, on postwar discourses about a "guilt complex": "All this talk, by the way, of a guilt complex displays something untruthful. Psychiatry, from which the phrase is borrowed ... implies that such guilt feelings are pathological, inadequate to reality: 'psychogenic' as analysts call it. With the help of the word 'complex' the impression is created that the guilt—which so many fend off, abreact, or deflect through the craziest rationalizations—is really no guilt at all, but exists only inside them, in their psychological makeup. So a real and terrible past is rendered harmless by being transformed this way—into a mere figment of the imagination of those who are affected by it. Or is guilt itself perhaps only a complex? Should we consider it pathological to burden oneself with the past, while the healthy and realistic person is absorbed in the present and its practical concerns? That would be to appropriate a moral from 'And it's as good as if it never happened,' which is written by Goethe but uttered by the devil at a decisive point in Faust to reveal his innermost principle: the destruction of memory" (Adorno 1986:117).

11. The moral issues arising from determining individual responsibility for acts committed in the context of war and by members of military organizations are considered by a host of philosophers in Cohen, Nagel, and Scanlon (1974), *War and Moral Responsibility*, and in French (1972), *Individual and Collective Responsibility: Massacre at My Lai*. The most comprehensive treatment of the issue is May (2004).

12. Henry Morgenthau Jr. was the son of the U.S. ambassador to the Ottoman Empire, Henry Morgenthau Sr., who, in vain, agitated for U.S. diplomatic intervention to

oppose the genocide of the Armenians in 1915. Like his father, he grasped the horror of genocide. See Samantha Power's moving account of Morgenthau Sr.'s response to the mass murder and the inaction of his state in Power (2002, ch. 1).

13. See the chapter on the struggles between Morgenthau Jr. and Henry Stimson with regard to the determination of U.S. policy for conquered Germany in Bass (2000).

14. This does not mean that Améry, for other reasons and in other contexts, was not a keen advocate of prosecution and punishment. For example, "I refuse any reconciliation with the criminals, and with those who only by accident did not happen to commit atrocities, and finally, all those who helped prepare the unspeakable acts with their words. . . . Too many criminals are spared by the letter of the law,... too many of the murderers in uniform, too many bloody judges of yesterday, are spending their last years in peace" (in Wiesenthal 1998:108).

15. See Hannah Arendt's "Organized Guilt and Universal Responsibility" from 1945 (in Arendt 1994:121–32).Cf. Primo Levi: "Almost all, but not all, had been deaf, blind, and dumb: a mass of 'invalids' surrounding a core of ferocious beasts" (Levi 1988:167). Levi too regards "the German people, on the whole" as fully culpable for the omission of resistance against the Nazi crimes (1988: 190). Cf. Grass in a speech in Jerusalem in 1967: "The Germans, those who did it and those who let it be done, killed six million human beings"(cited in Bar-on 1991:261).

16. In her "The Aftermath of Nazi Rule: Report from Germany" from 1950, Arendt referred to a similar kind of poster to press a similar point. She just adds to the picture a finger pointing at the spectator, and the text "You are guilty!" The finger is probably a figment of Arendt's imagination (perhaps, as Norbert Frei has suggested to me, with Uncle Sam posters as inspiration). But that the posters are claiming something indistinguishable, in my opinion, from the anyway vague thesis of collective guilt is documented in Herbert Marcuse's *Legacies of Dachau* where an example is reprinted. It shows photos of piles of corpses from Dachau below the headline, "Diese Schandtaten: Eure Schuld!" ("These Atrocities: Your Guilt!"). In the text below, two lines are in bold print: "Ihr habt zugesehen und es stillschweigend geduldet" ("You were witnesses and you tolerated it") and „Das ist Eure grosse Schuld—Ihr seid mitverantwortlich für dies grausame Verbrechen" ("This is your monumental guilt – you share responsibility for these cruel crimes" (Marcuse 2001:126, illustration 12).

17. Or as Améry put it in his response to Simon Wiesenthal's question about forgiveness: "too many criminals are spared by the letter of the law,... too many of the murderers in uniform, too many bloody judges of yesterday, are spending their last years in peace" (Wiesenthal 1998:198).

18. The question whether and why individuals and societies should remember also the crimes, victims, and horrors of the past has also been considered, for example, by Ricoeur (1995, 2004).

19. A very interesting and international anthology on the memory of mass crimes is *Verbrechen Erinnern* edited by Knigge and Frei (2002). An interesting global perspective is developed in Levy and Sznaider (2001). Finally, an anthology of articles on memory culture from a Danish perspective has been published (in Danish) in Brudholm and Mennecke (2004).

20. An awareness of collective liability emerges from the widespread guilty conduct of individuals in the past. It has nothing to do with the ascription of collective guilt (Habermas 2001b:31).

21. Roman Herzog represented the prevailing official opinion when he said that the majority of Germans living today bear no guilt for Auschwitz. But of course they have a particular responsibility to ensure that something like the Holocaust, like Auschwitz, never happens again (*Frankfurter Allgemeine Zeitung*, January 21, 1999, cited in Niven 2002:175).

CHAPTER 12 WISHFUL THINKING?

1. For an interesting article on the emotional aspect of reconciliation, see "Rehumanizing the Other: Empathy and Reconciliation," by Jody Halpern and Harvey M. Weinstein, in *Human Rights Quarterly* (2004).

2. ". . . die Auslöschung der Schande"(Améry 2002b:143). In the so-called Walser-Bubis debate in 1998, part of the debate turned on Martin Walser's use of the term *Schande* (disgrace) as the possible result of something that simply happens to one and, thus, as a term for evading the facing of responsibility (see Niven 2002:188).

3. The most notable point of reference in relation to such accounts of resentment is Jean Hampton (Murphy and Hampton 1988).

4. This idea, that the conflict is "our problem" and that its settlement would also be to the good of the Germans, is the Hegelian premise of Améry's deliberation (see Chaumont 1990:36).

5. The conjectural character of the "happy moments" of the essay was already indicated in relation to the example of Wajs, where Améry carefully wrote that he "would like to believe that . . ." and that "at least this is the way it seems to me now" (70 and 71).

6. The last essay contains several examples of the emphasis on an unbroken continuity between past and present. For example: "Being a Jew not only means that I bear within me a catastrophe that occurred yesterday and cannot be ruled out for tomorrow, it is—beyond being a duty—also *fear*. Every morning when I get up I can read the Auschwitz number one my forearm, something that touches the deepest and most closely intertwined roots of my existence. . . . Then I feel approximately as I did back then when I got a taste of the first blow from a policeman's fist" (94).

7. See "In den Wind gesprochen" (in Améry 1982:279–303), in particular: „Zorn erhält jung, sagt man. Ist er aber begleitet vom Gefühl völliger Ohnmacht, führt er hin zu einer Trauer, die keine ‚Trauerarbeit' im Sinne der Psychoanalyse ist, sondern Resignation. Und dies macht alt, zweifellos. Man spricht in den Wind. Die Stimme wird brüchig, muss erlöschen, noch ehe der Sprechende abtritt. Dennoch, der ohnmächtige Zorn ist da."(Amery 1982:279). In English: "Anger keeps one youthful, as the saying goes. But if it is accompanied by a feeling of sheer helplessness, it leads to a sort of sorrow that is not 'Trauerarbeit' [i.e. the work of mourning] in the sense of psychoanalysis but resignation. And resignation ages us, without doubt. We waste our breath. The voice becomes cracked and must extinguish even before the speaker makes his exit. Yet the helpless anger is there" (trans. Claudia Welz).

CHAPTER 13 A MULTIFARIOUS RECEPTION

1. In German: The essay is "'starker Tobak'—hoffentlich nicht allzu stark für Ihre Hörer. Nur ist es so, dass ein solcher Essay entweder mit völliger Aufrichtigkeit oder gar nicht geschrieben werden konnte" (cited in Heidelberger-Leonard 2004:123).

2. Philosophical works that broach Améry's concept of *ressentiment* but remain beyond the cluster of works especially pertinent here include the following: "Coexistence and Repair," by Elizabeth V. Spelman (2003) mentions Améry in its cautionary reflection on the limits of repair. Enzo Traverso broaches the meaning of *ressentiment* in a general comparison of Primo Levi and Jean Améry in *Die Intellektuellen und die Shoah Auschwitz Denken* (Traverso 2000). A comparison of Améry and Levi that is more focused on resentment can be found in Vetlesen (2006). Tzetan Todorov includes sporadic discussions of Améry in various places in his *Facing the Extreme: Moral Life in the Concentration Camps* (1997). W. G. Sebald has considered Améry in relation to the postwar German literary scene in "Against the Irreversible" (Sebald 2003). Panu Minkkinen includes Améry's essay in an interesting discussion of resentment and forgiveness in the context of transitional justice in "*Ressentiment* as Suffering: On Transitional Justice and the Impossibility of Forgiveness" (Minkkinen 2007). Studies of the background and reception of "*Ressentiments*" can be found in the excellent commentary to *Werke*, vol. 2 by Gerhard Scheitert (Améry 2002b) and in the first intellectual and recently published biography, *Jean Améry: Revolte in der Resignation* (Heidelberger-Leonard, I. 2004).

3. In German: "dass weit über Verbrechen und Bestrafung der unmittelbar Schuldigen hinaus jeder einzelne ein Interesse daran hat, die Verbindung zwischen den getrennten Teilen der Gesellschaft wiederherzustellen, weil ihre Unterbrechung die gemeinsame Grundlage ihrer Existenz verletz und folglich allen schadet" (Chaumont 1990:36).

4. See Chaumont (1990:36). According to Chaumont, the most relevant text lurking in the background is Hegel's "Der Geist des Christentums und sein Shicksal" ("The Spirit of Christianity and Its Destiny"; Hegel 1974). Another relevant source—if one was to trace the influence of Hegel in Améry—would be Hegel's *Elements of the Philosophy of Right* (Hegel 2003:97–99), in which the idea of the negation of the negation is also used in relation to the punishment of crimes.

5. The distance to Tutu's concept of *ubuntu*, as we were introduced to it in Chapter 5, is not far. The emphasis on interdependence is shared. Yet, there is at least one salient difference, and it has to do with a clear recognition that the *ressentiment* of the victim can be part of a conscientious attempt to repair relationships.

6. As Heyd writes, Tutu promotes a future-oriented view of restorative justice that is not blind to the past because it requires a "process of disclosure" (194).

7. The displacement of the forward-looking points of Améry's reasoning also obtains when Heyd identifies Améry's "moral daydream" (in parentheses) with the wish to inspire the entire society with the resentful perspective of the victim (191). This is, again, consistent with Heyd's picture of Améry's as a moral retrospectivist, but it is hardly compatible with Améry's promulgation of the dream of a Germany where even the surviving Nazi victims could feel at home again. Similarly, Heyd mentions Améry's demand that Germany internalize the Third Reich, but he only states that demand. He does not add the forward-looking vision of redemption or an overcoming of the past to explain why Améry raises so vehemently the demand for an internalization.

8. The place of Améry in Neiman and Agamben is, in both cases, limited to a couple of pages. Agamben and Neiman do not present readings of Améry, but simply pay attention to his essay as part of a larger argument.

9. "The wish to undo an evil that was done to you in the past is the very model of senseless obsession. If you cannot abandon it, you will be trapped in the sterile self-defeat

of rage without revenge, pain without relief. Just this picture capture the survivor—said Améry after examining himself" (Neiman 2002:265).

10. According to Agamben, "the ethics of the twentieth century opens with Nietzsche's overcoming of resentment" (99). The Nietzschean injunction to assume the past and to transform every "it was" into a "thus I wanted it to be" (cf. *Zarathrusta*, Nietzsche 1891/1969:161) does, however, not apply to Auschwitz. Agamben hammers out the point by reformulating the challenge to the will proposed by Nietzsche in *The Gay Science*: "Let us imagine repeating the experiment that Nietzsche, under the heading 'The Heaviest Weight,' proposes in *The Gay Science*. 'One day or night,' a demon glides beside a survivor and asks: 'Do you want Auschwitz to return again and again, innumerable times, do you want every instant, every single detail of the camp to repeat itself for eternity. . . . Do you want this to happen again, again and again for eternity?' This simple reformulation of the experiment suffices to refute it beyond all doubt, excluding even the possibility of its even being proposed" (Agamben 1999:99).

11. I would like to thank Margaret Walker for providing me with her manuscript to *Moral Repair* before it was published.

12. As Reemtsma puts it: "[W]enn eine Sozietät ihre Indolenz an beidem übt in dem, wie Améry es nannte, »unisono rundum erhobenen Friedensruf, der da aufgeräumt vorschlägt: Nicht rückwärts lasst uns schauen, sondern vorwärts, in eine bessere, gemeinsame Zukunft!«, dann wird sie sich mit dem Zerstörungswerk fortfahren (Reemtsma 1996:86).

CHAPTER 14 EPILOGUE

1. The excerpt is taken from a transcript of an interview of Eric Stover by Harry Kreisler, February 16, 1999 at Berkeley. The transcript and the interview can be retrieved from http://globetrotter.berkeley.edu/people/Stover/stover-con99-5.html (accessed April 21, 2007).

2. Among Stover's publications, *The Witnesses: War Crimes and the Promise of Justice in The Hague* (2005) is of particular relevance to the concerns of this book.

3. As noted in the *Wörterbuch*, the neutral use of the noun can be found in Molière's *Le Malade Imaginaire* (*The Imaginary Invalid*): "Souffrez, mon père . . . que j'embrasse pour vous témoigner mon ressentiment." That is, a daughter asks her father (whom she, falsely, believes to be dead) to allow her to kiss him to show him her *ressentiment*! In this case it is an intense and renewed feeling of genuine sorrow—not spite.

4. Améry's protest against the therapeutic reduction of his *ressentiment* has only become more important today. As Martha Minow has observed, "The striking prevalence of therapeutic language in contemporary discussions of mass atrocities stands in contrast to comparable debates fifty years ago" (1998:22).

APPENDIX 2 GENOCIDE AND CRIMES AGAINST HUMANITY

1. According to M. Cherif Bassiouni, the term "crimes against humanity" originated in the 1907 Hague Convention preamble (Bassiouni 1999:107). Yet, although the convention is important to the history of the *concept*, the actual *term* is not used in the preamble, only a reference to the "laws of humanity."

2. A philosophical analysis of the concept of "crimes against humanity" can be found in Geras (2005).

3. Antonio Cassese writes, "The wordings of the relevant provisions [in Charter of the International Military Tribunal, Article 6© and in Control Council Law No. 10, Article II(1c)] clearly shows that crimes against humanity encompassed genocide" (2002b:335).

4. Arendt even seems to identify "*the* crime against humanity" whose intent and purpose were unprecedented" (1987:275, italics added) with the Nazi genocide.

5. In Article 7.2, the enumerated criminal acts are further explained as follows:

(a) "Attack directed against any civilian population" means a course of conduct involving the multiple commission of acts referred to in paragraph 1 against any civilian population, pursuant to or in furtherance of a State or organizational policy to commit such attack.

(b) "Extermination" includes the intentional infliction of conditions of life, *inter alia* the deprivation of access to food and medicine, calculated to bring about the destruction of part of a population.

(c) "Enslavement" means the exercise of any or all of the powers attaching to the right of ownership over a person and includes the exercise of such power in the course of trafficking in persons, in particular women and children.

(d) "Deportation or forcible transfer of population" means forced displacement of the persons concerned by expulsion or other coercive acts from the area in which they are lawfully present, without grounds permitted under international law.

(e) "Torture" means the intentional infliction of severe pain or suffering, whether physical or mental, upon a person in the custody or under the control of the accused; except that torture shall not include pain or suffering arising only from, inherent in or incidental to, lawful sanctions.

(f) "Forced pregnancy" means the unlawful confinement of a woman forcibly made pregnant, with the intent of affecting the ethnic composition of any population or carrying out other grave violations of international law. This definition shall not in any way be interpreted as affecting national laws relating to pregnancy.

(g) "Persecution" means the intentional and severe deprivation of fundamental rights contrary to international law by reason of the identity of the group or collectivity.

(h) "The crime of apartheid" means inhumane acts of a character similar to those referred to in paragraph 1, committed in the context of an institutionalized regime of systematic oppression and domination by one racial group over any other racial group or groups and committed with the intention of maintaining that regime.

(i) "Enforced disappearance of persons" means the arrest, detention or abduction of persons by, or with the authorization, support or acquiescence of, a State or a political organization, followed by a refusal to acknowledge that deprivation of freedom or to give information on the fate or whereabouts of those persons, with the intention of removing them from the protection of the law for a prolonged period of time.

6. This does not mean that the prosecution must be able to prove that the accused was able to "anticipate all the specific consequences of his misconduct" (362). The

philosopher Larry May argues that convictions of persons accused of crimes against humanity should include a proof of special intent (like convictions for genocide). The "minor" player who has raped and tortured with the "mere" knowledge that his behavior was part of a widespread and systematic attack should *not* be prosecuted for crimes against humanity. The latter is only justifiable when the perpetrator has acted with *discriminatory intent*; that is when he intended to harm his victims because of their group membership. According to May, without the requirement of discriminatory intent, the connection between collective violence and the acts of the individual defendant will remain unclear and prosecutions will be unjustified (cf. May 2004).

7. Orentlicher refers to a 1946 article on crimes against humanity by Egon Schwelb: "'humanity' has at least two different meanings, the one connotating [sic] the human race or mankind as a whole, and the other humaneness, i.e. a certain quality of behaviour"(Orentlicher 1998:14).

8. The term combines the Greek "genos" (race, tribe) with the Latin "cide" (killing).

9. The incredible vehemence with which Lemkin fought to extend international law to include genocide is described vividly in Samantha Power's 2002 bestseller, *A Problem from Hell*.

10. Judgment, the Akayesu case, 2 September 1998 (ICTR-96-4-T, para. 16). Cf. also "the prime illustration of a crime against humanity"(the Justice Case under Control Council Law No. 10, quoted from Orentlicher 1998:18).

11. Meaning, respectively, that their principles are regarded as binding on states even without conventional obligation and that they constitute peremptory norms (i.e., they may not be derogated from by an international agreement; Cassese 2002b:338).

12. Actually, the only quantitative requirement that can be inferred from the definition of genocide in international law is, according to Cassese, "that genocide cannot exist when there is only one victim" (Cassese 2002b:348).

13. Lemkin's struggles to make the intentional destruction of entire groups recognized as a crime under international law began much earlier. In 1933 he had advocated for the adoption of two new crimes, that is "the crime of Barbarism" and the "crime of Vandalism" (cf. Lemkin 1933).

14. Thorough and authoritative legal examinations of the law in relation to the jurisprudence of the two ad hoc tribunals (ICTY and ICTR) and other sources can be found in Cassese (2002b) and Schabas (2000). Mennecke and Markusen (2003) consider the viability and appropriateness of the UN Convention.

15. ICTY in The Hague was established in 1993 and ICTR in Arusha in 1994. It is often stated that the first conviction of genocide was given in Arusha 1998. That is of course also correct, but in a broader perspective it is noteworthy that two Nazi defendants was found guilty of "the crime of genocide" in a tribunal working under Control Council Law No. 10 (Orentlicher 1998:18).

16. In David Scheffer's "Genocide and Atrocity Crimes" (2006), he presents and shapes a new policy term "atrocitiy crimes" and argues that the political use of the term "genocide" should be liberated from its legal definition as a crime of individual responsibility.

Works Cited

Acorn, Annalise. 2004. *Compulsory Compassion: A Critique of Restorative Justice.* Vancouver: UBC Press.

Adams, Robert M. 2002. *Finite and Infinite Goods: A Framework for Ethics.* New York: Oxford University Press.

Adorno, Theodor W. 1973. *Negative Dialectics,* trans. E. B. Ashton. London: Routledge.

———. 1986. What Does Coming to Terms With the Past Mean? In *Bitburg in Moral and Political Perspective,* ed. G. Hartman and trans. T. Bahti. Bloomington: Indiana University Press.

———. 2000. *The Adorno Reader,* ed. Brian O'Connor. Oxford: Blackwell.

Agamben, Giorgio. 1999. *Remnants of Auschwitz,* trans. D. Heller-Roazen. New York: Zone Books.

Akhavan, Payam. 2001. Beyond Impunity: Can International Criminal Justice Prevent Future Atrocities? *American Journal of International Law* 95 (7): 7–31.

Aldana, Raquel. 2006. A Victim-Centered Reflection on Truth Commissions and Prosecutions as a Response to Mass Atrocities. *Journal of Human Rights* 5 (1): 107–26.

Amann, Diane M. 2002. Group Mentality, Expressivism, and Genocide. *Netherland International Law Review* 2: 93–143.

Améry, Jean. 1976. *Hand an sich legen. Diskurs über den Freitod.* Stuttgart: Klett-Cotta.

———. 1977. Selbstmord—oder Freitod? *Meyers Enzyklopädisches Lexikon,* Vol. 21. Zürich: Bibliographisches Institut. Lexikonverlag: 547–50.

———. 1980. *Örtlichkeiten.* Stuttgart: Klett-Cotta.

———. 1982. *Weiterleben—aber wie? Essays 1968–1978,* ed. G. Lindemann. Stuttgart: Klett-Cotta.

___. 1984. *Radical Humanism*, trans. S. Rosenfeld and S.P. Rosenfeld. Bloomington: Indiana University Press.

___. 1966/1999. *At the Mind's Limits: Contemplations by a Survivor on Auschwitz and its Realities*, trans. S. Rosenfeld and S.P. Rosenfeld. London: Granta Books.

___. 2002a. *Jenseits von Schuld und Sühne: Bewältigungsversuche eines Überwältigten.* In *Jean Améry. Werke*, Vol. 2, ed. Gerhard Scheit. Stuttgart: Klett-Cotta.

___. 2002b. Jean Améry: *Ressentiments* (Werbe- und Klappentext-Entwurf, 1965/66). In *Jean Améry. Werke*, Vol. 2, ed. Gerhard Scheit. Stuttgart: Klett-Cotta: 623–24.

Amstutz, Mark R. 2005. *The Healing of Nations: The Promise and Limits of Political Forgiveness.* Lanham, MD: Rowham and Littlefield.

___. 2006. Restorative Justice, Political Forgiveness, and the Possibility of Political Reconciliation. In *Politics of Past Evil: Religion, Reconciliation, and the Dilemmas of Transitional Justice*, ed. D. Philpott. Notre Dame, IN: Notre Dame University Press.

Arendt, Hannah. 1965–66. Some questions of moral philosophy. In *Responsibility and Judgment: Hannah Arendt*, ed. Jerome Kohn. New York: Schocken Books: 49–146.

___. 1968a. Collective responsibility. In *Responsibility and Judgment: Hannah Arendt*, ed. Jerome Kohn. New York: Schocken Books: 147–58.

___. 1968b. *Men in Dark Times.* New York: Harcourt, Brace & World.

___. 1976. *The Origins of Totalitarianism.* New York: Harcourt.

___. 1978. *Eichmann in Jerusalem: A Report on the Banality of Evil.* New York: Penguin.

___. 1989. *The Human Condition.* Chicago: University of Chicago Press.

___. 1994. *Essays in Understanding: 1930–1954*, ed. Jerome Kohn. New York: Harcourt Brace.

___. 2003. *Responsibility and Judgment: Hannah Arendt*, ed. Jerome Kohn. New York: Schocken Books.

Aristotle. 1991. *The Nicomachean Ethics*, trans by D. Ross. Oxford: Oxford University Press.

Bacon, Francis. 1997/1625. *Essays.* Hertfordshire: Wordsworth.

Bandes, Susan A., ed. 1999. *The Passions of Law.* New York: New York University Press.

Barkan, Elazar. 2000. *The Guilt of Nations: Restitution and Negotiating Historical Injustices.* New York: W.W. Norton.

Bar-on, Zvi. 1985/1991. Measuring Responsibility. In *Collective Responsibility: Five Decades of Debate in Theoretical and Applied Ethics*, ed. L. May. Savage, MD: Rowman & Littlefield: 255–71.

Bass, Gary J. 2000. *Stay the Hand of Vengeance.* Princeton: Princeton University Press.

Bassioni, M.Cherif. 1999. Crimes Against Humanity. In *Crimes of War: What the Public Should Know*, ed. R. Gutman and D. Rieff. New York: W.W. Norton: 107–08.

Bauman, Zygmunt. 1989. *Modernity and the Holocaust.* New York: Cornell University Press.

Benjamin, Walter. 1988. Theses on the Philosophy of History. In *Illuminations*, trans. by H. Zohn. New York: Shocken Books: 253–64.

Berliner, Peter. 2006. Psykologi [Psychology]. In *Efter Folkedrab [After Genocide]*, ed. T. Brudholm and M. Mennecke. Copenhagen: DIIS Forlag: 181–204.

Bettelheim, Bruno 1980. *Surviving and Other Essays.* New York: Vintage Books.

Biggar, Nigel 2001. Forgiveness in the Twentieth Century: A Review of the Literature 1901–2001. In *Forgiveness and Truth*, ed. Alistair McFadyen and Marcel Sarot. Edinburgh: T&T Clark: 181–218.

Bonhoeffer, Dietrich. 1963. *The Cost of Discipleship*, trans. R.H. Fuller. New York: Macmillan.

Boraine, Alex. 2000. *A Country Unmasked: Inside South Africa's Truth and Reconciliation Commission.* Oxford: Oxford University Press.

Brudholm, Thomas. 2003. The Justice of Reconciliation. *Hypatia* 18 (2): 189–96.

———. 2005. *Resentment's Virtue: Jean Améry and the Morality of Unforgiving and Unreconciled Victims of Mass Atrocity.* Copenhagen: DPU Forlag.

———. 2006a. A Confiscated Past: Jean Améry on Home and Exile. *The Hedgehog Review* 7 (3): 7–19.

———. 2006b. Revisiting Resentments: Jean Améry and the Dark Side of Forgiveness and Reconciliation. *Journal of Human Rights* 5 (1): 7–26.

———. 2007b. Prosecuting Genocide. *Journal of Genocide Research* 9 (3).

———. 2007a: A light in the darkness: philosophical reflections on historians' assessments of the rescue of the Jews in Denmark in 1943, in R.M. Schott and Kirsten Klercke (eds.) *Philosophy on the border,* Copenhagen: Museum Tusculanum Press.

Brudholm, Thomas and Thomas Cushman, eds. 2006. A Special Issue on the Importance of Negative Emotions in Post-Conflict Societies. *Journal of Human Rights* 5 (1), 2006.

Brudholm, Thomas and Martin Mennecke. 2004. *Erindringens fremtid: Auschwitz-dag i Danmark* Copenhagen: Lindhardt og Ringhof.

Butler, Joseph. 1897. *Sermons by Joseph Butler, D.C.L. Sometime Lord Bishop of Furham.* Oxford: Clarendon Press.

Card, Claudia. 2002. *The Atrocity Paradigm: A Theory of Evil.* New York: Oxford University Press.

Carter, Chiara. 2006. Is the TRC Threatening to Become a Cold Case? *The Cape Argue.* 8: 15.

Caruth, Carly. 1995. *Trauma: Explorations in Memory.* Baltimore: Johns Hopkins University Press.

Cassese, Antonio. 2002a: Crimes Against Humanity. In *The Rome Statute of the International Criminal Court: A Commentary,* ed. A. Cassesse et al. Oxford: Oxford University Press: 353–78.

———. 2002b. Genocide. In *The Rome Statute of the International Criminal Court: A Commentary,* ed. A. Cassesse et al. Oxford: Oxford University Press: 335–51.

Cesarani, David. 2001. *Justice Delayed: How Britain Became a Refuge for Nazi War Criminals.* London: Phoenix Press.

———. 2004. Survivors, Liberation and Rebuilding Lives: Holocaust Memorial Day 2005, http://www.holocaustmemorialday.gov.uk (accessed 16 October 16, 2004).

Chapman, Audrey. 2001. Truth Commissions as Instruments of Forgiveness and Reconciliation. In *Forgiveness and Reconciliation,* ed. Raymond G. Helmick and Rodney L. Petersen. Philadelphia: Templeton Foundation Press.

Chaumont, Jean-Michel. 1990. Geschichtliche Verantwortung und menschliche Würde bei Jean Améry. In *Über Jean Améry,* ed., I. Heidelberger-Leonard. Heidelberg: Carl Winter Universitätsverlag: 29–47.

Chayes, Antonia and Martha Minow, eds. 2003. *Imagine Coexistence: Restoring Humanity After Violent Ethnic Conflict.* San Francisco: Jossey-Bass.

Claussen, Detlev. 1988. Nach Auschwitz: Ein Essay über die Aktualität Adornos. In *Die Zivilisationsbruch: Denken nach Auschwitz,* ed. D. Diner. Frankfurt am Main: Fischer Taschenbuch Verlag: 54–69.

Clendinnen, Inga. 1999. *Reading the Holocaust.* Cambridge: Cambridge University Press.

Cohen, David. 1999. Beyond Nuremberg: Individual Responsibility for War Crimes. In *Human Rights in Political Transitions: Gettysburg to Bosnia*, ed. Carla Hesse and Robert Post. New York: Zone Books: 53–92.

Cohen, Marshall, Thomas Nagel, and Thomas Scanlon, eds. 1974. *War and Moral Responsibility*. Princeton: Princeton University Press.

Constitutional Court of South Africa. 1996. *Azanian Peoples Organisation (AZAPO) and others v. The President of South Africa and others*, Case CCT 17/96, Judgment, July 25, 1996 (www.concourt.gov.za).

Crocker, D.A. 2000. Retribution and Reconciliation. Institute for Philosophy and Public Policy, http://www.puaf.umd.edu/IPPP/Winter-Spring00/retribution_and_reconciliation.htm (accessed December 3, 2004).

Deák, Istvan, Jan T. Gross, and Tony Judt, eds. 2000. *The Politics of Retribution in Europe. World War II and Its Aftermath*. Princeton: Princeton University Press.

Dembour, Marie-Bénédicte and Emily Haslam. 2004. Silencing Hearings? Victim-Witnesses at War Crimes Trials. *European Journal of International Law* 15 (1):151–77.

Derrida, Jacques. 2001. *On Cosmopolitanism and Forgiveness*, trans. M. Dooley and M. Hughes. London: Routledge.

Digeser, Peter E. 2001. *Political Forgiveness*. Ithaca: Cornell University Press.

Disch, Lisa J. 1993. More Truth Than Fact: Storytelling as Critical Understanding in the Writings of Hannah Arendt. *Political Theory* 21 (4): 665–94.

Dizdarevic, Zlatko. 1993. *Sarajevo: A War Journal*. New York: Fromm International.

Dostoyevsky, Fyodor. 1864/1993. *Notes From the Underground*, trans. R. Pevear and L. Volokhonsky. London: Vintage.

Douglas, Lawrence. 2001. *The Memory of Judgment: Making Law and History in the Trials of the Holocaust*. New Haven: Yale University Press.

Drakulic, Slavenka. 2004. *They Would Never Hurt a Fly: War Criminals on Trial in The Hague*. London: Abacus.

Dwyer, Susan. 1999. Reconciliation for Realists. *Ethics and International Affairs* 13: 81–98.

Edkins, Jenny. 2003. *Trauma and the Politics of Memory*. Cambridge: Cambridge University Press.

Etcheson, Craig. 2003. Beyond the Khmer Rouge Tribunal. *Phom Penh Post*, 12/22.

Falk, Richard A., Gabriel Kolko, and Robert J. Lifton, eds. 1971. *Crimes of War*. New York: Vintage Books.

Farmer, Sarah. 2000. Postwar Justice in France: Bordeaux 1953. In *The Politics of Retribution in Europe. World War II and Its Aftermath*, ed. Istvan Deák, Jan T. Gross, and Tony Judt. Princeton: Princeton University Press.

Fisher, Phillip. 2002. *The Vehement Passions*. Princeton: Princeton University Press.

Fischer, Thomas. 2003. Vorwort. In *Karrieren im Zwielicht: Hitlers Eliten nach 1945*, ed. Norbert Frei. München: Deutscher Taschenbuch Verlag: 7–12.

Fletcher, Laurel E. and Harvey M. Weinstein. 2004. Violence and Social Repair: Rethinking the Contribution of Justice to Reconciliation. *Human Rights Quarterly* 24: 573–639.

Forsberg, Tuomas. 2001. The Philosophy and Practice of Dealing With the Past: Some Conceptual and Normative Issues. In *Burying the Past: Making Peace and Doing Justice After Civil Conflict*, ed. N. Biggar. Washington, DC: Georgetown University Press: 57–72.

Frei, Norbert. 2000. *Von deutscher erfindungskraft oder: Die kollektivschuldthese in der nachkriegszeit*. In *Hannah Arendt revisited: "Eichmann in Jerusalem und die folgen,* ed. G. Smith. Frankfurt am Main: Suhrkamp: 163–76.

———.2002. *Adenauer's Germany and the Nazi Past: The Politics of Amnesty and Integration,* trans. J. Golb. New York: Columbia University Press.

———. ed. 2003. *Hitlers eliten nach 1945.* München: Deutscher Taschenbuch Verlag.

French, Peter A. 1972. *Individual and Collective Responsibility: Massacre at My Lai.* Cambridge MA:Schenkman Publishing.

———.2001 *The Virtues of Vengeance.* Lawrence, KS; University Press of Kansas.

Garrard, Eve. 2003. Forgiveness and the Holocaust. In *Moral Philosophy and the Holocaust,* ed. E. Garrard and G. Scarre. Aldershot: Ashgate.

Garrard, Eve and Geoffrey Scarre, eds. 2003. *Moral Philosophy and the Holocaust.* Aldershot: Ashgate.

Geras, Norman. 1999. *The Contract of Mutual Indifference: Political Philosophy After the Holocaust.* London: Verso.

———. 2005. Genocide and Crimes Against Humanity. In *Genocide and Human Rights: A Philosophical Guide,* ed. J.K. Roth. New York: Palgrave MacMillan.

Gerner, Kristian. 2003. Ambivalence, Bivalence and Polyvalence: Historical Culture in the German-Polish Borderlands. In *Echoes of the Holocaust: Historical Cultures in Contemporary Europe,* ed. K. Karlsson and U. Zander. Lund: Nordic Academic Press: 115–40.

Gilbert, Margaret. 2000. *Sociality and Responsibility.* Lanham, MD: Rowman and Littlefield.

Giordano, Ralph. 2000. *Die zweite schuld—oder Von der Last Deutscher zu sein.* Köln: KiWi.

Glover, Jonathan. 2001. *Humanity: A Moral History of the Twentieth Century.* New Haven: Yale University Press.

Goldie, Peter. 2002. *The Emotions: A Philosophical Exploration.* Oxford: Clarendon.

Govier, Trudy. 2002. *Forgiveness and Revenge.* London: Routledge.

Graybill, Lyn S. 2002. *Truth and Reconciliation in South Africa: Miracle or Model?* Boulder: Lynne Rienner Publishers.

Gready, Paul, ed. 2003. *Political Transition: Politics and Cultures.* London: Pluto Press.

Grøn, Arne. 2006. The Limits of Ethics—The Ethics of the Limit. Paper presented at the conference, "The Religious Responses to Mass Atrocity," Danish Institute for International Studies, Copenhagen, May 12–13.

Grunebaum-Ralph, Heidi Stier, and Oren Stier. 1999. Remains: Remembering Shoah, Forgetting Reconciliation. In *Facing the Truth: South African Faith Communities and the Truth & Reconciliation Commissions,* ed. J. Cochrane et al. Claremont, South Africa: David Phillips Publishers.

Gutman, Roy and David Rieff, eds. 1999. *Crimes of War: What the Public Should Know.* New York: W.W. Norton.

Habermas, Jürgen. 1987. *Eine Art Schadenabwicklung.* Frankfurt am Main: Suhrkamp.

———. 1989. *The New Conservatism,* trans. S.W. Nicholson. Cambridge, MA: MIT Press.

———. 1998. What Does Working off the Past Mean Today? In *A Berlin Republic: Writings on Germany,* trans. S. Rendall. Cambridge: Polity Press: 17–40.

———. 2001a. Der zeigefinger. Die Deutschen und ihr Denkmal. In *Zeit der Übergänge.* Frankfurt am Main: Suhrkamp: 47–59.

____. 2001b. *The Postnational Constellation*, trans. M. Pensky. Cambridge: Polity Press.

Haffner, Sebastian 2003. *Defying Hitler*, trans. O. Pretzel. New York: Picador.

Halpern, Jody and Harvey M. Weinstein. 2004. Rehumanizing the Other: Empathy and Reconciliation. *Human Rights Quarterly* 26: 561–83.

Hamber, Brandon. 1997. When Should Society Tire of the Voices of the Past? *Mail and Guardian*, January 17, http://brandonhamber.com (accessed November 15, 2004).

Hamber, Brandon and Richard Wilson. 2002. Symbolic Closure Through Memory, Reparation and Revenge in Post-Conflict Societies. *Journal of Human Rights* 1 (1): 35–53.

Harris, William V. 2001. *Restraining Rage: The Ideology of Anger Control in Classical Antiquity*. Cambridge, MA: Harvard University Press.

Hatzfeld, Jean 2005. *Into the Quick of Life: The Rwandan Genocide—The Survivors Speak*. London: Serpent's Tail.

____. 2006. *Machete Season: The Killers in Rwanda Speak*, trans. L. Coverdale. New York: Picador.

Hayner, Priscilla. 2002. *Unspeakable Truths: Facing the Challenge of Truth Commissions*. New York: Routledge.

Hegel, Friedrich. 1974. *Der Geist des Christentums und sein Shicksal*. Frankfurt am Main: Suhrkamp: 274–418.

____. 2001. *The Philosophy of History*, trans. J. Sibree. Kitchener, Ontario: Battoche Books.

____. 2003. *Elements of the Philosophy of Right*, trans. H.B. Nisbet. Cambridge: Cambridge University Press.

Heidelberger-Leonard, Irene. 2004. *Jean Améry: Revolte in der Resignation*. Stuttgart: Klett-Cotta.

Helmick, Raymond G. and Rodney L. Petersen, eds. 2001. *Forgiveness and Reconciliation: Religion, Public Policy, and Conflict Transformation*. Philadelphia: Templeton Foundation Press.

Herf, Jeffrey. 1997. *Divided Memory: The Nazi Past in the Two Germanys*. Cambridge, MA: Harvard University Press.

Herman, Judith L. 1992. *Trauma and Recovery*. New York: Basic Books.

Hermann, Ingo. 1992. *Jean Améry, der Grenzgänger: Gespräch mit Ingo Herman in der reihe: Zeugen des Jahrhunderts'.* Göttingen: Lamuv.

Hesse, Carla and Robert Post, eds. 1999. *Human Rights in Political Transitions: Gettysburg to Bosnia*. New York: Zone Books.

Heyd. David. 2004. Ressentiment and Reconciliation. Alternative Responses to Historical Evil. In *Justice in Time. Responding to Historical Injustice*, ed. L. H. Meyer. Baden-Baden: Nomos: 185–97.

Hieronymi, Pamela. 2001. Articulating an Uncompromising Forgiveness. *Philosophy and Phenomenological Research* 62: 529–56.

Hochschild. Adam. 1998. *King Leopold's Ghost*. London: Papermac.

Honneth, Axel. 1995. *The Struggle for Recognition: The Moral Grammar of Social Conflicts*, trans. J. Anderson. Cambridge: Polity Press.

Ignatieff, Michael. 2001. The Legacy of Raphael Lemkin. Lecture at the United States Holocaust Memorial Museum, December 13, http://www.ushmm.org/conscience/analysis/details.php?content=2000-12-13 (accessed April 19, 2007).

____. 2003. Afterword: Reflections on Coexistence. In *Imagine Coexistence: Restoring Humanity After Violent Ethnic Conflict*, ed. A. Chayes and M. Minow. San Francisco: Jossey-Bass: 325–34.

Interim Constitution of the Republic of South Africa. 1993. At http://www.doj.gov.za/trc/trc_frameset.htm (accessed April 19, 2007).

Jacoby, Susan. 1988. *Wild Justice: The Evolution of Revenge*. New York: Harper & Row.

Jankélévitch, Vladimir. 1986. *L'imprescriptible*. Paris: éditions du Seuil.

____. (1996). Should We Pardon Them? *Critical Inquiry* 22 (3): 552–72.

Jaspers, Karl. 2000. *The Question of German Guilt*, trans. E.B. Ashton. New York: Fordham University Press.

Jonas, Hans. 1984. *The Imperative of Responsibility*. Chicago: University of Chicago Press.

Judah, Tim. 2004. The Fog of Justice: *New York Times Review of Books*, January 15: 23–25.

Kaplan, Suzanne. 2002.*Children in the Holocaust: Dealing With Affects and Memory Images in Trauma and Generational Linking*. Stockholm: Department of Education, Stockholm University.

Karlsson, Karl and Ulf Zander, eds. 2003. *Echoes of the Holocaust: Historical Cultures in Contemporary Europe*. Lund: Nordic Academic Press.

Kearney, Richard, ed. 1996. *Paul Ricoeur: The Hermeneutics of Action*. London: Sage Publications.

Kellenbach, Katharina von. 2001a. Christian Discourses of Forgiveness and the Perpetrators. In *Remembering for the Future*, ed. J.K. Roth and E. Maxwell. Hampshire: Palgrave: 725–31.

____. 2001b. Future Directions for Christian Theology and Ethics After the Holocaust. In *Remembering for the Future*, ed. J.K. Roth and E. Maxwell. Hampshire: Palgrave: 656–60.

Kellenbach, Katharina von, Björn Krondorfer, and Norbert Reck, eds. 2001. *Von Gott reden im Land der Täter: Theologische Stimmen in der dritten Generation seit der Shoah*. Darmstadt: Wissenschaftlicher Buchverlag.

Krondorfer, Björn, Katharina von Kellenbach, and Norbert Reck. (2006). *Mit blick auf die Täter: Fragen an die deutche Theologie nach 1945*. München: Güterloher Verlagshaus.

Kenny, Anthony. 2003. *Action, Emotion and Will*. London: Routledge.

Kertesz, Imre. 1996. Die Panne: der Holocaust als Kultur. In *Jean Améry* [Hans Maier], ed. S. Steiner. Basel/Frankfurt am Main: Stroemfeld/Nexus: 13–24.

Kiss, Elizabeth. 2003. Moral Ambition Within and Beyond Political Constraints: Reflections on Restorative Justice. In *Truth v. Justice: The Morality of Truth Commissions*, ed. R.I. Rotberg and D. Thompson. Princeton: Princeton University Press: 68–98.

Knigge, Volkhard and Norbert Frei eds. 2002. *Verbrechen Erinnern*. München: C. H. Beck.

Kolnai, Aurel. 1973/74. Forgiveness. *Proceedings of the Aristotelean Society*, LXXIV.

Kritz, Neil, ed. 1995. *Transitional Justice: How Emerging Democracies Reckon With Former Regimes*, 3 vols. Washington, DC: U.S. Institute of Peace Press.

____. 2002. Progress and Humility: The Ongoing Search for Post-Conflict Justice. In *Post-Conflict Justice*, ed. M. S. Bassiouni. Ardsley, NY: Transnational Publishers: 55–87.

Krog, Antjie. 2000. *Country of My Skull: Guilt, Sorrow, and the Limits of Forgiveness in the New South Africa*. New York: Times Books.

Lamb, Sharon. 2006. Forgiveness, Women, and Responsibility to the Group. *Journal of Human Rights: A Special Issue on the Importance of Negative Emotions in Post-Conflict Societies* 5 (1), 2006: 45–60.

Lamb, Sharon and Jeffrey G. Murphy, eds. 2002. *Before Forgiving*. New York: Oxford University Press.

Landgren, Karin. 1998. Reconciliation: Forgiveness in the Time of Repatriation, World Refugee Survey, 20–26.

Landsman, Stephan. 2005. *Crimes of the Holocaust: The Law Confronts Hard Cases*. Philadelphia, PA: University of Pennsylvania Press, 2005.

Lang, Berel. 1999. *The Future of the Holocaust: Between History and Memory*. Ithaca: Cornell University Press.

___. 2005. *Post-Holocaust: Interpretation, Misinterpretation, and the Claims of History*. Bloomington: Indiana University Press.

Langer, Lawrence. 1991. *Holocaust Testimonies: The Ruins of Memory*. New Haven: Yale University Press.

___. 1998. *Preempting the Holocaust*. New Haven: Yale University Press.

___. 2006. Memory and Justice After the Holocaust and Apartheid. In *Using and Abusing the Holocaust*. Bloomington: Indiana University Press: 82–96.

Lanzmann, Claude 1986. *Shoah*. Düsseldorf: Claassen.

Lemkin, Raphael. 1933. Les actes constituant un danger général (interétatique) considérés comme délits des droits des gens. Explications additionnelles au Rapport spécial présentè à la V-éme Conférence pour l'Unification du Droit Penal à Madrid (14-2O.X.1933), http://www.preventgenocide.org/lemkin/

___. (1944). *Axis Rule in Occupied Europe*. Washington, DC: Carnegie Endowment for International Peace.

Levi, Primo. 1947. *If This is a Man*. New York: Penguin.

___. 1987. *Survival in Auschwitz*, trans. S. Woolf. New York: Collier Books.

___. 1988. *The Drowned and the Saved*, trans. R. Rosenthal. New York: Summit Books.

___. 1993. *The Reawakening*, trans. S. Woolf. New York: Collier Books.

___. 2001. *The Voice of Memory: Interviews 1961–1987*, ed. by M. Belpoliti and R. Gordon; trans. R. Gordon. New York: New Press.

Levy, Daniel and Natan Sznaider. 2001. *Erinnerung im globalen Zeitalter: der Holocaust*. Frankfurt am Main: Suhrkamp.

___. 2002. Memory Unbound: The Holocaust and the Formation of Cosmopolitan Memory. *European Journal of Social Theory* 5 (1): 87–106.

Lincoln, Bruce. 2003. *Holy Terrors: Thinking About Religion After September 11*. Chicago: Chicago University Press.

Lübbe, Hermann. 2001. *"Ich entschuldige mich": Das neue politische Bussritual*. Berlin: Siedler.

Maass, Peter. 1996. *Love Thy Neighbor: A Story of War*. New York: Alfred A. Knopf.

Maier, Charles. 1997. *The Unmasterable Past: History, Holocaust, and German National Identity*. Cambridge, MA: Harvard University Press.

Marcuse, Herbert. 2001. *Legacies of Dachau*. Cambridge: Cambridge University Press.

May, Larry, ed. 1991. *Collective Responsibility: Five Decades of Debate in Theoretical and Applied Ethics*. Savage, MD: Rowman & Littlefield.

___. 2004. *Crimes Against Humanity: A Normative Account*. New York: Cambridge University Press.

McFall, Lynne. 1991. What's Wrong With Bitterness? In *Feminist Ethics: Problems, Projects, Prospects*, ed. C. Card. Lawrence, KS: Kansas University Press: 147–60.

McGoldric, Dominic et al., eds. 2004. *The Permanent International Criminal Court: Legal and Policy Issues*. Oxford: Hart Publishing.

Mennecke, Martin and Eric Markusen. 2003. The International Criminal Tribunal for the Former Yugoslavia and the Crime of Genocide. In *Genocide: Cases, Comparisons and Contemporary Debates*, ed. S.L.B. Jensen. Copenhagen: Danish Center for Holocaust and Genocide Studies: 293–360.

Meyer, Lukas H., ed. 2004. *Justice in Time. Responding to Historical Injustice*. Baden-Baden: Nomos.

Minkkinen, Panu. (2007). *Ressentiment* as Suffering: On Transitional Justice and the Impossibility of Forgiveness. *Law and Literature* 19 (2).

Minow, Martha. 1998. *Between Vengeance and Forgiveness*. Boston: Beacon Press.

___. 1999. Institutions and Emotions: Redressing Mass Violence. In *The Passions of Law*, ed. S. A. Bandes. New York: New York University Press: 265–81.

___. 2002. *Breaking the Cycles of Hatred: Memory, Law, and Repair*, introduced and with commentaries edited by N. L. Rosenblum. Princeton: Princeton University Press.

Morris, Herbert. 1992. The Decline of Guilt. In *Ethics and Personality*, ed. J. Deigh. Chicago: University of Chicago Press.

Morton, Adam. 2004. *On Evil*. New York: Routledge.

Müller-Fahrenholz, Geiko. 1997. *The Art of Forgiveness—Theological Reflections on Healing and Reconciliation*. Geneva: World Council of Churches.

Murphy, Jeffrie G. 1999. Moral Epistemology, the Retributive Emotions, and the "Clumsy Moral Philosophy" of Jesus Christ. In *The Passions of Law*, ed. S. Bandes. New York: New York University Press.

___. 2000. Getting Even: The Role of the Victim. In *Philosophy of Law* (6th ed.), ed. J. Feinberg and J. Coleman. Belmont: Wadsworth: 788–98.

___. 2002. Forgiveness in Counseling: A Philosophical Perspective. In *Before Forgiving*, ed. S. Lamb and J. G. Murphy. New York: Oxford University Press.

___. 2003. *Getting Even: Forgiveness and Its Limits*. New York: Oxford University Press.

Murphy, Jeffrie G. and Jean Hampton. 1988. *Forgiveness and Mercy*. Cambridge: Cambridge University Press.

Neier, Aryeh. 1998. *War Crimes: Brutality, Genocide, Terror, and the Struggle for Justice*. New York: Random House.

___. 1999. Rethinking Truth, Justice, and Guilt After Bosnia and Rwanda. In *Human Rights in Political Transitions: Gettysburg to Bosnia*, ed. Carla Hesse and Robert Post. New York: Zone Books: 39–52.

Neiman, Susan. 1997. October 1978: Jean Améry Takes His Life. In *Yale Companion to Jewish Writing and Thought in German Culture 1096–1996*, ed. S.L. Gilman and J. Zipes. New Haven: Yale University Press: 775–82.

___. 2002. *Evil in Modern Thought*. Princeton: Princeton University Press.

Neu, Jerome. 2002. To Understand All Is to Forgive All—Or Is It? In *Before Forgiving*, ed. S. Lamb and J. Murphy. New York: Oxford University Press: 17–38.

Neuffer, Elizabeth. 2001. *The Key to My Neighbor's House: Seeking Justice in Bosnia and Rwanda*. New York: Picador.

Niebuhr, Reinhold. 1946. *Discerning the Signs of the Times: Sermons for Today and Tomorrow*. London: Charles Scribner's Sons.

Niederland, William G. 1980. *Volgen der Verfolgung: Das Überlebenden-Syndrom Seelenmord.* Frankfurt am Main: Suhrkamp.

Nietzsche, Friedrich. 1888/1979. *Ecce homo.* London: Penguin.

___. 1887/1998. *On the Genealogy of Morality,* trans. M. Clark and A.J. Swensen. Indianapolis: Hackett.

___. 1891/1969. *Thus Spoke Zarathustra,* trans. R. J. Hollingdale. London: Penguin Books.

Niven, Bill. 2002. *Facing the Nazi Past: United Germany and the Legacy of the Third Reich.* London: Routledge.

Nobel Committee. 2002. Why Imre Kertész Received the Nobel Prize in Literature, http://nobelprize.org/literature/laureates/2002/press.html.

Novick, Peter. 1999. *The Fall and Rise of the Holocaust: The Holocaust in American Life.* Boston: Houghton Mifflin.

Nussbaum, Martha. 1992. *Love's Knowledge.* New York: Oxford University Press.

___. 1994. *The Therapy of Desire.* Princeton: Princeton University Press.

___. 2001. *Upheavals of Thought.* Cambridge: Cambridge University Press.

___. 2004. *Hiding From Humanity: Disgust, Shame, and the Law.* Princeton: Princeton University Press.

Orentlicher, Diane. 1998. The Law of Universal Conscience: Genocide and Crimes Against Humanity. Paper presented at the Committee of Conscience Conference, "Genocide and Crimes Against Humanity: Early Warning and Prevention," at the U.S. Holocaust Memorial Museum.

Osiel, Mark. 2000. Why Prosecute? Critics of Punishment for Mass Atrocity. *Human Rights Quarterly* 22: 118–47.

Ozick, Cynthia. 1998. Notes Toward a Mediation on "Forgiveness." In *The Sunflower: On the Possibilities and Limits of Forgiveness,* ed. Simon Wiesenthal. New York: Schocken Books: 213–20.

Parfit, Derek. 1984. *Reasons and Persons.* Oxford: Clarendon Press.

Pendas, Devin O. 2006. *The Frankfurt Auschwitz Trial, 1963-1965: Genocide, History, and the Limits of Law.* New York: Cambridge University Press.

Phelps, Theresa G. 2004. *Shattered Voice: Language, Violence, and the Work of Truth Commissions.* Philadelphia: University of Pennsylvania Press.

Philpott, Daniel, ed. 2006. *The Politics of the Past: Religion, Reconciliation, and the Dilemmas of Transitional Justice.* Notre Dame: University of Notre Dame Press.

Posel, Deborah. and Graeme Simpson, eds. 2002. *Commissioning the Past.* Johannesburg: Witwatersrand University Press.

Power, Samantha. 2002. *"A Problem From Hell": America and the Age of Genocide.* New York: Basic Books.

Prager, Carol and Trudy Govier, eds. 2003. *Dilemmas of Reconciliation: Cases and Concepts.* Waterloo, Ontario: Wilfried Laurier Press.

Putnam, Hilary. 2004. *Ethics Without Ontology.* Cambridge, MA: Harvard University Press.

Rabinowitz, Dorothy. 1976. *New Lives: Survivors of the Holocaust Living in America.* New York: Alfred A. Knopf.

Reemtsma, Jan P. 1996. 172364: Gedanken über den gebrauch der ersten person singular bei Jean Améry. In *Jean Améry [Hans Maier],* ed. S. Steiner. Basel/Frankfurt am Main: Stroemfeld/Nexus: 63–86.

Richards, Norvin. 2002. In *Before Forgiving*, ed. S. Lamb and J. Murphy. New York: Oxford University Press.

Ricoeur, Paul. 1995. *Figuring the Sacred*. Minneapolis: Fortress Press.

———. 1996. Reflections on a New Ethos for Europe. In *Paul Ricoeur: The Hermeneutics of Action*, ed. R. Kearney. London: Sage Publications: 3–14.

———. 1998. *Das rätsel der vergangenheit*. Essen: Wallstein.

———. 2004. *Memory, History, Forgetting*, trans. K. Blamey and D. Pellauer. Chicago: University of Chicago Press.

Rigby, Andrew. 2001. *Justice and Reconciliation: After the Violence*. London: Lynne Rienner

Rome Statute of the International Criminal Court. 1998. At http://www.un.org/law/icc/ (accessed November 27, 2004).

Rorty, Richard. 1998. *Truth and Progress: Philosophical Papers*. Cambridge: Cambridge University Press.

Rosenblum, Nancy L. 2002. Memory, Law, and Repair. In *Breaking the Cycles of Hatred: Memory, Law, and Repair*, ed. Martha Minow. Princeton: Princeton University Press: 1–13.

Rotberg, Robert I. and Dennis Thompson, eds. 2000. *Truth v. Justice: The Morality of Truth Commissions*. Princeton: Princeton University Press.

Roth, John K. 1999. The Holocaust and Philosophy. In *Lessons and Legacies*, Vol. III, ed. P. Hayes. Evanston, IL: Northwestern University Press.

Roth, John K. and Elisabeth Maxwell. 2001. *Remembering for the Future: The Holocaust in an Age of Genocide, Volume 2, Ethics and Religion*. London: Palgrave

Sarat, Austin. 1999. Remorse, Responsibility, and Criminal Punishment: An Analysis of Popular Culture. In *The Passions of Law*, ed. S. Bandes. New York: New York University Press: 169–90.

Sartre, Jean-Paul. 1939/1977. *Sketch for a Theory of the Emotions*, trans by P. Mairet. London: Methuen.

Schaap, Andrew. 2005. *Political Reconciliation*. London: Routledge.

Schabas, William A. 2000. *Genocide in International Law*. Cambridge: Cambridge University Press.

———. 2006. The "Odious Scourge": Evolving Interpretations of the Crime of Genocide. *Genocide Studies and Prevention* 1 (2): 93–106.

Scheler, Max. 1915/1998. *Ressentiment*, trans. L. B. Coser and W. W. Holdheim. Milwaukee: Marquette University Press.

———. 1992. Negative Feelings and the Destruction of Values: Ressentiment. In *On Feeling, Knowing, and Valuing: Selected Writings*, ed. H. J. Bershady. Chicago: University of Chicago Press: 116–43.

Schimmel, Solomon. 2002. *Wounds Not Healed by Time: The Power of Repentance and Forgiveness*. New York: Oxford University Press.

Schwan. 2001. *Politik und Schuld: Die Zerstörishe Macht des Schweigens*. Frankfut am Main: Fisher.

Sebald, Winfried G. 2003.Against the Irreversible. In *On the Natural History of Destruction*. New York: Random House.

Seneca. 1970. *Moral Essays*, trans. J. W. Basore. Cambridge, MA: Harvard University Press.

Shaw, Rosalind. 2005. *Rethinking Truth and Reconciliation Commissions: Lessons From Sierra Leone*. Special Report No. 130, United States Institute of Peace, http://www.usip.org/pubs/specialreports/sr130.html (accessed April 19, 2007).

Smedes , Lewis. 1997. *The Art of Forgiving*. New York Ballantine Books.

Smith, Adam. 1854/2000. *The Theory of Moral Sentiments*. New York: Prometheus Books.

Smith, Barbara Herrnstein. 1988. *Contingencies of Value: Alternative Perspectives for Critical Theory*. Cambridge, MA: Harvard University Press.

____. 1997. *Belief and Resistance: Dynamics of Contemporary Intellectual Controversy*. Cambridge, MA: Harvard University Press.

Smith, James. 2004. *Option Papers Drafted for Conference Workshops at the Stockholm International Forum: Preventing Genocide; Threats And Responsibilities*, http://www.preventinggenocide.com (accessed November 24, 2004).

Solomon, Robert C. 1999. Justice v. Vengeance: On Law and the Satisfaction of Emotion. In *The Passions of Law*, ed. S. Bandes. New York: New York University Press: 123–48.

____. ed. 2003. *What Is an Emotion? Classic and Contemporary Readings* (2nd ed.). New York: Oxford University Press.

Spelman, Elizabeth. V. 2003. Coexistence and Repair. In *Imagine Coexistence: Restoring Humanity After Violent Ethnic Conflict*, ed. A. Chayes and M. Minow. San Francisco: Jossey-Bass: 235–51.

Spinoza. 1677/2000. *Ethics*, ed. and trans. G.H.R. Parkinson. Oxford: Oxford University Press.

Staub, Ervin and Pearlman, Laurie A. 2001. Healing, Reconciliation, and Forgiving After Genocide and Other Collective Violence. In *Forgiveness and Reconciliation*, ed. R. G. Helmick and R. L. Petersen. Philadelphia: Templeton Foundation Press: 205–28.

Staub, Ervin, Laurie Pearlman, Alexandria Gubin, and Athanese Hagengimana. 2005. Healing, Reconciliation, Forgiving and the Prevention of Violence After Genocide or Mass Killing: An Intervention and Its Experimental Evaluation in Rwanda. *Journal of Social and Clinical Psychology* 24 (3): 297–334.

Steiner, Stephan, ed. 1996. *Jean Améry [Hans Maier]*. Basel/Frankfurt am Main: Stroemfeld/Nexus.

Stover, Eric. 2005. *The Witnesses: War Crimes and the Promise of Justice in The Hague*. Berkeley: Human Rights Center.

Strawson, Peter F. 1974. *Freedom and Resentment and Other Essays*. London: Methuen.

Tal, Kali. 2004. *Worlds of Hurt: Reading the Literatures of Trauma*. New York: Cambridge University Press.

Taylor, Charles. 1979. *Hegel and Modern Society*. Cambridge Mass.: Cambridge University Press.

____. 1989. *Sources of the Self. The Making of the Modern Identity*. Cambridge: Cambridge University Press.

____. 1994. The Politics of Recognition. In *Multiculturalism*, ed. A. Gutman. Princeton: Princeton University Press.

Taylor, Gabriele. 2006. *Deadly Vices*. Oxford: Clarendon Press.

Teitel, Ruti. 2000. *Transitional Justice*. New York: Oxford University Press.

____. 2004. Transitional Historical Justice. In *Justice in Time*, ed. L. H. Meyer. Baden-Baden: Nomos Verlagsgesellschaft.

Terreblanche, Christelle. 2006. Apartheid Victims and State Clash. *The Sunday Independent*, June 22: 3.

Theissen, Gunnar and Brandon Hamber. 1998. A State of Denial: White South African's Attitudes to the Truth and Reconciliation Commission, http://www.und.ac.za/und

Thomas, Joshua and Garrod, Andrew. 2002. Forgiveness After Genocide? Perspective From Bosnian Youth. In *Before Forgiving*, ed. S. Lamb and J. Murphy. New York: Oxford University Press: 192–210.

Thomas, Laurence. 2003. Forgiving the Unforgivable? In *Moral Philosophy and the Holocaust*, ed. E. Garrard and G. Scarre. Aldershot: Ashgate: 201–30.

Tobias, Jim G. and Zinke, Peter. 2000. *Nakam—Jüdische Rache an NS-Tätern*. Hamburg: Konkret Litteratur Verlag.

Torpey, John. 2002. Making Whole What Has Been Smashed: Reflections on Reparations. In *Post-Conflict Justice*, ed. M. S. Bassiouni. Ardsley, NY: Transnational Publishers: 217–42.

Torrance, Alan J. 2006. The Theological Grounds for Advocating Forgiveness and Reconciliation in the Sociopolitical Realm. In *Politics of Past Evil: Religion, Reconciliation, and the Dilemmas of Transitional Justice*, ed. D. Philpott. Notre Dame: Notre Dame University Press.

Traverso, Enzo. 2000. *Auschwitz denken: die intellektuellen und die Shoah*, trans H. Dahmer. Hamburg: Hamburger Edition.

Truth and Reconciliation Commission of South Africa. 1998. *Truth and Reconciliation Commission of South Africa Final Report*. Cape Town: Juta.

Tudor, Steven. 2001. *Compassion and Remorse: Acknowledging the Suffering of Others*. Leuven: Peeters.

Tutu, Desmond M. 1998. Contribution to Symposium. In *The Sunflower: On the Possibilities and Limits of Forgiveness*, ed. Simon Wiesenthal. New York: Schocken Books.

———. 1999. *No Future Without Forgiveness*. New York: Doubleday.

———. 2002. Foreword. In *Forgiveness and Reconciliation*, ed. R. Helmick and R. Petersen. Philadelphia: Templeton Foundation Press: ix–xiii.

Tzetan, Todorov. 1997. *Facing the Extreme: Moral Life in the Concentration Camps*. New York: Henry Holt.

U.S. Catholic. 2000. *No Forgiveness, No Future: An Interview With Archbishop Desmond Tutu*. Clarentian Publications.

Verdoolaege, Annelies. 2006. Managing Reconciliation at the Human Rights Violations Hearings of the South African TRC. *Human Rights and Negative Emotions: Special Issue of Journal of Human Rights* 5 (1): 61–80.

Vetlesen, Arne J. 2006. A Case for Resentment: Jean Améry Versus Primo Levi. *Human Rights and Negative Emotions: Special Issue of Journal of Human Rights* 5 (1): 27–44.

Villa-Vicencio, Charles. 2000. Getting on With Life: A Move Towards Reconciliation. In *Looking Back Reaching Forward: Reflections on the Truth and Reconciliation Commission of South Africa*, ed. C. Villa-Vicencio and W. Verwoerd. Cape Town: University of Cape Town Press.

Villa-Vicencio, Charles and Wilhelm Verwoerd, eds. 2000. *Looking Back Reaching Forward: Reflections on the Truth and Reconciliation Commission of South Africa*, ed. C. Villa-Vicencio and W. Verwoerd. Cape Town: University of Cape Town Press.

Walker, Margaret U. 2006a. The Cycle of Violence. *Human Rights and Negative Emotions: Special Issue of Journal of Human Rights* 5 (1): 81–105.

___. 2006b. *Moral Repair: Reconstructing Moral Relations After Wrongdoing.* New York: Cambridge University Press.

Wallace, Richard. Jay. 1994. *Responsibility and the Moral Sentiments.* Cambridge, MA: Harvard University Press.

Walzer, Michael. 1994. Thick and Thin: Moral Argument at Home and Abroad. Notre Dame, Indiana, University of Notre. Dame Press.

___. 1997. *On Toleration.* New Haven: Yale University Press.

Wasserstrom, Richard. 1974. The Relevance of Nuremberg. In *War and Moral Responsibility*, ed. M. Cohen et al. Princeton: Princeton University Press: 134–58.

Weine, Stevan M. 1999. *When History Is a Nightmare: Lives and Memories of Ethnic Cleansing in Bosnia-Herzegovina.* New Brunswick, NJ: Rutgers University Press.

Weissmark, Mona S. 2004. *Justice Matters: Legacies of the Holocaust and World War II.* New York: Oxford University Press.

Wiesenthal, Simon. 1998. *The Sunflower: On the Possibilities and Limits of Forgiveness.* New York: Schocken Books.

Williams, Bernard. 1973. *Problems of the Self: Philosophical Papers, 1956–72.* Cambridge: Cambridge University Press.

Wilson, Richard. 2001. *The Politics of Truth and Reconciliation in South Africa: Legitimizing the Post-Apartheid State.* Cambridge: Cambridge University Press.

Wilson, Stuart. 2001. The Myth of Restorative Justice: Truth, Reconciliation and the Ethics of Amnesty. *South African Journal of Human Rights* 17(4): 531–62.

Young, James E. 1993. *The Texture of Memory: Holocaust, Memorials and Meaning.* New Haven: Yale University Press.

Index

226 / Index

negative emotions: (cont.)
challenge to South Africans on, 36–37. *see also* anger; resentment; vengeance; vindictiveness
Neher, André, 134
Neier, Aryeh, 136
Neiman, Susan, 111, 161, 192n.4, 192n.10, 198n.8, 204n.8–9; critique of Améry's "*Ressentiments*," 166–68
nested resentments, 58
Neuffer, Elisabeth, 171, 194n.5
The Nichomachean Ethics (Aristotle), 87
Niebuhr, Reinhold, 49–50
Niederland, William, 197n.5, 199n.8; on hypermnesia, 107; reality of trauma and, 195n.17
Nietzsche, Friedrich, 167, 174, 205n.10; Améry's critique of, 195n.13; on predicament of the human will, 108–9; on redemption, 111; *ressentiment* and, xi, 11, 12, 70–71, 91–93, 109, 195n.14–16; on spirit of revenge, 126
Niven, Bill, 147, 203n.2
nonacknowledgment. *see* misrecognition; nonrecognition
nonforgiveness: Améry and, 132, 151–53; Améry defends, 151–53; attempts to change victims' attitude toward, 31–32, 189n.9; in Bosnian context, 190n.5; contextual approach to, 14; legitimacy of, xi; as moral protest, 171; of Nazi victims, 89–90; Tutu on, 43, 46–50
nonrecognition: harm inflicted by, 121; *ressentiment* as weapon against, 123
Notes From the Underground (Dostoyevsky), 11–12
nursing a grudge, blame and, 86–87
Nussbaum, Martha, 191n.8, 197n.26; on anger and humanity relationship, 97; on emotional specificity, 14; on moral remainders, 60; philosophy of emotion and, 187n.14; recounts Elie Wiesel story, 96–97

objective attitude: Améry against, 123; Améry's experience of, 94–95; bias against, 121–22; Strawson on, 11, 94, 122; *vs.* subjective attitude, 123
On Cosmopolitanism and Forgiveness (Derrida), 188n.4
On the Genealogy of Morals (Nietzsche), 11
"On the Necessity and Impossibility of Being a Jew" (Améry), 157
"On the Psychology of the German People" (Améry), 67–68

open letter, by Améry, 144
opposition, Arendt on, 194n.8
optimism, 175–76
Oradour massacre, France, 189n.2
Orentlicher, Diane, 179, 180, 206n.7
The Orestia (Aeschylus), 60
The Origins of Totalitarianism (Arendt), 148
Osiel, Mark, 139
overcoming the past: concept of, 71–72, 193n.11; and German memory culture, 72–73; postwar Germany and, Améry's demand for, 114–15, 146–47, 159

Palm, Roland, 187n.1
Parfit, Derek, 197n.3
passing of time: amoral nature of, 130–31; German memory culture and, 72–73, 98–99; holding a grudge and, 87; moral significance of, 5, 186n.6; in *ressentiment,* 106–7; victim's inability to respond to, 108–11. *see also* overcoming the past
passion, *ressentiment* as, 105
passivity: of bystanders, and loneliness of victim, 122; as form of human subjugation, 130
past and present: interweaving of, 155–56, 203n.6; and irreversibility of the past, 108–11, 113; and moral rehabilitation of German people, 152–53; and nullification of the past, 119–20; Ricoeur and, 112
Paul (apostle), 49–50; on anger, 50, 187n.15
Pendas, Devin O., 76, 192n.8, 198n.7
The Periodic Table (Levi), 105
perpetrators, of mass crimes: abandonment experience of, 126; discriminatory intent and, 206n.6; Govier on, 198n.6; just punishment for, xi; moral truth and, 126; negation and coordination with victims, 119–22; objective attitude and, 122; repentance of, victim forgiveness and, 52–54, 55; TRC requirements and, xi; victim's desire for punishment of, 36
persecution, defined, 206n.5
personal bitterness. *see* bitterness
Petersen, ?, 190n.3, 191n.14
Pfäfflin, Friedrich, 192n.4
Phelps, Theresa G., 4, 23, 29
philosophical abstraction, 15
Philpott, Daniel, 190n.2
political expurgations, in postwar Germany, 73
"The Politics of Recognition (Taylor), 121
polling data, in postwar Germany, 73–74
Posel, Deborah, 36

Thomas Brudholm holds a PhD in Philosophy and is Associate Professor of Minority Research Theory at the University of Copenhagen.